Impulse Control Disorders

Impulse Control Disorders

A Clinician's Guide to Understanding
and Treating Behavioral Addictions

Jon E. Grant

W. W. Norton & Company
New York • London

BP 53

For information about permission to reproduce
selections from this book, write to Permissions,
W. W. Norton & Company, Inc.
500 Fifth Avenue, New York, NY 10110

For information about special discounts for bulk purchases, please contact
W. W. Norton Special Sales at specialsales@wwnorton.com or 800-233-4830

Manufacturing by Courier Westford
Production manager: Devon Zahn

Library of Congress Cataloging-in-Publication Data

Grant, Jon E.
    Impulse control disorders : a clinician's guide to understanding and treating behavioral
addictions / Jon E. Grant.—1st ed.
        p. ; cm.
"A Norton Professional Book."
Includes bibliographical references and index.
ISBN 978-0-393-70521-8 (hardcover)
1. Impulse control disorders. I. Title.

[DNLM: 1. Impulse control disorders. 2. Behavior, Addictive.
WM 190 G762i 2008]

RC569.5.I46G72 2008
616.85'84–dc22   2007029115

W. W. Norton & Company, Inc., 500 Fifth Avenue, New York, N.Y. 10110
www.wwnorton.com

W. W. Norton & Company Ltd., Castle House, 75/76 Wells St., London W1T 3QT

1 3 5 7 9 0 8 6 4 2

7/28/10

Contents

Preface

The idea for this book started brewing 9 years ago when I began research on impulse control disorders. At that time, some limited information was available on a few of these disorders, but most remained largely unexamined, with only anecdotal reports. Much has happened since then, including a greater understanding of these disorders, a deeper knowledge of their biological and psychological aspects, and most important, a growth in promising treatment options.

Still considered, unfortunately, by many researchers to be only of limited interest, research has generated a remarkable amount of data supporting the claim that the impulse control disorders are truly common and disabling behaviors. Having now seen thousands of people with these disorders, my goal has been to educate clinicians about their seriousness, and to help the millions of people who suffer from them.

I am grateful to the many people who have helped me think about and examine impulse control disorders over the years. My interactions with them have had tremendous influence on me. These include colleagues of mine at the University of Minnesota (Suck Won Kim, Gary Christenson, Kyle Williams, Brian Odlaug, and S. Charles Schulz), at Brown University and Butler Hospital (Maria Mancebo, Steve Rasmussen, Jane Eisen, Katharine Phillips, Lawrence Price, Stephen Correia, and Martin Keller), and at other institutions, including Marc Potenza at Yale University, Donald Black at the University of Iowa, Eric Hollander at Mount Sinai Medical School, Patrick Marsh at the University of South Florida, and Carlos Blanco at Columbia University.

I am most grateful to the people suffering from impulse control disorders who let me ask intimate questions of them. Although I use clinical cases throughout this book, these cases do not represent any actual patient or research subject I have known. To protect the confidentiality of my patients or research subjects, the cases are merely fictional composites of various characteristics of the disorders.

Without the openness and courage of my patients and research subjects to discuss their struggles, this book could not have been written. It is for all of these people that I wrote it.

Introduction

Several disorders have been classified together in the American Psychiatric Association's (2000) *Diagnostic and Statistical Manual of Mental Disorders* (4th Edition) as impulse control disorders, grouped together based on perceived similarities in clinical presentation and hypothesized similarities in pathophysiology. These disorders include pathological gambling, kleptomania, intermittent explosive disorder, trichotillomania, and pyromania. Several other disorders have been proposed as belonging to this same category: compulsive Internet use, compulsive sexual behavior, pathological skin picking, and compulsive buying.

Although they are grouped together, some controversy exists regarding the precise categorization of these disorders. Are they impulse disorders? If so, why do we call so many of them "compulsive" problems? Are they related to obsessive-compulsive disorder? Isn't gambling considered an addiction? And if so, are the others addictions as well? Some people shop excessively when they are depressed. Are these disorders related to mood disorders? Which category do these disorders belong in? Do all the impulse disorders belong in the same category?

These questions raise more than just theoretical debates. Without clear knowledge of what causes these disorders, their conceptualization has implications for prevention as well as treatment. Consider the following case.

Sylvia, a 36-year-old single female, described herself as compulsive. She reported a history, beginning in late adolescence, of uncontrollable shoplifting. Over the course of a few months, she became obsessed with stealing, thinking about it all day. The shoplifting started when she stole candy with friends and, over a period of a few months, developed into an almost daily ritual that she did by herself. Sylvia reports that she currently shoplifts one to two times each week. She feels a high or a rush each time. She primarily steals hygiene products such as shampoo and soap, usually taking multiple versions of the same item. Sylvia reports having boxes of the same shampoo and soap hidden in her closet. She does not use the stolen shampoo and soap, and instead buys her preferred shampoo and soap at another store. When asked why she does not discard them, Sylvia reports that having these products comforts her. Shoplifting may consume 2 to 3 hours at a time. Sylvia also describes daily thoughts and urges to shoplift that preoccupy her for 3 to 4 hours each day. She may even leave work early with projects unfinished so that she can get to a store and steal something. In addition, she lies to her fiancé and family, telling them that she buys the items she steals. Sylvia reports feeling compelled to shoplift items.

Does Sylvia suffer from kleptomania? Does she have obsessive-compulsive disorder? Is there a difference? Is her behavior compulsive, impulsive, or both? If we understand how to categorize Sylvia, does that help us treat her? And if so, how do we treat this behavior?

An understanding of impulse control disorders allows clinicians the opportunity to address common and disabling behaviors that a large number of people struggle with on a daily basis. An examination of the biology and psychology of these behaviors also affords clinicians greater comprehension of how and why people find any number of behaviors rewarding. The impulse control disorders are extreme versions of behaviors that people have engaged in for centuries—gambling, sex, acquiring possessions, and so on. In their pathological versions, these disorders are experienced by approximately 5–15% (a conservative estimate) of the U.S. population. This means that between 14 and 42 million Americans have struggled with these behaviors. It would therefore be difficult to find someone who has not known a close friend or family member who suffers from an impulse control disorder.

Beyond academic interest, clinicians need to understand these behaviors and how to address them. For example, Sylvia was originally diagnosed with obsessive-compulsive disorder and treated with a serotonergic medication. Although usually beneficial for obsessive-compulsive disorder, the medication did not help Sylvia. In fact, after the failed trial of medication, Sylvia became more despondent, believing she was incapable of being helped. When more appropriately diagnosed with kleptomania, she was started on an opioid antagonist, naltrexone, and responded within a few weeks.

Clinical ignorance surrounds these disorders and may reflect their complexity. What does it mean that someone cannot stop a behavior? Some may argue that people with these behaviors must not be trying hard enough to control themselves or that they lack will power or have a character flaw. Many clinicians may not even consider these disorders to be legitimate psychiatric conditions. Some might argue that psychiatrists are attempting to pathologize poor judgment or personal deficits beyond the scope of medicine.

These complaints show a misunderstanding of impulse control disorders and the growing evidence of the neurobiology of these disorders. Although we have many unanswered questions, strong evidence supports a genetic and neurochemical basis underlying these behaviors. Such complaints also further stigmatize these behaviors and the people who suffer from them. The embarrassment associated with these disorders makes it difficult for people to voluntarily offer information about their behaviors. Clinicians therefore need to ask about these disorders and do so in a knowledgeable and supportive manner. This book provides the information clinicians need to begin addressing these problems.

This book provides an overview of impulse control disorders from a clinical perspective. It describes the clinical manifestations of multiple impulse control disorders and their relationship to other psychiatric disorders such as obsessive-compulsive disorder and substance use disorders. A greater understanding of the clinical features of these problematic behaviors results in a more comprehensive assessment and treatment plan. In addition, clinicians need to be aware of the similarities and differences of impulse control disorders to other disorders so that treatments can more effectively target the impulsive behavior and any comorbid disorders.

The book also investigates risk factors for the development of impulse control disorders. Because one explanation is biological, the book examines neurochemical and genetic evidence for developing impulse control disorders. Another explanation involves developmental and psychological perspectives. Developmental, psychological, personality and gender, and cognitive aspects are reviewed.

Because many clinicians are unfamiliar with impulse control disorders, the book provides a detailed method of assessing and treating these behaviors. A screening instrument is provided, along with evidence-based approaches to both pharmacological and psychosocial treatment interventions. Problems with keeping people in treatment and the role of the family are also examined. In addition, many impulse control disorders raise legal issues that often make clinicians uncomfortable. The book therefore examines some common legal problems associated with some of these disorders.

This book is designed to serve as a guide for both new and experienced clinicians who work with people with a wide range of impulse control disorders. Given its scope and the up-to-date references, the book is also a resource for researchers. The scientific study of impulse control disorders is still in its infancy. New research continues on a fairly constant basis and will continue to inform the topics covered in this book. This text should therefore be seen, not as the final word on this subject, but as a starting point for continued research and clinical care.

Impulse Control Disorders

CHAPTER 1

Clinical Characteristics of Impulse Control Disorders

IMPULSIVITY HAS BEEN defined as a predisposition toward rapid, unplanned reactions to either internal or external stimuli without regard for negative consequences (Moeller et al., 2001). Given this definition of impulsivity, multiple psychiatric disorders might be characterized as exhibiting problems with impulse control. In the 4th edition of the *Diagnostic and Statistical Manual of Mental Disorders* (*DSM-IV-TR*), the category of Impulse Control Disorders Not Elsewhere Classified currently includes pathological gambling, kleptomania, trichotillomania, pyromania, intermittent explosive disorder, and impulse control disorders not otherwise specified (American Psychiatric Association, [APA] 2000). Other specific disorders have been proposed for inclusion based on perceived phenomenological, clinical, and possibly biological similarities: pathological skin picking, compulsive buying, compulsive Internet use, and nonparaphilic compulsive sexual behavior. There might also be other disorders—self-injurious behavior, binge eating, and hoarding—that share features with impulse control disorders. The extent to which any or all of these impulse control disorders share clinical, genetic, phenomenological, and biological features continues to be debated.

Many of the impulse control disorders share common core qualities: (1) repetitive or compulsive engagement in a behavior despite adverse consequences; (2) diminished control over the problematic behavior; (3) an appetitive urge or craving state prior to engagement in the problematic behavior; and (4) a hedonic quality during the performance of the problematic behavior (Grant and Potenza, 2004a).

1

Pathological Gambling

Robert, a 34-year-old divorced male, started gambling at 18 years of age. He began playing poker with friends for money, and by the age of 30, he was gambling alone at casinos. Robert reported that his urges to gamble were often triggered by advertisements for the local casino and fantasies of winning large amounts of money. For the past 2 years, Robert has played blackjack approximately 4 nights a week, usually spending 6 hours per night and losing up to $800. In addition, he began gambling with larger amounts of money. Although a successful self-employed businessman, his work suffered as a result of his gambling. In addition, because of the lying and time spent away from home, Robert's wife filed for divorce.

Some form of gambling addiction or compulsivity has been recognized since the days of the ancient Romans and has been discussed in the medical literature since the early 1800s (Petry, 2005). With recognition of the problem came various attempts to control it (e.g., laws and prison terms, limits on what one could bet). Nonetheless, excessive gambling behavior and the resultant personal and social consequences (e.g., criminal behavior, suicide) have continued for centuries.

Pathological gambling is the psychiatric term for what might more generally be understood as gambling addiction or compulsive gambling. Pathological gambling is characterized by persistent and recurrent maladaptive patterns of gambling behavior and is associated with impaired functioning, reduced quality of life, and high rates of bankruptcy, divorce, and incarceration (Grant and Kim, 2001). It affects an estimated 0.9–1.6% of people in the United States (National Opinion Research Center, 1999).

Pathological gambling usually begins in adolescence or early adulthood, with males tending to start at an earlier age (Shaffer et al., 1999; Ibanez et al., 2003). In epidemiological studies, women represent approximately 32% of the pathological gamblers in the United States (Volberg, 1994). Although prospective studies are largely lacking, pathological gambling appears to follow a trajectory similar to substance dependence, with high rates in adolescent and young adult groups, lower rates in older adults, and periods of abstinence and relapse (Grant and Potenza, 2005b). Pathological gambling is a serious psychiatric disorder, but there is evidence that approximately one-third of individuals with pathological gambling experience natural recovery (i.e., without treatment; Slutske, 2006).

Unique gender differences are seen in individuals with pathological gambling. For example, male pathological gamblers appear more likely to report problems with strategic or face-to-face forms of gambling such as blackjack or poker. Female pathological gamblers, on the other hand, tend to report problems with nonstrategic, less interpersonally interactive forms of gambling such as slot machines or bingo (Potenza et al., 2001). Both female and male gamblers report that advertisements are a common trigger of their urges to gamble, although females are more likely to report that feeling bored or lonely may also trigger their urges to gamble (Grant and Kim, 2001). Financial and marital problems are common (Grant and Kim, 2001). Many pathological gamblers engage in illegal behavior, such as stealing, embezzlement, and writing bad checks to fund their gambling (Potenza et al., 2000) or in an attempt to pay off past gambling losses (Argo and Black, 2004). Usually due to the financial and legal problems, suicide attempts are common and have been reported in 17% of individuals in treatment for pathological gambling (Petry and Kiluk, 2002).

Kleptomania

Maria, a 44-year-old married female, described a history, beginning in late adolescence, of uncontrollable shoplifting. Over the course of a few months, she thought about stealing "all the time" and was only rarely able to control her behavior when she entered a store. Maria reports that she currently shoplifts one to two times each week. She describes a rush each time she steals. The rush is short-lived and when she leaves the store she usually throws away the stolen item or leaves it outside the store. She steals various items, none of which she cares about and all of which she could easily afford. Maria's shoplifting may consume anywhere from minutes to a couple of hours at a time. Maria also describes daily thoughts and urges to shoplift that preoccupy her for at least 2 hours each day. In addition, she lies to her husband, telling him that she buys the items she steals. The behavior and the lying cause significant depression and feelings of worthlessness. Maria has tried to commit suicide on three occasions, never telling anyone the reason behind her suicide attempts.

Shoplifting appears to date back centuries. In fact, for as long as people have been selling merchandise, there have been people stealing it (Murphy, 1986). In 1816, Andre Matthey, a Swiss physician, used the word *klopemanie* (from the Greek words *kleptein*, to steal, and *mania*, insanity) to describe the behavior of a distinct group of thieves that would impulsively or compulsively steal worthless or unneeded objects (McElroy et al., 1991; Segrave, 2001). In 1838, two French physicians, Jean-Etienne Esquirol (Matthey's mentor) and C. C. Marc (Esquirol's pupil), changed the term to *kleptomanie* and included it among the monomanias, a group of disorders characterized by involuntary and irresistible actions that were mental diseases, not moral depravity (Abelson, 1989).

In the 19th and early 20th centuries, kleptomania was discussed alongside insanity and female pelvic disorders, as doctors referred to three groups of disease—epilepsy, insanity, and hysteria—as diseases of uterine organs. Although episodic mention is made of kleptomania in the scientific literature of the early 20th century, it would not generate concentrated scientific interest again until the early 1990s.

Kleptomania is characterized by repetitive, uncontrollable stealing of items not needed for personal use (APA, 2000). Although kleptomania typically has its onset in early adulthood or late adolescence (Goldman, 1991; McElroy et al., 1991), the disorder has been reported in children as young as 4 years and in adults as old as 77 years (Grant, 2006). The literature clearly suggests that the majority of patients with kleptomania are women. Of the four independent studies that have assembled large numbers of patients with kleptomania, 68 of 108 (63.0%) total subjects were female (McElroy et al., 1991; Sarasalo et al., 1996; Grant and Kim, 2002a; Presta et al., 2002). One explanation for this gender disparity may be that women are more likely to present for psychiatric evaluation or that courts are more likely to send male shoplifters to prison (Goldman, 1991). The severity of kleptomania symptoms and the clinical presentation of symptoms do not appear to differ based on gender (Grant and Kim, 2002a). Intense guilt and shame are commonly reported by those suffering from kleptomania. Items stolen are typically hoarded, given away, returned to the store, or thrown away (McElroy et al., 1991). Many individuals with kleptomania (64–87%) have been apprehended at some time due to their stealing behavior (Grant, 2006).

Trichotillomania

> Stephanie began pulling her hair at the age of 12 years. She is now 40 years old and has pulled fairly consistently over the last 28 years. She pulls from her head and her eyebrows. After pulling, she plays with the hair, inspects it, and eats the root. She often spends an hour each day pulling. Although she wears a wig to cover the bald spots and pencils in her missing eyebrows, she cannot stop the behavior. She does not swim (a favorite pastime) or socialize for fear of someone seeing her bald spots or lack of eyebrows. She lives each day tormented by a behavior she does not understand.

Pathological hair pulling, or trichotillomania, has been defined as repetitive, intentionally performed pulling that causes noticeable hair loss and results in clinically significant distress or functional impairment (APA, 2000). Accounts of hair pulling are found in the Bible, Homer's *Iliad*, and the plays of William Shakespeare (Christenson and Mansueto, 1999). Although Hippocrates noted that hair pulling should be assessed by all physicians, particularly in the context of grief, the idea of hair pulling as a medical syndrome appears to have originated in the 19th century. The term *trichotillomania* dates back to Hallopeau's 1889 account of a young man who pulled every hair out of his body. Hallopeau described the behavior as chronic and lacking a cure; his attempt to treat hair pulling with mentholated camphor and wrapping the person in rubber apparently failed (Christenson and Mansueto, 1999).

Although 17–23% of people with clinically meaningful hair pulling fail to meet the *DSM-IV* criteria, which require either tension immediately before pulling or pleasure, gratification, or relief when pulling (Christenson et al., 1991), trichotillomania appears relatively common with an estimated prevalence of 1–3% (Christenson et al., 1991). Trichotillomania has traditionally been considered to predominantly affect females (Swedo and Leonard, 1992).

The mean age at onset for trichotillomania is approximately 13 years (Christenson and Mansueto, 1999). Although prospective studies are lacking, the onset of trichotillomania has been associated with scalp disease and stressful life events (Christenson and Mansueto, 1999). People report pulling from any body area, although the scalp is the most common. The feel of the hair's texture is a frequent trigger.

Hair pulling is subject to great fluctuations in severity, with worsening of symptoms often related to stress. Individuals with trichotillomania often pull for more than 1 hour each day, may pull hair from spouses or children, and often have rituals surrounding the pulling. For example, they may play with the hair, rub it on their faces, or occasionally eat the root or hair shaft. Significant social and occupational disability is common, with 34.6% of individuals reporting daily interference with job duties and 47% reporting avoidance of social situations such as dating or participating in group activities (Woods et al., 2006).

Pyromania

> Jonathan, a 20-year-old single college student, reported a 3-year history of setting fires. Initially starting by burning things in his room or in the backyard, his behaviors gradually progressed to burning small, empty buildings throughout the town. Jonathan described the fires as intoxicating. He would spend hours planning, setting, and watching the fires. He often would miss classes because of the planning, which could take up to 4 hours each day. Jonathan set a fire approximately once per month. Although he enjoyed the fires, the behavior left him feeling guilty and depressed. Due to the time he spent setting fires, Jonathan became socially isolated and eventually attempted suicide.

Pyromania has been discussed in the medical literature for almost 200 years. One of the first descriptions in medical texts was by Esquirol, who described "incendiary monomania," a symptom complex including exalted mood and increased energy (Esquirol, 1845). Since that time, surprisingly little has been written about pyromania.

The *DSM-IV-TR* describes pyromania as a preoccupation with fire setting and characterizes the behavior with the following diagnostic criteria: (1) deliberate and purposeful fire setting on more than one occasion; (2) tension or affective arousal before the act; (3) fascination with, interest in, curiosity about, or attraction to fire and its situational contexts; and (4) pleasure, gratification, or relief when setting fires or when witnessing or participating in their aftermath (APA, 2000).

In one study suggesting the rare nature of pyromania, the authors found that only 3 (3.3%) of 90 arson recidivists had pure pyromania and that an additional 9 subjects met *DSM* criteria for pyromania only when intoxicated at the time of the fire setting (Lindberg et al., 2005). Several studies of clinical, noncriminal samples, however, have found that pyromania may not be that uncommon. One study of 107 patients with depression found that 3 (2.8%) met current *DSM-IV* criteria for pyromania (Lejoyeux et al., 2002). A study of 204 psychiatric inpatients revealed that 3.4% (*n* = 7) endorsed current symptoms and 5.9% (*n* = 12) had lifetime symptoms meeting *DSM-IV* criteria for pyromania (Grant et al., 2005). Small studies of individuals with compulsive buying (*n* = 20) and kleptomania (*n* = 20) have also found rates of 10% (*n* = 2) and 15% (*n* = 3), respectively, for lifetime pyromania (McElroy et al., 1991, 1994). Although adolescent fire setting may be a symptom of various psychiatric disorders, a recent study of 102 adolescent psychiatric inpatients found that after excluding those patients who set fires due to conduct disorder, substance use disorders, bipolar disorder, psychotic disorders, or developmental disorders, 7 (6.9%) met criteria for current pyromania (Grant et al., in press).

Although long thought to be a disorder primarily affecting men, more recent research suggests that the gender ratio is equal in adults and may be slightly higher among females in adolescence (Grant et al., in press). Mean age of onset is generally late adolescence, and the behavior appears chronic if left untreated (Grant et al., in press). Urges to set fires are common in individuals with this behavior, and the fire setting is almost always pleasurable. Severe distress follows the fire setting, and individuals with pyromania report significant functional impairment (Grant et al., in press).

Intermittent Explosive Disorder

David, a 34-year-old married stockbroker, has had problems with his temper since adolescence. As an adult, his temper has been particularly unstable when driving. Easily angered by a slow car or a perceived slight by another driver (such as a car cutting him off in traffic), David is filled with uncontrollable rage. David describes it as "going from 0 mph to 100 mph in no time." On many occasions he has tried running another driver off the road or throwing items at another car. On one occasion, David got the other

driver to pull off to the side of the road and then began a physical alterca-
tion. These episodes might only last 30 minutes, but David has been
arrested on two occasions and his wife has threatened to leave him
because of his anger. After each episode, David feels remorseful, realizes
his behavior is out of proportion, and wishes he could control his outbursts.

Although anger outbursts may be a sign of depression, manic
depression, substance addiction, personality pathology, or immaturity,
the idea of a specific syndrome for unique anger outbursts was not recognized by the American Psychiatric Association until 1980.

Intermittent explosive disorder is characterized by recurrent, significant outbursts of aggression, often leading to assaultive acts against
people or property, which are disproportionate to outside stressors and
not better explained by another psychiatric diagnosis (APA, 2000).
Research suggests that intermittent explosive disorder may be common, with 6.3% of a community sample meeting criteria for the disorder (Coccaro et al., 2004).

Intermittent explosive disorder symptoms tend to start in adolescence (approximately age 16) and appear to be chronic (McElroy et al.,
1998; Coccaro et al., 2004). The disorder appears to be somewhat
more common in males, although some research suggests that the gender ratio is equal (Coccaro and Danehy, 2006). Individuals suffering
from intermittent explosive disorder regard their behavior as distressing and problematic (McElroy et al., 1998). Outbursts are generally
short lived (usually less than 30 minutes in duration) and frequent
(multiple times per month; McElroy et al., 1998). Legal and occupational difficulties are common (McElroy et al., 1998).

Pathological Skin Picking

Yvonne, a 30-year-old married female, picked at the bridge of her nose
every day. Although she had previously picked at her face, the nose had
been the primary focus for the past 3 years. Her picking was so intense (up
to 3 hours each day) that she picked a hole right through the bridge of her
nose, requiring cosmetic surgery. She had also picked at the rest of her

face, leaving it scarred and covered with scabs. Touching and feeling her face triggered the urge to pick, and she felt unable to resist.

Yvonne started picking her face when she was 22 years old. Because of the time she spent picking, she missed a significant amount of high school and could not graduate. Since then, because of the facial scarring, Yvonne has avoided going out in public, working, or socializing. She lives at home, alone, on medical disability. She had never sought help for her picking until she had plastic surgery.

Pathological skin picking is characterized by the repetitive or compulsive picking of skin to the point of causing tissue damage. Proposed diagnostic criteria for pathological skin picking include the following: (1) recurrent skin picking resulting in noticeable tissue damage; (2) preoccupation with impulses or urges to pick skin, which is experienced as intrusive; (3) feelings of tension, anxiety, or agitation immediately prior to picking; (4) feelings of pleasure, relief, or satisfaction while picking; (5) the picking is not accounted for by another medical or mental disorder (e.g., cocaine or amphetamine use disorders, scabies); and (6) the individual suffers significant distress or social or occupational impairment.

Pathological skin picking has an estimated prevalence rate of 4% in the collegiate population and 2% in dermatology clinic patients (Griesemer, 1978; Gupta et al., 1987; Keuthen et al., 2000). The afflicted person frequently reports shame and embarrassment and the avoidance of social situations (Arnold et al., 2001). People who engage in this behavior typically spend a significant amount of time picking, often several hours each day. Most often they pick the face, but any body part may be the focus—torso, arms, hands, or legs.

Although pathological skin picking generally has its onset in adolescence, it may occur at any age (Arnold et al., 2001; Odlaug and Grant, 2007). In fact, the onset of pathological skin picking often begins with a dermatological condition such as acne, eczema, or psoriasis (Wilhelm et al., 1999). The picking behavior may result in significant tissue damage and scarring, sometimes even warranting reconstructive surgery, and in rare cases can be life threatening. Individuals with pathological skin picking rarely seek dermatological or psychiatric treatment due to embarrassment or the mistaken belief that their condition is untreatable (Wilhelm et al., 1999; Grant et al., in press). In a study of 31 patients with pathological skin picking, only 14 (45%) had ever sought treatment and only 6 (19.4%) had ever received dermatological treatment despite the infections and deep craters their picking behavior had produced (Wilhelm et al., 1999).

Compulsive Buying

Jeffrey has been buying books for many years. In fact, Jeffrey has a storage locker dedicated to housing only his books. He buys new, used, and rare books. When interested in an author, he feels a need to buy all of that author's books. Until every book by a particular author is purchased, he feels uncomfortable. Jeffrey often buys multiple copies of the same books. Most of the books go unread and not even perused. Jeffrey reports a feeling of completeness from his purchases. He also enjoys the interactions with store clerks, reporting that the interactions make him feel important, well known, and special. Jeffrey has significant credit card debt ($80,000) due to these purchases. Although he has a successful business, he has recently lost his home due to an inability to pay the mortgage.

Uncontrollable spending behavior has been documented throughout history. Marie Antoinette, Mary Todd Lincoln, and William Randolph Hearst are but a few of the famous figures in history who exhibited uncontrollable buying (Black, 2006). Emil Kraepelin in 1915 used the term *oniomania* to describe compulsive buying that leads to senseless debts and financial catastrophe (Black, 2006). Compulsive buying was considered an "impulsive insanity" (Black, 2006).

Although not specifically recognized by the American Psychiatric Association, the following diagnostic criteria have been proposed for compulsive buying: (1) maladaptive preoccupation with or engagement in buying (evidenced by frequent preoccupation with or irresistible impulses to buy, or frequent buying of items that are not needed or not affordable, or shopping for longer periods of time than intended); (2) preoccupations or buying lead to significant distress or impairment; and (3) the buying does not occur exclusively during hypomanic or manic episodes (McElroy et al., 1994). A random-sample study of

2,513 adults in the United States found that 5.8% of those surveyed screened positive for compulsive buying (Koran et al., 2006).

The onset of compulsive buying typically occurs during late adolescence or early adulthood (Black, 1996). The disorder appears more common among females (Christenson et al., 1994; Black, 1996). Individuals with compulsive buying report repetitive, intrusive urges to shop that are often triggered by being in stores and worsen during times of stress, emotional difficulties, or boredom. Compulsive buying regularly results in substantial financial debt, marital or family disruption, and legal consequences (Christenson et al., 1994). Guilt, shame, and embarrassment typically follow the buying episodes. Most items are not used or even removed from the packaging (Christenson et al., 1994).

Compulsive Sexual Behavior

Brian, a 26-year-old married man who owned his own business, reported that he felt strong daily urges to masturbate to Internet pornography. The urges were described as uncontrollable. Brian detailed a history with thousands of hours spent on the Internet, each episode followed by feelings of remorse and guilt. On average, Brian was spending at least 3 hours per day looking at pornography. In addition, Brian reported that the preoccupation with looking at pornography consumed him daily. Brian reported that this behavior caused significant guilt and interfered with his marriage. In addition, because of his inability to control his behavior at work, he was dismissed from his job.

Brian's compulsive sexual behavior started at the age of 20. Getting married and having regular sexual activity with his wife did not dampen the urges. Brian reported symptoms consistent with depression that started only after several years of compulsive sexual behavior. Brian sought psychiatric treatment after his wife threatened to leave him.

Compulsive sexual behavior is characterized by inappropriate or excessive sexual behaviors or thoughts that lead to subjective distress or impaired functioning (Black et al., 1997). Although not currently included in *DSM-IV*, compulsive sexual behavior may be relatively common. No epidemiological studies of compulsive sexual behavior have been performed, but the prevalence of the disorder in adults is estimated to range from 3–6% (Coleman 1992). A study of patients admitted to a psychiatric hospital found that 4.4% suffered from current compulsive sexual behavior (Grant et al., 2005). The disorder is believed to predominantly affect men. In the three large case series that have been published to date, men accounted for 77 of 87 subjects, or 88.5% (Kafka and Prentky 1994; Black et al., 1997; Raymond et al., 2003). In a study of adolescents ($n = 102$), the disorder was also common (4.9%) but was found exclusively among adolescent females (Grant et al., in press). Compulsive sexual behavior may be underreported in women because they may feel more social stigma associated with sexual behavior.

Compulsive sexual behavior can involve a wide range of sexual behaviors, often including a mixture of paraphilic and nonparaphilic behaviors (Coleman, 1992; Kafka and Prentky, 1994). Nonparaphilic compulsive sexual behavior involves conventional sexual behaviors (e.g., masturbation, promiscuity, pornography) that have become excessive or uncontrolled. Many people with compulsive sexual behavior may also satisfy criteria for one of the paraphilias, such as exhibitionism, voyeurism, sexual masochism and sadism, or transvestic fetishism. Although the compulsive sexual acts are gratifying, the behavior is followed by remorse or guilt (Barth and Kinder, 1987). The behavior is often driven by either pleasure seeking or anxiety reduction (Coleman, 1992).

Internet Addiction

Scott is a single, 28-year-old male who reports that he uses the Internet for at least 6 hours each day. Although currently unemployed, Scott is not using the Internet to look for work, gamble, or even look at pornography. Scott enjoys the endless searches of a variety of subjects. He enjoys the stimulation from the Internet and the interactive quality of blogs and chat rooms. Scott reports that he tries to stop using the Internet, but instead, he keeps telling himself repeatedly and unsuccessfully that "this is the last topic I will search." Often on the Internet late into the evening, Scott lost his job due to his inability to arrive at work on time. He quit dating and spending time with friends due to his Internet use.

Internet addiction, also called problematic Internet use or compulsive computer use (Black et al., 1999; Lin and Potenza, 2007), is characterized by either irresistible preoccupations with the Internet or excessive use of the Internet for longer periods of time than planned (Shapira et al., 2003). The use or preoccupation leads to clinically significant distress or impaired functioning (Shapira et al., 2003). Although frequently discussed in the medical literature over the last several years, there have been no epidemiological studies of Internet addiction. Clinical samples, however, suggest that the disorder may be somewhat more prevalent in men (Black et al., 1999; Shapira et al., 2000).

The majority of people who suffer from Internet addiction have some college education and are employed (Black et al., 1999; Shapira et al., 2000). Individuals suffering from this disorder have reported a mean of 27 hours per week spent on the Internet for nonessential purposes (Black et al., 1999). Consequently, these individuals tend to report significant social impairment, financial difficulties, and vocational impairment (Shapira et al., 2000). They report that the behavior allows distraction from other concerns, helps them feel more social, and relieves anxiety (Black et al., 1999).

Self-Injurious Behavior

Susan, a 28-year-old single attorney, cut herself every 2 or 3 days and has been doing so for the past 12 years. She cut herself on her shoulders, reporting that the blood trickling down her arms made her feel calm. With a long history of sexual abuse while growing up, Susan reports that she used multiple means of comforting herself, including sex, alcohol, and cutting. She never told anyone about the cutting as it deeply embarrassed her. Although bothered by her behavior, she felt unable to control it and missed cutting when she tried not to do so. She had never had thoughts of suicide but on one occasion the cutting was deep and required emergency care. This led her to psychiatric treatment.

The term *self-injurious behavior* encompasses a category of harmful acts deliberately inflicted upon oneself without the overt intent to die. Due to the wide variety of behaviors that result in self-injury, previous authors have suggested a classification system that divides self-injurious behaviors into four categories: stereotypic, major, compulsive, and impulsive (Simeon and Favazza, 2001). The stereotypic (rhythmic, contentless) and major (e.g., castration, amputation) self-injurious behaviors are typically components of psychotic and mental retardation syndromes, and are thus less prevalent. Compulsive self-injury is conceptualized as repetitive, ego-dystonic behavior (e.g., hair pulling, nail biting, skin picking) which an individual feels compelled to perform to relieve mounting anxiety. Finally, impulsive self-injury is characterized by episodic desires to harm oneself, a loss of control preceding the act, and a sense of gratification following the injury. Impulsive self-injurious behavior is arguably the most recognizable form of deliberate self-injury, and includes self-cutting, burning, and choking (Simeon and Favazza, 2001).

A large-scale community sample of young women found a high lifetime prevalence of 24% for both impulsive and compulsive self-injurious behaviors (Favaro et al., 2007). Yet impulsive self-injury (primarily self-cutting, self-burning, and self-hitting) was reported by 5% of the patients who self-injured, and these behaviors were more strongly associated with childhood rape, substance abuse, and lower socioeconomic status than patients engaging in compulsive self-injurious behaviors (Favaro et al., 2007). The regulation of negative affective states has been consistently identified as a motivating factor for self-injurious behavior, in particular impulsive self-injury (Lloyd-Richardson, et al., 2007; Nock and Prinstein, 2005; Rodham et al., 2004; Kumar et al., 2004).

Binge Eating Disorder

Patricia is a 58-year-old married female who reports a 20-year period of excessive eating. Unable to cite any emotional reasons for the eating, Patricia simply states that she cannot stop eating, even when she does not feel hungry. Patricia is aware of how the eating has affected her life—she is embarrassed to socialize, unable to wear shorts or a bathing suit in the summer, and has poor self-esteem—and yet is unable to control her behavior. Patricia eats enormous amounts of food in a very short time (approximately 1-hour sittings) and then regrets her behavior. Her weight has created health problems such as diabetes and hypertension. Patricia and her husband have not been intimate for the past 10 years.

Binge eating, or pathological overeating, has been reported in the medical literature at least since 1903 (McElroy and Kotwal, 2006). Although not well studied, rates of binge eating have been estimated as ranging from 1–4.6% (McElroy and Kotwal, 2006), with rates slightly higher among females.

An episode of binge eating has been defined as: (1) eating in a discrete period of time (generally 2 hours) an amount of food that is definitely larger than most people would eat; and (2) a sense of lack of control over eating during that period. In addition, the diagnosis requires that the binges are highlighted by at least three of the following: (1) eating more rapidly than normal; (2) eating until feeling uncomfortable; (3) eating large amounts of food when not physically hungry; (4) eating alone due to embarrassment; and (5) feeling disgusted with oneself (APA, 2000).

Binge eating has been associated with mounting tension or anxiety prior to the act, pleasure from the binge, and then guilt or self-disgust afterward. People rarely seek treatment for binge eating or admit to it on direct questioning. The complications of binge eating—excessive weight and related health problems (e.g., diabetes, pulmonary and cardiac problems)—are the typical reasons people seek treatment (Dingemans et al., 2002). Many people with binge eating disorder appear to recover without treatment (McElroy and Kotwal, 2006).

Conclusion

Clinicians evaluating patients with impulse control disorders should assess the circumstances that led them to seek help. In most psychiatric disorders, patients seek treatment because they are troubled by their symptoms. Patients with impulse control disorders, however, continue to struggle with the desire to engage in the behavior and their need to stop because of the mounting social, occupational, financial, or legal problems.

This chapter has presented several behavioral problems that have or could be included among disorders of impulse control. Which disorders to include, however, has been a matter of some debate. For example, drug addiction could be considered an impulse control disorder. The person has urges to use drugs, enjoys the drug use, and then feels guilty and unable to stop. It is therefore possible that one common neurobiological dysfunction may give rise to multiple behavioral symptoms. Some support for this notion comes from the fact that many people with one impulse control disorder also will report problems with another impulse disorder during their lives. In fact, many individuals switch from one behavior to another. This suggests that the same pathology may be causative in several disorders. A counterargument to this theory, however, is that many people have only one impulse disorder and never have any urge to engage in other behaviors. If the same biology underlay these behaviors, wouldn't most people switch back and forth between several behaviors? What is the role of environment in this equation? Without a clear understanding of the neurobiology that underlies these behaviors, it is not yet possible to say which behaviors share a common etiology.

CHAPTER 2

Models for Understanding Impulse Control Disorders

UNTIL RECENTLY, THERE was very little research on impulse control disorders. Although clinicians generally had seen cases of these behaviors, they had only anecdotal reports on which to base their diagnoses and treatment decisions. Without clear evidence of pathophysiology, many clinicians and researchers have used various models to understand the impulse control disorders and thereby refine treatment approaches. This has entailed examining clinical characteristics, family history, comorbidity, and treatment response and then using these data to compare impulse disorders to other more thoroughly researched disorders. Various questions are still being examined: Are the impulse control disorders similar to obsessive-compulsive disorder, or are they more like substance use disorders? Other models have suggested that perhaps the impulse control disorders are really just symptoms of, or responses to, other disorders such as bipolar disorder, major depressive disorder, or attention-deficit/hyperactivity disorder (ADHD). Further complicating this picture is that, given the heterogeneity between and within impulse control disorders, any or all of these models may in fact be appropriate for certain individuals.

Obsessive-Compulsive Spectrum Model

As seen in the case of Sylvia (from the introduction), kleptomania, like all of the impulse control disorders, is characterized by a repetitive behavior and impaired inhibition. The irresistible and uncontrollable shoplifting characteristic of kleptomania suggests a similarity to the frequently excessive, unnecessary, and unwanted rituals of obsessive-compulsive disorder. The behaviors of impulse control disorders, like the compulsive behavior in obsessive-compulsive disorder, are often urge-driven and characterized by lack of control. Furthermore, impulse control behaviors, like the compulsions of obsessive-compulsive disorder, often provide a reduction in tension that is described as rewarding (Ettelt et al., 2007).

Studies examining rates of comorbid disorders in impulse control disorders have found that 5–35% of individuals with an impulse control disorder have co-occurring obsessive-compulsive disorder (Christenson et al., 1991; Schlosser et al., 1994; Black et al., 1997; McElroy et al., 1998), with some having much higher rates than others (35% of compulsive buyers have obsessive-compulsive disorder compared to only 4.5% of pyromaniacs). Subjects with impulse control disorders may also score high on measures of compulsivity (Blanco et al., 2004). Additionally, individuals with some impulse control disorders (kleptomania, compulsive buying) frequently report hoarding symptoms that resemble those of individuals with obsessive-compulsive disorder (Goldman, 1991; Christenson et al., 1994).

There are, however, some clear differences between impulse control disorders and obsessive-compulsive disorder. For example, most individuals with impulse control disorders report their behaviors as pleasurable (Stanley and Cohen, 1999; Schlosser et al., 1994; Black et al., 1997; McElroy et al., 1998; Grant and Kim, 2002a; Grant et al., 2006) and rarely elicited by an obsession (Grant and Potenza, 2006). In addition, neurobiological studies suggest that individuals with impulse control disorders may have neural features (relatively decreased activation within cortical, basal ganglionic, and thalamic brain regions) distinct from brain activation patterns observed in cue-provocation studies of obsessive-compulsive disorder (relatively increased cortico–basal ganglionic–thalamic activity). Individuals with impulse control disorders are generally sensation seeking, whereas individuals with obsessive-compulsive disorder are generally harm avoidant with a compulsive risk-aversive end point to their behaviors (Kim and Grant, 2001). Perhaps most important, however, is that the response of impulse control disorders to pharmacotherapy (particularly serotonergic medications) has been, unlike that of obsessive-compulsive disorder, equivocal at best (Grant and Potenza, 2006).

Although the obsessive-compulsive spectrum model has multiple strengths, the failure of impulse control disorders to respond as robustly to treatment has therefore raised the question of whether other reasonable alternative understandings of these disorders should be entertained. Of course, the diagnostic categories of impulse control disorders and obsessive-compulsive disorder may be too broad and thereby complicate our understanding of the relationship of these disorders. Research has suggested that the obsessive-compulsive spectrum disorders may have various clusters that cohere based on clinical and possibly genetic grounds (Lochner et al., 2005). Further research examining various abnormalities of the impulsive-compulsive neurocircuitry may lead us to finding that there is a subtype of impulse control disorder that is more like a subtype of obsessive-compulsive disorder, whereas other impulse control subtypes have more in common with other disorders such as addictions.

Behavioral Addiction Model

To examine whether impulse control disorders should be considered addictions, clinical similarities between these disorders and substance use disorders can be considered. For many but not all individuals with impulse control disorders, their behavior shares common features with the core elements of addictions: (1) an urge to engage in a behavior with negative consequences; (2) mounting tension unless the behavior is completed; (3) rapid but temporary reduction of the urge after completion of the behavior; (4) return of the urge over hours, days, or weeks; (5) external cues unique to the behavior; (6) secondary conditioning by external and internal cues (dysphoria, boredom); and (7) hedonic feeling early in the addiction (Marks, 1990). These features have led to a description of impulse control disorders as "addictions without the drug" or "behavioral addictions."

Unlike compulsions in obsessive-compulsive disorder, impulse behaviors have a pleasurable quality. The person might look forward to getting home at the end of the day to go gamble or shoplift. Many people with an impulse disorder report an urge or craving state prior to their behavior, as do individuals with substance use disorders prior to drinking or using drugs. Additionally, the impulse behavior decreases anxiety as drinking often does, for example, in alcohol use disorders.

Similar to individuals with substance use disorders, many people with impulse control disorders also have problems inhibiting or delaying impulses. Phenomenological data further support a relationship between impulse control disorders and substance addictions; for example, high rates of impulse control disorders and drug addictions have been reported during adolescence and young adulthood, and the telescoping phenomenon (defined as the rapid rate of progression from initial to problematic behavioral engagement) in women as compared with men, initially described for alcoholism, has been applied to impulse control disorders such as pathological gambling.

Sylvia described her shoplifting as a rush or a high. The behavior was intensely pleasurable. In fact, when she compared it to either sexual satisfaction or previous use of cocaine, she would always affirm that shoplifting was her greatest high. Sylvia's high, however, was short-lived, usually lasting only a few minutes after she left a store. Intense despair and shame followed. Because of the pleasurable quality of the behavior, Sylvia would have urges to shoplift on a daily basis. Although aware of the possible negative consequences and the distress that followed the shoplifting, Sylvia continued to shoplift because the intensity of the rush, albeit short-lived, always seemed to overwhelm her better judgment regarding negative consequences.

The best evidence for thinking of impulse control disorders as addictions comes from genetic and pathophysiology studies. A possible genetic link between impulse control disorders and substance abuse is supported by data that substance use disorders are more common in relatives of subjects with impulse control disorders than in the general population. Studies that have used control groups (for trichotillomania, pathological gambling, kleptomania, and compulsive buying) have found that the first-degree relatives of impulsive subjects were significantly more likely to have substance use disorders (Schlosser et al., 1994; Grant, 2003a; Black et al., 1998; Black et al., 2006).

Consistent with the notion that impulse control disorders share possible neurobiological links with drug addictions, studies have demonstrated the high comorbidity of some impulse control disorders (e.g., pathological gambling) with substance use disorders, with rates of nicotine dependence approaching 70%, alcohol abuse or dependence in the range of 50% to 75%, and other drug use problems nearing

40%. In addition, a growing body of literature implicates multiple neurotransmitter systems (e.g., serotonergic, dopaminergic, noradrenergic, opioidergic) as well as familial and inherited factors in the pathophysiology of impulse control disorders, which is consistent with previous research on drug addictions.

Impulse control disorders have also demonstrated response to opioid antagonists, which have been successful in treating substance use disorders (Grant et al., 2006; Kim et al., 2001). The finding that impulse control disorders may be responsive to antiaddiction medications may support the inclusion of impulse control disorders within an addictive spectrum.

Ultimately, an assessment of the relationship of impulse control disorders to established addictive disorders needs to consider the respective etiologies. Unfortunately, knowledge of these psychiatric disorders is not yet advanced enough to answer this question. Nonetheless, evidence suggests that corticostriatal circuitry mediates reward processes via dopamine activity within the ventral striatum, and this has been supported by research in the field of addictions (Chambers et al., 2003). There is also evidence that dopaminergic agonists increase the symptoms of impulse control disorders consistent with the neurobiology of drug addiction (Grant and Potenza, 2006). The compulsive behavior of impulse control disorders could therefore be conceptualized for some individuals as due to disruptions of this reward circuitry.

Affective Disorder Models

Although much data from diverse sources support a close relationship between impulse control disorders and either obsessive-compulsive disorder or substance use disorders, other models that are not mutually exclusive have been proposed. The association of impulse control disorders with mood disorders has led to their grouping as an affective spectrum disorder (McElroy et al., 1992, 1996). This affective spectrum model hypothesizes that impulse control disorders may in fact share a common pathophysiology with major depressive disorder or bipolar disorder (McElroy et al., 1996).

Many people with impulse control disorers report that the pleasurable yet problematic behaviors alleviate negative emotional states.

Although many individuals with impulse control disorders may report that depression drives the behavior, one must consider the possibility of a mixed manic state. Also, are impulsive behaviors associated with an affective state merely symptoms of the primary mood disorder? Currently no research has described whether impulse control behaviors differ when they are secondary to mood disorder, compared to being independent disorders. Although mood symptoms are common in individuals with impulse control disorders, it is not always clear whether the mood symptoms precede the impulse control disorder or may be considered reactive.

Because the behaviors are risky, dangerous, and self-destructive, the question has also been raised whether impulse control disorders reflect subclinical mania or cyclothymia (McElroy et al., 1996). In addition, both impulse control disorders and bipolar disorder include impulsive thinking—that is, acting without considering the long-term consequences of the behavior. After the impulsive behavior is performed, individuals will often describe a depressed mood or guilt following the act, resembling the affective instability and mood swings seen in bipolar disorder (McElroy et al., 1996). The elevated rates of co-occurrence between impulse control disorders and depression and bipolar disorder may further support their inclusion within an affective spectrum. Additional support for the affective disorders model comes from early reports of treatment response to antidepressants and mood stabilizers (McElroy et al., 1991, 1996).

Several issues complicate the argument for an affective disorders model. Depression in impulse control disorders, however, may be distinct from primary or uncomplicated depression; for example, depression in impulse control disorders may represent a response to shame and embarrassment (Grant and Kim, 2002a). In addition, rates of co-occurrence of impulse control disorders and bipolar disorder may not be as high as initially thought. Finally, the response to antidepressants and mood stabilizers is not as robust as initially anticipated (McElroy et al., 1991), and impulse control disorders respond to opioid antagonists, which have not demonstrated efficacy in mood disorders.

Nonetheless, brain imaging studies have found common regional brain activity differences distinguishing bipolar subjects from controls and pathological gambling subjects from controls during a cognitive task involving attention and response inhibition (Blumberg et al.,

TABLE 2.1

Lifetime Rates of Affective Disorders in Impulse Control Disorders

Impulse Control Disorder	Lifetime Rates of Major Depressive Disorder (%)	Lifetime Rates of Bipolar Disorder (%)
Pathological gambling	50	20
Intermittent explosive disorder	37	11–55
Kleptomania	59–75	9–27
Pyromania	48	14
Compulsive buying	28–50	10–35
Compulsive sexual behavior	39	14
Trichotillomania	39–57	5

2003; Potenza et al., 2003). For these reasons, the relationship between impulse control disorders and mood disorders requires clarification, particularly as appropriate classification has implications for treatment development.

Sylvia's shoplifting responded to naltrexone, an opioid antagonist, but had failed to respond to an antidepressant. Her kleptomania appears to have greater similarities to substance use disorders than affective disorders. Of course, the two are not mutually exclusive. In fact, individuals like Sylvia may have a co-occurring depression or bipolar disorder that exacerbates their shoplifting but is not the cause of the behavior (Table 2.1). In those cases, an opioid antagonist in combination with an antidepressant or mood stabilizer may be most beneficial.

Attention-Deficit/Hyperactivity Disorder (ADHD) Model

The ADHD model for impulse control disorders is just beginning to generate research attention. The main symptoms of ADHD in adults are impulsiveness and inattention (APA, 2000). An early study of pathological gambling found that 24% of subjects suffered from co-occurring ADHD (compared to a 3–7% lifetime rate in the general population; Specker et al., 1996). One study also found that 15% of individuals with kleptomania have met criteria for ADHD in their lifetime (Presta et al., 2002). No further studies of the possible clinical relationship of ADHD to impulse control disorders have been published as of this writing.

Anecdotal reports of the use of stimulant medications in the treatment of a subset of pathological gamblers who appear to have an inattentive, impulsive drive to gamble support the hypothesis that in a subset of individuals, impulse control disorders may be functionally related to ADHD. An open-label study of bupropion (a medication found to be effective in treating adults with ADHD) in pathological gambling found that subjects responded well to medication, independent of its antidepressant effects (Black, 2004), although a double-blind follow-up study failed to confirm these earlier results (Black et al., 2007).

Heterogeneity of Impulse Control Disorders

Although people with impulse control disorders share various features in common, our understanding of which model will be most effective may be complicated by failing to understand the heterogeneity of impulse control disorders. On the diagnosis level, perhaps some impulse control disorders would be better served by an addiction model, while others may have more in common with obsessive-compulsive disorder. Toward that end, research has tried to find similarities between various impulse control disorders. A cluster analysis has demonstrated that kleptomania, compulsive buying, and intermittent explosive disorder may belong to an impulsive subgroup, while trichotillomania, pathological gambling, and compulsive sexual behavior may belong to a reward deficiency group (Lochner et al., 2005). But even this type of analysis may be too simple.

On an individual level, perhaps some people with pathological gambling have more in common neurobiologically with some people with compulsive sexual behavior than they do with other gamblers. Neurobiology may cut across disorders. This may explain why one person with pathological gambling seems to fit the affective model well but another fits the ADHD model. A particular impulse behavior, such as gambling, may be a manifestation of several pathophysiologies. Family history, comorbidity, genetics, neuroimaging, and treatment response may all be means by which this complexity can be better understood.

Effective Treatment May Depend Upon Proper Conceptualization

Although not a direct measure of pathophysiology, responses to pharmacotherapy may suggest different or shared neurobiologies. As with obsessive-compulsive disorder, addictions, and psychiatric disorders in general, treatment for impulse control disorders has largely focused on pharmacological and behavioral interventions.

Various pharmacological agents have shown benefit for impulse control disorders, and these findings underscore the importance of the conceptualization. Opioid antagonists are efficacious and FDA approved for the treatment of alcohol and opioid dependence. If a disorder for a particular person is conceptualized as an addiction, the opioid antagonists may be an effective choice. In two studies of pathological gambling where enrollment was based on having urges to gamble (a parallel to alcohol or drug craving), an opioid antagonist (naltrexone, nalmefene) was shown effective in reducing gambling urges, thoughts, and behaviors (Kim et al., 2001; Grant et al., 2006). Behaviorally, opioid antagonist administration leads to diminished urges and longer periods of abstinence consistent with a mechanism of action involving ventral striatal dopamine systems. For naltrexone to be effective, however, these urges seem to need to be triggered by an anticipated positively reinforcing stimulus instead of an aversive stimulus such as the ones that are triggered when an obsessive patient touches an unclean item. The efficacy of opioid antagonists and by extension the hypothesized underlying neurobiology would suggest a pathophysiology for some people with impulse control disorders distinct from that hypothesized to underlie obsessive-compulsive disorder or major depressive disorder. Therefore, it is important to pay attention to the presenting clinical symptomatology as it might guide treatment choice or predict treatment outcome. For example, those people with impulse control disorders who respond to opioid antagonists may preferentially be those who derive pleasure from the behavior, have family histories of substance use disorders, and have cravings.

A study of lithium for pathological gamblers with some bipolar spectrum disorder was found effective in a double-blind design (Hollander et al., 2005). The study examined the idea that not all pathological gamblers had the same pathophysiology underlying their gambling symptoms. Pathological gamblers with a bipolar spectrum comorbidity might better fit the affective disorder model than the addiction model. It is possible that treating those subjects with naltrexone or nalmefene would have failed. In that case, we might believe that lithium was not helpful for pathological gambling. Instead, we are beginning to understand that clinical presentation (as a proxy for pathophysiology) should dictate choice of medication option.

It is likely that heterogeneity exists in impulse control disorders, and that some individuals with impulse control disorders might be more similar to those with obsessive-compulsive disorder and respond to a serotonergic medication while others might be more similar to those with addictions and may respond to opioid antagonists. While these notions remain speculative and require additional studies to examine their appropriateness, the approach of using clinical symptomatology, including symptoms relating to co-occurring disorders, to guide pharmacological treatment selection is gaining empirical support for impulse control disorders.

Similarly, it could be hypothesized that behavioral therapy might be selected in part by clinical symptomatology. For example, prominent urges and withdrawal symptoms may suggest the use of relapse prevention techniques. Further research is needed to empirically validate specific treatments for individuals with impulse control disorders and help guide the selection of specific treatments for specific groups of people with the disorder. Subtyping impulse control disorders based on clinical similarities to other disorders (e.g., ADHD), existence of co-occurring conditions (e.g., bipolar disorder), or core features of the behavior (e.g., cravings) may all be useful ways to decide on treatment interventions. Although subtyping needs more research, the early studies suggest that looking beyond the *DSM-IV* diagnostic criteria and examining what maintains impulse control behaviors may be clinically helpful.

Conclusion

Sylvia's case illustrates not only the similarities between impulse control disorders, obsessive-compulsive disorder, and addictive disorders, but also the complexity of impulse behaviors in general. Currently, there are no pharmacological treatments for impulse control disorders that have consistently demonstrated efficacy. The distress of patients with impulse control disorders highlights the importance of exploring alternative models to explain these disorders. Further exploration into the neurobiology of impulse control disorders is necessary to substantiate the hypotheses presented in this chapter. More comprehensive information, which could be gleaned from such studies, has significant potential to advance prevention and treatment strategies for those who suffer from disorders characterized by impaired impulse control.

CHAPTER 3

The Compulsive-Impulsive Spectrum: The Compulsive Aspects of Impulse Control Disorders

BARBARA, A 28-YEAR-OLD single female, reports a history (beginning in late adolescence) of uncontrollable buying. Over the course of a few months, she became preoccupied with buying things and thought about shopping all day. Barbara currently shops three to four times each week. She reports a thrill when she is in the store followed by a "sense of calm or peace" as she leaves the store after purchasing her items. She primarily buys clothing and jewelry. She usually purchases multiple versions of the same item and keeps them unused in her closet. She describes the items as providing a sense of security, and she feels unable to part with any of the unused items. Barbara enjoys the interaction with store clerks and feels important and "taken seriously" due to her purchases. Barbara often shops for hours at a time. She may even leave work early with projects unfinished in order to get to a store and buy something. In addition, she lies to her husband about the amount she is spending and hides the credit card bills. Unable to pay the minimum due on her bills, and unable to admit her behavior to her husband, Barbara reports extreme despair and stress.

Barbara suffers from compulsive buying, but many clinicians would diagnose her with obsessive-compulsive disorder. On the one hand, she displays repetitive buying, with preoccupation, and the buying reduces a feeling of anxiety. Her behavior, therefore, shares some of the same features as obsessive-compulsive disorder. In addition, she hoards the items she buys and feels comforted by having multiple copies of items. Does the diagnosis even matter? Evidence suggests that selective serotonin reuptake inhibitors, the first-line pharmacological treatment for obsessive-compulsive disorder, have not shown benefit in treating compulsive buying. Although these antidepressants may help with Barbara's despair, they may not aid in reducing her compulsive buying behavior. Also, therapies beneficial for obsessive-compulsive disorder (such as cognitive behavioral therapy) need dramatic modifications when used to treat compulsive buying. Therefore, although impulse control disorders share features with obsessive-compulsive disorder, proper diagnosis of the impulse control disorder may have treatment implications.

The American Psychiatric Association defines compulsivity as the performance of repetitive behaviors with the goal of reducing or preventing anxiety or distress, not providing pleasure or gratification (APA, 2000). Although obsessive-compulsive disorder may have the most obvious compulsive features, compulsivity is often a prominent symptom in multiple psychiatric disorders such as substance use disorders, personality disorders, or schizophrenia (Goldstein and Volkow, 2002).

The domains of impulsivity and compulsivity have been considered by some as being diametrically opposed, but the relationship appears more intricate. Compulsivity and impulsivity may co-occur simultaneously in the same disorders or at different times within the same disorders, thereby complicating both our understanding and treatment of certain behaviors. In fact, impulse control disorders have recently been found to have features of compulsivity.

Historically, one conceptualization of impulse control disorders has been as part of an obsessive-compulsive spectrum (Hollander, 1993). This initial understanding of impulse control disorders was based on available data on the clinical characteristics of these disorders, patterns of familial transmission, and responses to pharmacological and psychosocial treatments. Data from studies of impulse control disorders, however, suggest a complex relationship between impulse control disorders and obsessive-compulsive disorder, heterogeneity within the impulse control disorders, and a complicated overlap between impulsivity and compulsivity.

Pathological Gambling

Compulsivity refers to repetitive behaviors performed according to certain rules or in a stereotyped fashion, and pathological gambling is associated with many features of compulsivity. Pathological gambling is characterized by the repetitive behavior of gambling and impaired inhibition of the behavior. People who pathologically gamble often describe gambling as difficult to resist or control, and in this respect it appears on the surface to be similar to the frequently excessive, unnecessary, and unwanted rituals of obsessive-compulsive disorder. Additionally, individuals with pathological gambling often have specific rituals for luck associated with their gambling—for example, wearing certain clothes when gambling or gambling on particular slot machines. Another putative link between pathological gambling and obsessive-compulsive disorder is the propensity of individuals with pathological gambling to engage in excessive, possibly harmful behavior that leads to significant impairment in social or occupational functioning and causes personal distress (Grant and Potenza, 2004b). As with obsessive-compulsive disorder, the compulsive behavior of pathological gambling (i.e., the gambling) is often triggered by aversive or stressful stimuli (Potenza et al., 2003). Individuals with pathological gambling often report that their urges to gamble are triggered by feelings of anxiety, sadness, or loneliness (Grant and Kim, 2001; Ladd and Petry, 2002).

Studies consistently find that individuals with pathological gambling have high rates of lifetime mood (60–76%), anxiety (16–40%), and other (23%) impulse control disorders (Black and Moyer, 1998; Crockford and el-Guebaly, 1998; Argo and Black, 2004). Rates of co-occurrence between pathological gambling and obsessive-compulsive disorder, however, have been largely inconsistent. For example, in samples of pathological gambling subjects, rates of co-occurring obsessive-compulsive disorder have ranged from 1% to 20% (Argo and Black, 2004), with some but not all studies finding higher rates of obsessive-compulsive disorder than estimated for the general population (approximately 2%). However, the St. Louis Epidemiologic Catchment Area study found no significant relationship between problem gambling and obsessive-compulsive disorder (an odds ratio of 0.6 for obsessive-compulsive disorder in problem gamblers as compared with nongamblers; Cunningham-Williams et al., 1998). Although this study collected data in the 1980s, it is the only study published to date in which a community sample was assessed for *DSM*-based diagnoses for both obsessive-compulsive disorder and pathological gambling.

Studies of pathological gambling among individuals with obsessive-compulsive disorder have reported little if any relationship between the disorders. Although studies of small obsessive-compulsive disorder samples have reported pathological gambling rates of 2.2–2.6% (Fontenelle et al., 2005; Matsunaga et al., 2005), a study of a large sample of subjects with primary obsessive-compulsive disorder (n = 293), found rates of current (0.3%) and lifetime (1.0%) pathological gambling (Grant et al., 2006) that were no greater than those in the general population (0.7–1.6%). These more recent findings are consistent with those from a sample of over 2,000 individuals with obsessive-compulsive disorder, in which lifetime rates of pathological gambling were under 1% (Jaisoorya et al., 2003). Similarly, a family study of obsessive-compulsive disorder probands did not find evidence of a significant relationship between obsessive-compulsive disorder and pathological gambling or obsessive-compulsive disorder and impulse control disorders in general, with the exception of trichotillomania and pathological skin picking (Bienvenu et al., 2000).

Family history studies of pathological gambling subjects are limited. Black and colleagues examined 17 subjects with pathological gambling and 75 of their first-degree relatives (Black et al., 2003). The study found that 1% of the first-degree relatives had obsessive-compulsive disorder (similar to rates in the community) and 0% in the control group. Although the sample was small, the study used a control group as well as structured interviews for the subjects and first-degree relatives. As in the study of obsessive-compulsive disorder probands, the family study of pathological gambling subjects and their relatives failed to find a link between the two disorders.

Assessing compulsivity in obsessive-compulsive disorder and in pathological gambling and other impulse control disorders has the potential to clarify the role of compulsivity in each disorder. Although many studies have assessed impulsivity and related constructs (e.g., sensation seeking) in pathological gambling, relatively few have explored the construct of compulsivity in pathological gambling. In one study, pathological gamblers scored higher than normal controls on a measure of compulsivity (Padua Inventory; Blaszczynski, 1999). A study attempting to understand the compulsive and impulsive dimensions of pathological gambling examined 38 subjects with the Padua Inventory before and after 12 weeks of treatment with paroxetine (Blanco et al., 2004). The Padua Inventory measures obsessions and compulsions and contains four factors: (1) impaired control over mental activities, which assesses ruminations and exaggerated doubts; (2) fear of contamination; (3) checking; and (4) impaired control over motor activities, which measures urges and worries related to motor behavior, such as violent impulses (Sanavio, 1988). At baseline, pathological gambling symptom severity was associated with features of both impulsivity and compulsivity (specifically, Factors 1 and 4 of the Padua Inventory). During treatment, overall scores on measures of impulsivity and compulsivity diminished, with significant decreases in Factor 1 (impaired control over mental activities) and the impulsiveness subscales of the Eysenck Impulsivity Questionnaire. This study suggests that compulsivity and impulsivity in pathological gambling interact in a complex fashion, and that measures of impulsivity and compulsivity have relevance with respect to treatment outcome. A corollary of this finding is that compulsivity or impulsivity (or specific aspects of each) might represent treatment targets for pathological gambling.

Although pathogenesis is arguably the most valid indicator of whether disorders are related, research on possible neurobiological correlates of pathological gambling has been sparse and the evidence suggests a different pathology from that seen in obsessive-compulsive disorder. A functional magnetic resonance imaging (MRI) study of gambling urges in male pathological gamblers suggests that pathological gambling has neural features (relatively decreased activation within cortical, basal ganglionic, and thalamic brain regions in pathological gambling subjects as compared to control) distinct from the brain activation pattern observed in cue provocation studies of obsessive-compulsive disorder (relatively increased cortico–basal ganglionic–thalamic activity; Saxena and Rauch, 2000; Potenza et al., 2003). Until more systematic comparison studies of these two disorders are conducted, the neurobiological relationship of pathological gambling and obsessive-compulsive disorder remains to be clarified.

Originally there was a suggestion that pathological gambling, like obsessive-compulsive disorder, might demonstrate a preferential response to serotonin reuptake inhibitors. Data from double-blind randomized pharmacotherapy trials of serotonin reuptake inhibitors in the treatment of pathological gambling, however, have been inconclusive (Grant and Potenza, 2006c). In addition, pathological gambling has demonstrated responses to opioid antagonists (Kim et al., 2001b; Grant et al., 2006c), drugs that have not been shown to be effective in treating obsessive-compulsive disorder.

Cognitive and behavioral treatments that address the compulsive aspect of pathological gambling have shown early benefit (Hodgins and Petry, 2004). The cognitive behavioral therapy for pathological gambling, however, differs from the exposure and response prevention treatment used for obsessive-compulsive disorder (Simpson and Fallon, 2000). In pathological gambling, cognitive therapy focuses on changing the patient's beliefs regarding perceived control over randomly determined events. Cognitive therapy helps the patient understand that the laws of probability, not ritualistic behavior, control the outcome of gambling. In one study, individual cognitive therapy resulted in reduced gambling frequency and increased perceived self-control over gambling when compared with a wait list (Hodgins and Petry, 2004). A second study that included relapse prevention also produced improvement in gambling symptoms compared to a wait list (Hodgins and Petry, 2004).

Although on the surface pathological gambling shares many phenomenological features with obsessive-compulsive disorder, the majority of data suggest that the co-occurrence of these disorders is not elevated, different neurobiology likely underlies the two disorders, and treatment approaches differ. Thus it seems that pathological gambling has multiple compulsive features and yet is not associated with obsessive-compulsive disorder. One reason for this observation may involve limitations of categorical diagnoses. An alternate explanation that is not mutually exclusive is that although compulsive features are observed in each disorder, the underlying biologies differ. Another consideration is that aspects of compulsivity may differ between the disorders.

Trichotillomania

The repetitive motor behavior of hair pulling with perceived diminished control bears a striking resemblance to obsessive-compulsive disorder. In contrast to obsessive-compulsive disorder, in which compulsions occur in a variety of situations, individuals with trichotillomania tend to pull most often when engaged in sedentary activities (Stanley and Cohen, 1999). Although the hair pulling in trichotillomania decreases anxiety, as do compulsions in obsessive-compulsive disorder, it may also produce feelings of pleasure, whereas the compulsions of obsessive-compulsive disorder typically do not.

Trichotillomania has traditionally been considered to predominantly affect females (Swedo and Leonard, 1992, whereas obsessive-compulsive disorder has a 1:1 gender ratio. Rates of other psychiatric disorders are elevated in individuals with trichotillomania: generalized anxiety disorder (27–32%) and substance abuse (15–20%). In particular, rates of co-occurring obsessive-compulsive disorder are significantly higher (13–27%); Christenson and Mansueto, 1999) than those found in the community (1–3%), and this finding raises the possibility of an underlying common neurobiological pathway for the compulsivity seen in these two disorders. Interestingly, trichotillomania is not associated with higher rates of obsessive-compulsive symptoms, with scores generally in the normal range (Stanley and Cohen, 1999). Neurocognitive testing has also demonstrated a lack of a relationship, with trichotillomania subjects demonstrating poor motor inhibition, whereas obsessive-compulsive subjects exhibited motor and cognitive inflexibility (Chamberlain et al., 2006).

Rates of trichotillomania among individuals with obsessive-compulsive disorder are inconsistent across studies. Three studies of small samples of obsessive-compulsive subjects have reported rates ranging from 4.6% to 7.1% (Matsunaga et al., 2005; Fontenelle et al., 2005; du Toit et al., 2005). One larger study of 293 subjects with obsessive-compulsive disorder reported lifetime and current rates of trichotillomania of 1.4% and 1.0% respectively (Grant et al., 2006). As with pathological gambling, the question remains whether it would be more valuable to examine the domain of compulsivity across these disorders as a means of understanding potential pathophysiology.

A relationship between trichotillomania and obsessive-compulsive disorder is partially supported by findings that obsessive-compulsive disorder is common in relatives of subjects with trichotillomania. Although family history studies of trichotillomania are limited, one study involved 22 subjects with trichotillomania and 102 first-degree relatives. When compared to a control group (n = 33 with 182 first-degree relatives), there were significantly more relatives of the trichotillomania probands who had obsessive-compulsive disorder (2.9%) compared to the control group (Schlosser et al., 1994). A family study of obsessive-compulsive probands found a higher proportion of case subjects with trichotillomania than control subjects with the disorder (4% vs. 1%), although the difference was not statistically significant given the sample size (Bienvenu et al., 2000).

Treatments evaluated for trichotillomania include pharmacological and behavioral interventions. It is well established that the pharmacological first-line treatment for obsessive-compulsive disorder is a serotonin reuptake inhibitor (e.g., clomipramine, fluvoxamine, fluoxetine). The data regarding the efficacies of such drugs for trichotillomania, however, are less convincing. Although clomipramine has shown benefit for trichotillomania (Swedo et al., 1989), other serotonin reuptake inhibitors have demonstrated mixed results in three randomized trials of trichotillomania (O'Sullivan et al., 1999). Other pharmacological agents (e.g., naltrexone, lithium, olanzapine) that have shown benefit for trichotillomania have not been effective for obsessive-compulsive disorder and therefore question the overlap between these disorders. Both obsessive-compulsive disorder and trichotillomania respond to behavioral interventions; however, the mode of behavioral treatment differs quite substantially for trichotillomania.

Kleptomania

Like obsessive-compulsive disorder, kleptomania usually first appears during late adolescence or early adulthood (Grant and Kim, 2002a). The repetitive shoplifting behavior seen in kleptomania is suggestive of a compulsion. In addition, the majority of individuals with kleptomania (63%) hoard particular items that they steal (Grant and Kim, 2002a).

Unlike obsessive-compulsive disorder, however, women are twice as likely to suffer from kleptomania as are men (Grant, 2006). Personality examinations of individuals with kleptomania suggest, however, that they are generally sensation seeking (Grant and Kim, 2002c) and impulsive (Bayle et al., 2003) and thereby differ from individuals with obsessive-compulsive disorder, who are generally harm avoidant with a compulsive risk-aversive end point to their behaviors. Unlike individuals with obsessive-compulsive disorder, people with kleptomania may also report an urge or craving state prior to engaging in the stealing and a hedonic quality during the performance of the thefts (McElroy et al., 1991).

High rates of other psychiatric disorders have been found in patients with kleptomania. Rates of lifetime comorbid affective disorders range from 59% to 100% (Grant, 2006). Studies have also found high lifetime rates of comorbid anxiety disorders (60–80%) and substance use disorders (23–50%; Grant, 2006). The extent to which obsessive-compulsive disorder and kleptomania co-occur is not well understood. Rates of obsessive-compulsive disorder in samples of individuals with kleptomania have ranged from 6.5% (Grant, 2003a) to 60% (Presta et al., 2002). Conversely, rates of kleptomania in obsessive-compulsive disorder samples suggest a higher rate of co-occurrence than found in the community (2.2–5.9%; Matsunaga et al., 2005; Fontanelle et al., 2005). A study of 293 subjects with obsessive-compulsive disorder reported current and lifetime rates of kleptomania (0.3% and 1.0%) (Grant et al., 2006) that were lower than rates found in a population of general psychiatric inpatients (7.8% and 9.3% respectively; Grant et al., 2005). Large psychiatric epidemiological studies have typically excluded measures of kleptomania, thus limiting the available knowledge regarding its prevalence and patterns of co-occurrence with other psychiatric disorders.

A family history study compared 31 individuals with kleptomania and 152 first-degree relatives with 35 control subjects and 118 of their first-degree relatives (Grant, 2003). The study found that 0.7% of the kleptomania probands' relatives suffered from obsessive-compulsive disorder, compared to 0% in the control families—a comparison that was not statistically different.

Unlike obsessive-compulsive disorder, there does not appear to be a preferential response of kleptomania to serotonergic medications. In one open-label study followed by double-blind discontinuation, escitalopram was not different from placebo during the double-blind phase (Koran et al., 2007a). In the only other formal trial of medication for kleptomania, 9 of 10 subjects treated with naltrexone for 12 weeks in an open-label design demonstrated improvement (Grant and Kim, 2002b).

Other Impulse Control Disorders

Fewer studies have examined the relationship of the other impulse control disorders to obsessive-compulsive disorder. In general, the impulse control disorders (pyromania, compulsive sexual behavior, pathological skin picking, compulsive buying, internet addiction, and binge eating) share a similar age of onset with obsessive-compulsive disorder (usually late adolescence or early adulthood). Also, the other impulse disorders (except, arguably, intermittent explosive disorder) are characterized by their repetitive behaviors (fire setting, skin picking, sexual behavior, spending, bingeing, Internet use), which share phenomenological similarities to the compulsions of obsessive-compulsive disorder. In the case of compulsive buying, there is also an element of hoarding that is seen in kleptomania and obsessive-compulsive disorder.

TABLE 3.1

Rates of Obsessive-Compulsive Disorder in Individuals with Impulse Control Disorders

Impulse Control Disorders	Rate of Co-occurring Obsessive-Compulsive Disorder (%)
Pathological gambling	1–20
Kleptomania	6.5–60
Pyromania	4.5
Intermittent explosive disorder	22
Trichotillomania	13–27
Pathological skin picking	6–52
Binge eating disorder	0–1
Compulsive sexual behavior	14
Internet addiction	0–15
Compulsive buying	4–35

In the cases of compulsive buying, binge eating disorder, and pathological skin picking, women are overrepresented, which is not the case with obsessive-compulsive disorder. Unlike obsessive-compulsive individuals, people with compulsive sexual behavior, compulsive buying, pyromania, and Internet addiction may report urges or cravings prior to engaging in the behavior.

Rates of obsessive-compulsive disorder in samples of individuals with these other impulse control disorders have either been mixed, as in the case of compulsive buying (McElroy et al., 1994; Schlosser et al., 1994), or only slightly elevated compared to rates in the community (Table 3.1; Black et al., 1997). Controlled family studies with these other impulse control disorders are currently lacking, and therefore any putative familial link between these disorders and obsessive-compulsive disorder cannot be determined. As with the other impulse control disorders, there does not appear to be a preferential response of compulsive buying, compulsive sexual behavior, pathological skin picking, or binge eating disorder to serotonergic medications (Black et al., 2000; Ninan et al., 2000a; McElroy and Kotwal, 2006; Koran et al., 2007a & b;) as compulsive buying and compulsive sexual behavior have responded to naltrexone (Grant 2003b; Raymond et al. 2002), binge eating has responded to topiramate (McElroy et al., 2003), and pathological skin picking has shown improvement with lamictal (Grant et al., in press).

If a relationship exists between impulse control disorders and obsessive-compulsive disorder, there should be evidence either that obsessive-compulsive disorder is overrepresented in patients with impulse control disorders or that impulse control disorders are over-represented in patients with obsessive-compulsive disorder. As shown above, the studies examining rates of obsessive-compulsive disorder in patients with impulse control disorders have reported inconsistent results, with some impulse control disorders showing relatively high rates of comorbidity with obsessive-compulsive disorder (trichotillo-mania, compulsive buying), others demonstrating low rates (intermittent explosive disorder, pathological gambling, and compulsive sexual behavior), and others (kleptomania, pathological skin picking) with wide ranges that suggest possible biases in ascertainment of comorbidity (Table 3.1).

Conversely, studies examining rates of impulse control disorders among obsessive-compulsive subjects demonstrate an equally complex picture, with elevated rates of some impulse control disorders (skin picking, trichotillomania), and low rates of others (kleptomania, compulsive sexual behavior, pathological gambling; Table 3.2).

TABLE 3.2

Rates of Current Impulse Control Disorders in Individuals With Obsessive-Compulsive Disorder

| Impulse Control Disorder | Obsessive-Compulsive Disorder Subjects | | | | | |
	$n = 45$ (Fontenelle et al., 2005)	$n = 293$ (Grant et al., 2006)	$n = 153$ (Matsunaga et al., 2005)	$n = 85$ (du Toitet al., 2001)	$n = 75$ (Cullen et al., 2001)	$n = 60$ (Lejoyeux et al., 2005)
Skin picking	6 (13.3)	26 (8.9)	18 (11.8)	19 (22.4)	18 (24.0)	N/A
Trichotillomania	3 (6.7)	4 (1.4)	7 (4.6)	6 (7.1)	N/A	N/A
Compulsive sexual behavior	1 (2.2)	N/A	3 (2.0)	4 (4.7)	N/A	N/A
Kleptomania	1 (2.2)	3 (1.0)	9 (5.9)	2 (2.4)	N/A	N/A
Compulsive buying	1 (2.2)	N/A	10 (6.5)	9 (10.6)	N/A	14 (23.3)
Pathological gambling	1 (2.2)	3 (1.0)	4 (2.6)	0	N/A	N/A
Intermittent explosive disorder	1 (2.2)	N/A	11 (7.2)	9 (10.6)	N/A	N/A
Pyromania	N/A	1 (0.3)	N/A	N/A	N/A	N/A
Binge eating disorder	N/A	4 (1.4)	N/A	N/A	N/A	N/A

Note. All values are n (%). N/A = not available.

Heterogeneity of Impulse Control Disorders

One reason for the conflicting data regarding the relationship of obsessive-compulsive disorder to impulse control disorders may be that not everyone with the same impulse control disorder shares similar phenomenology or biology. Subtyping of the various impulse control disorders has been recently examined in the case of pathological gambling and trichotillomania.

In the case of pathological gambling, subtyping has been done for the past several years. For example, one study reported four factors that may reflect different subtypes of pathological gambling: psychological distress, sensation seeking, crime and liveliness, and impulsivity and antisocial behavioral patterns (Steel and Blaszczynski, 1996). Another means of subtyping gambling is based on the primary drive seen clinically: depression or anxiety, impulsivity, and urges or cravings. Yet another means of subtyping pathological gambling might be based on patterns of comorbidity and family history: bipolar spectrum, addiction, and obsessive compulsive (Hollander et al., 2005). Subtyping may explain why certain individuals with pathological gambling respond to serotonergic medications while others respond to opioid antagonists or lithium.

In the case of trichotillomania, one area of research has focused on whether those who pull unconsciously are a different subtype from those who pull with full awareness (Christenson et al. 1991). We have proposed an addiction subtype for certain individuals who pull hair. Hair pulling, like drugs, has a pleasurable quality for some individuals (Arzeno et al., 2006). In fact, 39% of individuals with trichotillomania report a pleasurable feeling when pulling their hair (Grant et al., 2007). Some people with trichotillomania may report an urge or craving state prior to hair pulling, as do individuals with substance use disorders, and naltrexone has demonstrated benefit in reducing the urges to pull (O'Sullivan et al., 1999). Additionally, the hair pulling in trichotillomania decreases anxiety, as alcohol often does. One of the few studies that has used a control group found that the first-degree relatives of trichotillomania subjects were significantly more likely to have substance use disorders (21.6% alcohol use disorders and 14.7% drug use disorders) than relatives of well comparison subjects (Schlosser et al., 1994).

Further examination of possible subtypes of impulse control disorders might lead us to a finding that there is a subtype of impulse control disorders that is more like a subtype of obsessive-compulsive disorder, whereas other trichotillomania subtypes have more in common with other disorders such as addictions.

Heterogeneity of Obsessive-Compulsive Disorder

Although many instances of impulse control disorders may share features with obsessive-compulsive disorder, understanding the relationship between impulsivity and compulsivity may be further complicated by failing to account for the heterogeneity of obsessive-compulsive disorder (Calamari et al., 1999; Mataix-Cols et al., 2005; Chamberlain et al., 2007). Factor and cluster analyses have demonstrated four robust and temporally stable symptom dimensions in obsessive-compulsive disorder: contamination obsessions with cleaning compulsions; harm-related aggressive, sexual, and religious obsessions with checking compulsions; symmetry obsessions with arranging and repeating compulsions; and hoarding or saving symptoms (Leckman et al., 1997; Miguel et al., 2005). Individuals with various disorder subtypes present with a range of obsessions and compulsions (Calamari et al., 1999), experience different co-occurring disorders (Rasmussen and Eisen, 1992), may have unique genetic transmission (Mataix-Cols and van den Heuval, 2006), appear to have distinct but overlapping neuropathologies, and vary in their response to both psychosocial and pharmacological treatments (Mataix-Cols and van den Heuval, 2006). It is therefore possible that certain subtypes of obsessive-compulsive disorder may have more in common with certain subtypes of impulse control disorders while other subtypes have greater commonality with anxiety disorders.

Some support for this hypothesis comes from two studies of obsessive-compulsive disorder subjects wherein impulsivity was significantly associated with aggressive obsessions and hoarding obsessions and compulsions (Grant et al., 2006). Compulsive hoarding is characterized by the accumulation of or failure to discard possessions of little use or value. Hoarding has historically been considered more resistant to treatment with either cognitive behavioral therapy or selective serotonin reuptake inhibitors than other subtypes of obsessive-compulsive disorder. Furthermore, genetic studies suggest that hoarding is more prevalent in families with hoarding than in nonhoarding families (Samuels et al., 2007). These findings suggest that hoarding may in fact be an etiologically discrete phenotype (Saxena, 2007).

Hoarding appears to have several similarities to impulse control disorder. Like impulse control disorders, hoarding is usually ego-syntonic (Steketee and Frost, 2003; Grant and Potenza, 2006). In addition, individuals with hoarding score high on measures of impulsivity (Grisham et al., 2007), which is also seen in pathological gambling, kleptomania, and compulsive buying (Lejoyeux et al., 1997; Petry, 2005; Bayle et al., 2003). One study of impulse control disorders in individuals with obsessive-compulsive disorder found that the presence of an impulse control disorder was most robustly associated with hoarding obsessions and compulsions (Grant et al., 2006). These findings are consistent with studies that found high rates of compulsive buying in individuals with hoarding behavior (Frost et al., 1998; Winsberg et al., 1999). Rates of hoarding have also been shown to be much higher in certain impulse control disorders such as pathological gambling, kleptomania, and compulsive buying (Frost et al. 2001; Grant and Kim, 2002a).

Understanding how obsessive-compulsive disorder subtypes, such as hoarding, share common clinical features and possibly pathophysiology with certain impulse control disorders may improve treatment outcome. For example, assessments may wish to focus on the overlap between shopping and hoarding. Psychotherapy may wish to target problems with decision making that exist in both behaviors, while pharmacotherapy may focus on the impulsivity demonstrated in both behaviors.

Conclusion

As seen in the case of Barbara, impulse control disorders are characterized by repetitive behaviors and impaired inhibition of these behaviors. The characteristic difficult-to-control behaviors suggest a similarity to the frequently excessive, unnecessary, and unwanted rituals of obsessive-compulsive disorder. There are, however, differences between the two types of disorders such as the urge or craving state, the hedonic quality during the performance of impulsive behavior, and the sensation-seeking personality type often seen in individuals with impulse control disorders. Despite these differences, features of compulsivity have been observed in association with impulse control disorders, and preliminary data suggest that features of compulsivity as well as impulsivity might represent important targets for further subtyping of impulse control disorders to maximize treatment outcome.

Because research is limited and shows varied findings, it seems premature to identify impulse control disorders too closely with obsessive-compulsive disorder. The extent to which there exist specific impulse control disorders or subtypes that are more closely associated with obsessive-compulsive disorder remains to be investigated more systematically. In addition, the construct of compulsivity as related to impulse control disorders and obsessive-compulsive disorder warrants additional investigation not only to identify the similarities and differences but also to examine the implications for prevention and treatment strategies. Future investigations are needed to determine whether specific subgroups (e.g., individuals with pathological gambling with specific features of compulsivity or impulsivity) respond better to specific treatments. Similarly, specific aspects of compulsivity might represent a target for behavioral interventions for impulse control disorders.

CHAPTER 4

The Relationship of Impulse Control Disorders to Drug and Alcohol Addiction

ALTHOUGH THERE EXISTS some controversy regarding the precise categorization of impulse control disorders, mounting evidence supports phenomenological, clinical, epidemiological, and biological links between impulse control disorders and drug addictions. In fact, impulse control disorders might be thought of as nonsubstance or behavioral addictions. It seems increasingly important that individuals involved in the prevention and treatment of substance use disorders have a current understanding of impulse control disorders and the potential for future research findings to guide prevention and treatment efforts for addictions in general.

Core Features of Behavioral and Drug Addictions

Behavioral and drug addictions share common core qualities: (1) a craving state prior to behavioral engagement, or a compulsive engagement; (2) impaired control over the problematic behavior; and (3) continued engagement in the behavior despite adverse consequences (Potenza, 2006). If, as it appears, these are the core elements of addictions, then impulse control disorders deserve consideration as behavioral addictions (Holden, 2001).

Diagnostic Criteria

The impulse control disorders share multiple clinical characteristics with substance use disorders. Impulsivity—defined as a predisposition toward unplanned reactions to internal or external stimuli without regard for negative consequences—is a core element of multiple psychiatric disorders, including substance use and impulse control disorders (Moeller et al., 2001; Potenza, 2006). Impulse control disorders are not currently grouped with substance use disorders in the *DSM-IV-TR*, a decision that may in part have been due to the limited information on impulse control disorders that was formerly available. Unfortunately, other than pathological gambling, there is still little systematic research on these disorders compared to substance use disorders. Because pathological gambling is better studied than the other impulse control disorders, it is the focus of this chapter. Other impulse disorders are discussed but limitations of our knowledge are highlighted.

The clinical similarities between pathological gambling and substance use disorders are best reflected in the diagnostic criteria for pathological gambling. Criteria for pathological gambling share common features with those for substance use disorders: interference in major areas of life functioning, tolerance, withdrawal, and repeated unsuccessful attempts to cut back or stop (APA, 2000). People with pathological gambling, like many with a substance use disorder, experi-

TABLE 4.1
Lifetime Rates of Substance Use Disorders in Impulse Control Disorders

Impulse Control Disorder	Lifetime Rate of Substance Use Disorder (%)
Pathological gambling	35–63
Kleptomania	23–50
Pyromania	33
Intermittent explosive disorder	48
Trichotillomania	22
Pathological skin picking	38
Binge eating disorder	28
Compulsive sexual behavior	64
Internet addiction	38
Compulsive buying	21–46

ence an intense wish to engage in the behavior (Castellani and Rugle, 1995). Those with pathological gambling may also experience withdrawal symptoms such as irritability and agitation (Wray et al., 1981) and the equivalent of tolerance (i.e., the need to gamble with larger amounts of money to attain the same rush; Blanco et al., 2001). Preoccupation of the gambler, like that of the substance abuser, can lead to the abandonment of other interests and negative social and occupational consequences (Wray and Dickerson, 1986).

Epidemiology and Comorbidity

Although most nationally representative samples have not included an assessment of the impulse control disorders, existing epidemiological data also support a relationship between pathological gambling and substance use disorders, with high rates of co-occurrence in each direction. Data from the St. Louis Epidemiologic Catchment Area study indicate that high rates of co-occurrence exist for substance use disorders (including nicotine dependence) and pathological gambling, with the highest odds ratios generally observed between gambling, alcohol use disorders, and antisocial personality disorder (Cunningham-Williams et al., 1998). These data suggest that pathological gambling is linked to externalizing disorders (i.e., disorders characterized by being at odds with society) such as substance use disorders (Kessler et al., 2004). Pathological gambling and other impulse control disorders also share with externalizing disorders a disinhibited personality style and lack of constraint (Krueger et al., 2002). A study of over 43,000 individuals, however, found that a broad range of psychiatric disorders frequently co-occur with pathological gambling (Petry et al., 2005), and so the way that gambling and other impulse disorders fit within the structure of other mental health disorders and addictions is not completely understood.

A Canadian epidemiological survey estimated that the relative risk for an alcohol use disorder is increased 3.8 times when disordered gambling is present (Grant et al., 2002). Among individuals with substance dependence, the risk of moderate-to-high severity gambling was 2.9 times higher (El-Guebaly et al., 2006). Odds ratios ranging from 3.3 to 23.1 have been reported between pathological gambling and alcohol use disorders in U.S. population-based studies (Cunningham-Williams et al., 1998; Welte et al., 2001).

Clinical samples of the other impulse control disorders suggest that co-occurrence with substance use disorders is common (Table 4.1). The rates of co-occurring substance use disorders, however, are not uniform across all impulse control disorders. The lowest rate of co-occurrence appears to be in individuals with trichotillomania. This finding may suggest that only certain impulse control disorders share clinical features and possible neurobiology with substance use disorders or that only certain individuals with any impulse control disorder share these features with substance use disorders (Grant et al., 2007).

Moderating Variables

Additional comorbidities involving other psychiatric disorders may further complicate understanding of the relationship between substance use disorders and impulse control disorders. For example, studies have shown that individuals with ADHD are at increased risk for developing a substance use disorder (Biederman et al., 1995). In addition, studies have demonstrated that individuals with impulse control disorders (e.g., pathological and compulsive sexual behavior) have an increased prevalence rate of comorbid ADHD (Specker et al., 1996; Kafka and Hennen, 2002). Although little relevant research has been conducted, a reasonable hypothesis for further study is that some psychiatric conditions may mark those who are more likely to develop both a substance use disorder and an impulse control disorder. Such a finding might point toward factors common to the etiology of both substance addictions and impulse control disorders.

Temporal Relationship

When attempting to understand the comorbidity between substance use disorders and impulse control disorders, establishing the temporal relationship of the two is appealing. If one disorder consistently precedes the other, that would be consistent with a direct causal relationship. If there is heterogeneity in the order, however, that suggests a third variable might serve as a common cause for both. One study found that pathological gambling began after nicotine, alcohol, and cannabis dependence in 56% to 68% of cases (Cunningham-Williams and Cottler, 2001). This study suggests that neither the impulse control disorder nor the alcohol use disorder routinely precedes the other in cases of comorbidity.

Further complications arise from the fact that causal associations may manifest on an event level (e.g., alcohol use disinhibits a range of inappropriate behaviors including the impulse behavior) or on a syndrome level (e.g., an impulse control behavior starts after alcoholism treatment, possibly as a substitute for drinking). One study of 464 problem gamblers found that those with frequent alcohol use had greater gambling severity and more psychosocial problems resulting from gambling than those without alcohol use histories (Stinchfield et al., 2005). A similar finding was reported in the context of nicotine use. In a study of 225 adults with pathological gambling, those who were current or prior smokers had significantly stronger urges to gamble (Grant and Potenza, 2005). Problem gamblers who use tobacco daily are more likely to have alcohol and drug use problems (Potenza et al., 2004). In adolescents, those who are moderate-to-high frequency drinkers are more likely to gamble frequently (Duhig et al., 2007).

Clinical Characteristics

Phenomenological data further support a relationship between behavioral and drug addictions. In the cases of pathological gambling, pyromania, and intermittent explosive disorder, higher rates have been observed in adolescent and young adults and lower rates among older adults, which suggests a natural history similar to that observed in substance use disorders (Chambers et al., 2003; Grant et al., 2005; Grant et al., in press). The natural histories of certain impulse control disorders (e.g., pathological gambling) and substance use disorders suggest they are chronic, relapsing conditions (Potenza et al., 2001), but that many people recover on their own (Potenza, 2006).

Like substance use disorders, impulse control disorders have a pleasurable quality. Many people with such disorders report an urge or craving state prior to initiating the behavior, as do individuals with substance use disorders prior to drinking or using drugs. Additionally, the impulsive behavior often decreases anxiety, as drinking often does, for example, in alcohol use disorders. One study examined whether cravings were the same in impulse control disorders as in alcohol dependence. In that study, 50 pathological gamblers were compared to 42 alcohol-dependent subjects regarding craving. The study found that craving for either gambling or alcohol had a significant association with emotional state. Gambling craving, however, was more dependent upon external factors and related to an unpleasant dearousing state, whereas alcohol craving was linked with unpleasant arousing state. Emotional dysregulation played a large role in cravings in both disorders (de Castro et al., 2007).

Research on pathological gambling (arguably the most thoroughly studied of the impulse control disorders) provides further insight into the relationship of impulse control disorders and substance use disorders. Pathological gambling usually begins in childhood or adolescence, with males tending to start at an earlier age (Grant and Kim, 2001; Chambers and Potenza, 2003), and this finding mirrors those from substance use disorders. In addition, higher rates of pathological gambling are observed in men, with a telescoping phenomenon observed in females (i.e., women have a later initial engagement in the addictive behavior but foreshortened time period from initial engagement to addiction; Potenza et al., 2001). The telescoping phenomenon has been extensively documented in a variety of substance use disorders (Brady and Randall, 1999).

Other gender-related differences in pathological gambling have been described, and they bear striking parallels to those seen in substance use disorders. Female as compared with male pathological gamblers tend to have problems with nonstrategic forms of gambling such as slot machines and bingo, whereas men are more likely than women to have problems with strategic forms such as sports and card gambling (Potenza et al., 2001). As with specific substance use disorders, the extent to which problems with specific forms of gambling might relate to prevention and treatment efforts requires further investigation. Both female and male gamblers, like their counterparts with substance use disorders, report that advertisements are a common trigger of their urges to gamble, although females are more likely to report that feeling bored or lonely may also trigger their urges to gamble (Grant and Kim, 2001; Ladd and Petry, 2002; Dawson et al., 2005; Collins et al., 2007).

As in substance use disorders, financial and marital problems are common in pathological gamblers (Grant and Kim, 2001). Individuals with pathological gambling, like those with drug addictions, will frequently commit illegal acts, such as stealing, embezzlement and writing bad checks, to either fund their addictive behavior or cope with the consequences of the behavior (Potenza et al., 2000; Grant and Kim, 2001).

Personality

Individuals with impulse control disorders (e.g., pathological gambling, kleptomania, compulsive sexual behavior, and compulsive buying) and those with substance use disorders both appear to score high on self-report measures of impulsivity and sensation-seeking (Lejoyeaux et al., 1997; Kim and Grant, 2001; Grant and Kim, 2002a; Raymond et al., 2003; Kelly et al., 2006). In contrast to these impulsive behaviors, individuals with obsessive-compulsive disorder score high on measures of harm avoidance (Kim and Grant, 2001). Impulsivity and compulsivity are of course not mutually exclusive. Individuals with impulse control disorders also score high on measures of compulsivity, but it appears limited to impaired control over mental activities and worries about losing control over motor behaviors (Blanco et al., in press). Impaired inhibition of motor responses (impulsivity) has been found in individuals with obsessive-compulsive disorder and trichotillomania (an impulse control disorder with arguably closer phenomenological links to obsessive-compulsive disorder), whereas cognitive inflexibility (thought to contribute to compulsivity) was limited to obsessive-compulsive disorder (Chamberlain et al., 2006).

Neurocognition

Cognitive features have also been reported as common to both impulse control disorders and substance use disorders. Both pathological gamblers and people with substance use disorders have been found to have high rates of temporal discounting of rewards (Petry and Casarella, 1999) and to perform disadvantageously on decision-making tasks (Bechara, 2003). Individuals with pathological gambling have shown disadvantageous performances on the Iowa Gambling Task, a paradigm that assesses risk-reward decision making (Cavedini et al., 2002). In people with substance use disorders, a poor performance on the Iowa

Gambling Task correlates with adverse functioning (Bechara, 2003). A study using a comprehensive neurocognitive battery in 49 pathological gamblers, 48 abstinent alcohol-dependent subjects, and 49 controls found that gamblers and alcoholics both showed diminished performance on tests of inhibition, cognitive flexibility, and planning tasks. There were no differences on tests of executive functioning between the pathological gamblers and the alcoholics (Goudriaan et al., 2006).

Common Neurobiological Processes

A growing body of literature implicates multiple neurotransmitter systems (e.g., serotonergic, dopaminergic, noradrenergic, opioidergic), as well as familial and inherited factors, in the pathophysiology of impulse control disorders and substance use disorders.

Many disorders characterized by impaired impulse control appear to share similar dysfunction of the serotonin system, a system that may assist in inhibiting behaviors. The most consistent findings involve the serotonin (5-hydroxyindole or 5-HT) system, believed to underlie impulse control (Potenza, 2001). Evidence for serotonergic involvement in impulse control and substance use disorders comes in part from studies of platelet monoamine oxidase B activity, which correlates with cerebrospinal fluid levels of 5-hydroxyindolacetic acid (5-HIAA, a metabolite of 5-HT) and is considered a peripheral marker of 5-HT function. Low 5-HIAA levels have been found to correlate with high levels of impulsivity and sensation seeking and have been found in pathological gambling and substance use disorders (Potenza, 2001). Pharmacological challenge studies that measure hormonal response after administration of serotonergic drugs also provide evidence for serotonergic dysfunction in both impulse control and substance use disorders (Potenza, 2001).

The repetitive use of substances or engagement in an impulsive behavior following an urge may reflect a unitary process. Preclinical and clinical studies suggest that an underlying biological mechanism for urge-driven disorders involves the processing of incoming reward input by a specific brain system. This system is the ventral tegmental area–nucleus accumbens–orbital frontal cortex circuit. The ventral tegmental area contains neurons that release dopamine to the nucleus accumbens and orbital frontal cortex (Koob and Bloom, 1988). Alterations in dopaminergic pathways have been proposed as underlying the seeking of rewards (gambling, drugs) that trigger the release of dopamine and produce feelings of pleasure.

Neurocircuitry

Although few neuroimaging studies have been performed for impulse control disorders, evidence supports a shared neurocircuitry of impulse control and substance use disorders. Diminished activity of the ventro-medial prefrontal cortex (vmPFC) has been associated with impulsive aggression and may play a large role in impulse regulation across a spectrum of disorders (Dougherty et al., 2004). The vmPFC has been implicated in decision making in risk-reward assessments and has been shown to exhibit abnormal functioning in subjects with substance use disorders (London et al., 2000). In the case of pathological gambling, decreased activation of the vmPFC has been shown when the subjects were presented with gambling cues (Potenza et al., 2003). This same

TABLE 4.2

Family History of Substance Use Disorders in Individuals with Impulse Control Disorders

Impulse Control Disorder	First-Degree Relatives With Substance Use Disorder
Trichotillomania (Schlosser et al., 1994)	21.6% had alcoholism and 14.7% had a drug use disorder, compared to 7.7% and 2.2%, respectively, in control group; both statistically significant ($p < .001$).
Kleptomania (Grant, 2003a)	15.1% had alcohol use disorder compared to 5.1% in control group; statistically significant ($p = .008$)
Compulsive buying (Black et al., 1998)	19.7% had alcohol use disorder and 5.1% had drug use disorder compared to 4.3% and 1.3%, respectively, in the control group; both significantly different ($p = .0001$ and $p = .03$)
Pathological gambling (Black et al., 2006)	32.7% had a substance use disorder compared to 14.8% in the control group; significantly different ($p = .0003$)

finding also distinguished subjects with bipolar disorder from controls (Blumberg et al., 2003).

The dopaminergic mesolimbic pathway from the ventral tegmental area to the nucleus accumbens has been a central focus of addiction research as this area has been implicated in reward-seeking behaviors. Brain imaging research suggests that this area is involved in substance use disorders as well as pathological gambling. In a study involving a guessing task, subjects with pathological gambling demonstrated less ventral striatal activity than controls (Reuter et al., 2005), which is similar to the response seen in a study of alcohol-dependent subjects (Potenza, 2006). This decreased ventral striatal activation may be implicated in the cravings associated with substance and nonsubstance addiction. In a study of cravings in pathological gambling and cocaine dependence, decreased activation of the ventral striatum was significantly greater in those subjects with addictions than in controls (Potenza, 2006).

Family History and Genetics

A relationship between impulse control disorders and substance use disorders would be supported by data that substance use disorders are more common in relatives of subjects with impulse control disorders than in the general population. Only a few impulse control disorders have been studied using control groups (Table 4.2). In one study, first-degree relatives of trichotillomania subjects were significantly more likely to have substance use disorders (21.6% alcohol use disorders and 14.7% drug use disorders) than relatives of comparison subjects (Schlosser et al., 1994). A family study comparing 31 pathological gambling probands to 31 control probands found that relatives of pathological gamblers had significantly higher lifetime rates of a problem with gambling, alcohol use disorders, and any substance use disorder (Black et al., 2006). A study of first-degree relatives of kleptomania subjects found that both alcohol use disorders and any psychiatric disorder were present at significantly greater rates in the probands' families (Grant, 2003a). Similarly, a study of compulsive buyers also found that first-degree relatives were significantly more likely to suffer from substance use disorders, depression, and any psychiatric disorder (Black et al., 1998). These controlled family studies support the view that impulse control disorders may have a genetic relationship to other substance use disorders. Although various psychiatric disorders were more common in first-degree relatives of impulse disorder probands, the most robust finding, and the most consistent across the impulse disorders, was substance use.

Researchers can estimate the extent of genetic versus environmental contributions to specific behaviors and conditions by contrasting their concordance between identical (i.e., monozygotic) and fraternal (i.e., dizygotic) twin pairs. In a study using the Vietnam Era Twin Registry, examining male twin subjects, 12–20% of the genetic variation in risk for pathological gambling and 3–8% of the nonshared environmental variation in risk for pathological gambling was accounted for by risk for alcohol use disorders (Slutske et al., 2000). Additionally, 64% of the co-occurrence between pathological gambling and alcohol use disorders appears attributable to genes that simultaneously influence both disorders, suggesting some overlap in the genetically transmitted underpinnings of both conditions. These findings are similar to those suggesting common genetic contributions to a range of drug use disorders (Tsuang et al., 1998).

Further similarities between impulse control disorders and substance use disorders have been suggested by research in molecular genetics. The *D2A1* allele of the *D2* dopamine receptor gene (*DRD2*) has been shown to increase in frequency from nonaddicted to pathological gambling and co-occurring pathological gambling and substance use disorder groups (Comings, 1998). Genetic studies are currently lacking for the other impulse control disorders, but this area of enquiry may shed more light on the relationships of these disorders to each other as well as to substance use disorders.

Responsiveness to Treatment

Based on the view that impulse control disorders and substance use disorders share common causal and maintaining factors, one could predict that these disorders would respond positively to the same treatments. In fact, various nonmedical treatment modalities that are effective in treating substance use disorders are also helpful in treating impulse control disorders. For example, 12-step approaches have been used for pathological gambling, compulsive sexual behavior, kleptomania, and compulsive buying. Cognitive behavioral therapies have also demonstrated benefit in controlled studies of pathological gambling, trichotillomania, pathological skin picking, and compulsive buying (Ninan et al., 2000; Petry and Roll, 2001; van Minnen et al., 2003; Petry et al., 2005; Woods et al., 2005; Mitchell et al., 2006; Teng et al., 2006; Twohig et al. 2006). In addition, several influential psychosocial interventions for both impulse control disorders and substance use disorders rely on a relapse prevention model that encourages abstinence by identifying patterns of abuse, avoiding or coping with high-risk situations, and making lifestyle changes that reinforce healthier behaviors.

Although research has only recently explored pharmacological treatment for impulse control disorders, these studies have shown a similar response for substance use disorders and impulse control disorders. Historically, the results of using serotonergic medications for substance use disorders have not been impressive (Kranzler et al., 1995; Kabel and Petty, 1996). Similarly, numerous controlled studies of serotonergic medications in the treatment of impulse control disorders also support their use but in a limited fashion (Black et al., 2000a & b; Ninan et al., 2000a,b; Grant et al., 2003; Koran et al., 2007a,b).

No medications are currently approved for the treatment of impulse control disorders, but other medications that have shown promise in treating substance use disorders have also shown promise in treating impulse control disorders. Given their ability to modulate dopaminergic transmission in the mesolimbic pathway, opioid receptor antagonists (naltrexone and nalmefene) have also been investigated in the treatment of impulse control disorders.

Naltrexone, approved by the Food and Drug Administration for the treatment of alcoholism and opioid dependence, has been effective in reducing the frequency and amount of drinking in patients with alcohol use disorders (O'Malley et al., 1992; Volpicelli et al., 1992; Anton et al., 1999). Studies evaluating the efficacy of naltrexone in the treatment of pathological gambling have also demonstrated its benefit in reducing gambling urges (Crockford and el-Guebaly, 1998; Kim and Grant, 2001; Kim et al., 2001). Although controlled studies are still lacking, naltrexone has shown promise in treating compulsive buying (Grant, 2003b), compulsive sexual behavior (Raymond et al., 2002), and kleptomania (Grant and Kim, 2002b). As in the case of substance use disorders, naltrexone appears to target urges in impulse control disorders. The drug also appears to be at its most efficacious in individuals reporting higher intensity urges (Kim et al., 2001).

Nalmefene, another opioid antagonist, has similarly shown promise in treating substance use disorders (Mason et al., 1999). A multi-center study further demonstrated the efficacy of nalmefene in the treatment of pathological gambling. In a sample of 207 subjects, nalmefene demonstrated statistically significant improvement in gambling symptoms compared to placebo in a 16-week double-blind trial (Grant et al., 2006b).

Because dopaminergic systems, which influence rewarding and reinforcing behaviors, have been implicated in addictions, agents that can improve glutamatergic tone within the nucleus accumbens (and thereby affect dopamine) may also reduce reward-seeking behavior in addictions (Kalivas et al., 2006). Studies examining cocaine addiction in rats demonstrate that N-acetylcysteine, an amino acid, restores extracellular glutamate concentration in the nucleus accumbens, blocks reinstitution of compulsive behaviors, and decreases cravings (Baker et al., 2003). One study examining N-acetylcysteine in pathological gambling found that the medication could reduce gambling urges and behavior (Grant et al., in press).

The positive outcomes in both substance use and impulse control disorders when treated with certain medications (opioid antagonists and possible glutamatergic agents) provide evidence that the dopamine and possibly glutamate systems affected by these drugs play roles in both conditions.

Treatment Implications

Regardless of the specific causal association linking impulse control disorders and substance use disorders, the fact that they frequently co-occur raises important treatment issues. Treatment of either an impulse control or substance use disorder could be complicated by the presence of the other untreated condition. Treating one disorder alone may not be effective if the second disorder is exerting a causal or maintaining influence on the treated condition. Even in the event that impulse control disorders and substance use disorders are associated via the influence of a third variable that can promote both disorders, treating one but not the other condition would be potentially problematic. Furthermore, more intense treatment may be required for patients with comorbid conditions because they are likely to have more functional impairment and poorer prognosis than those with either condition alone.

Conclusion

Prospective studies of the temporal association of impulse control disorders and substance use disorders are virtually absent from the literature, but would be suited to the important goal of clarifying the natural history and temporal relationships of these disorders. It is important to catch people early in the window of risk for both disorders (i.e., early adolescence). Because one's substance use status can change rapidly, prospective assignments necessary to document interactions between these conditions should be frequent. Reliable information concerning key interactions of these disorders may not be obtainable without prospective studies.

Another question that has not been addressed is whether different subtypes of substance use and impulse control disorders are more likely to manifest as comorbid conditions. For example, perhaps only some pathological gamblers with strong urges share neurobiological underpinnings with some cocaine-dependent individuals with strong urges. Disorder subtypes may be associated with neurobiological processes that overlap for both impulse control and substance use disorders, whereas other subtypes may have a different etiology that is unrelated to the comorbid condition. Research findings from genetic and brain imaging studies may help identify key subgroup variables and serve as a methodology for identifying common biological substrates associated with both impulse control disorders and substance use disorders.

Understanding the relationship of impulse control disorders and substance use disorders will help refine views of the psychopathology and taxonomy of these conditions. In addition, by unraveling the shared and unique etiologies of these disorders, research may be better able to develop and test treatment and prevention strategies.

CHAPTER 5

Intermittent Explosive Disorder: Relationship to Impulse Control Disorders

IN SEVERAL PSYCHIATRIC disorders, impulsivity is linked to aggression. Impulsive aggression has been defined as a deliberate, non-premeditated aggressive act, either verbal or physical, that is directed against another person, an object, or the self (Coccaro, 1998). Perhaps the disorder that best reflects this link between impulsivity and aggression is intermittent explosive disorder, a behavioral disorder characterized by impulsive aggression. Not all impulsive acts, however, are aggressive, and in fact most of the other impulse control disorders do not appear to be characterized by aggression. Is there a relationship between intermittent explosive disorder and the rest of the impulse control disorders? If so, what is it?

Intermittent explosive disorder is characterized by discrete episodes of failing to resist aggressive impulses that result in serious assaultive acts or destruction of property (APA, 2000). Also, the degree of aggression expressed during an episode is grossly out of proportion to the precipitating psychosocial stressor (APA, 2000).

Among adults, intermittent explosive disorder has been found to be costly and relatively common in the community, with a U.S. prevalence estimate of 7.3% for lifetime intermittent explosive disorder (Kessler et al., 2006). In the community, intermittent explosive disorder frequently co-occurs with other psychiatric disorders and typically precedes the onset of other psychiatric disorders, with a mean age of onset of 14 years (Kessler et al., 2006). Intermittent explosive disorder is characterized by an approximately 2:1 male predominance (Kessler et al., 2006).

In a study of adolescent psychiatric inpatients ($n = 102$), intermittent explosive disorder was the most commonly seen impulse control disorder, with a current prevalence of 12.7% (Grant et al., in press). Compared with adulthood, adolescence is a time of intense emotional and physical changes (Dahl, 2003). Control mechanisms over often widely fluctuating emotions and related physical responses may be relatively immature, leading to problems with aggressive outbursts characteristic of intermittent explosive disorder (Kessler et al., 2006). The fact that lifetime proportions of intermittent explosive disorder appear lower in adults than among adolescents raises the possibility of age-related developmental differences (e.g., development of the prefrontal cortex during the transition to adulthood allowing for greater inhibition of impulses), cohort effects (e.g., violent outbursts being more tolerated in present-day society than previously), or other factors (e.g., early death of violent or aggressive individuals).

> Stephen is a 37-year-old male reporting an inability to manage his anger and outbursts. He reports a long history of easily losing his temper in spite of relatively small provocations. For example, Stephen describes how, after waiting for a doctor's appointment for 30 minutes, he became verbally abusive to the receptionist. He threw magazines, threatened violence, and couldn't control himself. The police came and he was given a citation. After he calmed down, he was extremely embarrassed and remorseful over his actions. He describes anger episodes as "uncontrollable rage" that are never planned but instead just happen. He reports a type of amnesic dissociative state during the outbursts with only partial memory of the particular details. Due to these outbursts, he has had numerous legal problems and his finances and relationships are quite strained. He is on probation currently and is required to receive treatment.

Phenomenological Links to Impulse Control Disorders

Conceptualizing intermittent explosive disorder as an impulse control disorder has historically been based on their shared clinical characteristics. Impulsivity has been defined as a predisposition to rapid, unplanned reactions to either internal or external stimuli without regard for negative consequences (Moeller et al., 2001); this definition certainly applies to the aggressive outbursts seen in intermittent explosive disorders. People with this disorder, like those with other impulse control disorders, experience tension and relief when engaging in the behavior (McElroy et al., 1998). In addition, impulse control disorders generally involve a hedonic quality—sex, stealing, and gambling all are associated with a rush or a high (Grant and Potenza, 2006c). The aggressive behaviors associated with intermittent explosive disorder are also often gratifying and accompanied by excitement (McElroy et al., 1998). In this respect, the behaviors are similar to those seen in most of the other impulse control disorders.

Upon closer examination of intermittent explosive disorder, however, we see some clear differences between it and other impulse control disorders. As discussed for other impulse control problems, individuals can experience an urge to engage in the behavior and it may be rewarding, as in the case of pathological gambling, or develop out of habit, as with trichotillomania. Most individuals with intermittent explosive disorder, however, do not appear to obtain similar benefits (e.g., reward) from acting on their impulsive tendencies, but rather experience tension reduction alone (McElroy et al., 1998). All subjects with intermittent explosive disorder in a case series experienced an irresistible impulse to be aggressive prior to the aggressive acts (McElroy et al., 1998). For subjects in this small case study, aggressive impulses were associated with a buildup in tension (88%), and the aggressive acts were associated with a relief of tension (75%), but only in a minority of cases (48%) did individuals experience pleasure following the aggressive acts.

Studies have demonstrated that mood disorders and anxiety disorders, not impulse control disorders, are the most common comorbidities seen in individuals with intermittent explosive disorder (Coccaro and Danehy, 2006). Individuals with intermittent explosive disorder commonly have comorbid psychiatric disorders: 93% of subjects have a lifetime mood disorder and 48% have anxiety disorders. These high rates of co-occurring mood and anxiety disorders suggest possible impairment in stress management skills, particularly the ability to tolerate negative emotion.

Additionally, different neurocircuitry may be involved in intermittent explosive disorder than in other impulse control disorders. Finally, although treatment studies for intermittent explosive disorder are lacking, it seems to respond to serotonergic medications, an intervention that has generated mixed results for most impulse control disorders.

TABLE 5.1
Comorbidity of Intermittent Explosive Disorder With Other Impulse Control Disorders

Impulse Control Disorder	Lifetime Rate of Intermittent Explosive Disorder (%)
Compulsive sexual behavior (Black et al., 1997)	3
Compulsive buying (Christenson et al., 1994; Schlosser et al., 1994)	4–22
Pathological gambling (Grant and Kim, 2003)	2.1
Kleptomania (Grant and Kim, 2002a)	4.5

Comorbidity Studies

If a relationship exists between intermittent explosive disorder and other impulse control disorders, one would expect to see elevated rates of intermittent explosive disorder in subjects with the other impulse control disorders (Table 5.1). In fact, with the exception of one study in compulsive buying, studies of this co-occurrence have not found significantly higher rates of intermittent explosive disorder with other impulse control disorders compared to its rates in the general community.

Conversely, when examining rates of impulse control disorders in a sample of subjects with intermittent explosive disorder, only 7.5% had a lifetime disorder (Coccaro et al., 2005). Instead, substance use disorders and personality disorders (antisocial and borderline) were common (Coccaro et al., 1998, 2005).

Family History and Genetics

Although few studies have examined the family history or genetics of intermittent explosive disorder, studies have demonstrated that impulsive aggressive behaviors follow a familial transmission. Several lines of research suggest that sociopathy and aggression may be familial and are associated with central serotonin dysfunction (Halperin et al., 2003). A genetic linkage study found that an allelic version of the serotonin 1B receptor gene was associated with alcoholism in impulsively aggressive people who had either intermittent explosive disorder or antisocial personality disorder (Lappalainen et al., 1998).

Neurobiology

Impulsive aggression is likely due to multiple neurotransmitters and brain regions. Preclinical research has implicated testosterone, gamma-aminobutyric acid, nitric oxide, monoamine oxidase, glutamate, dopamine, and serotonin (Olivier and Young, 2002). Data implicate the 5-HT 1B receptor in impulsive aggression in mice, with knockout mice lacking the receptor showing marked physical aggression (Saudou et al., 1994). Human studies have implicated the same receptor in impulsive aggression in alcoholics (Lappalainen et al., 1998).

One study using magnetic resonance spectroscopy in human adolescents with and without intermittent explosive disorder found no differences between groups with respect to myoinositol measures (Davanzo et al., 2003). Other human studies in impulsive aggression have implicated opiates, vasopressin, testosterone, dopamine, norepinephrine, and 5-HT. One replicated finding is that low levels of central 5-HT is associated with impulsive aggression (Coccaro and Siever, 2002). This finding has been replicated in studies of cerebrospinal fluid, physiological responses to serotonin agonists, and platelet measures of serotonin activity (Coccaro and Danehy, 2006).

Individuals with impulsive aggression have shown relatively decreased activity in the ventromedial prefrontal cortex, a region responsible for decision making and social and moral judgments (Coccaro and Danehy, 2006). The dysfunction of the ventromedial prefrontal cortex furthermore appears linked with 5-HT dysfunction as serotonin stimulations resulted in blunted glucose utilization in intermittent explosive disorder subjects who also suffered from borderline personality disorder (Coccaro and Danehy, 2006).

The brain regions implicated in impulsive aggression mirror those examined in other impulse control disorders, particularly pathological gambling. This suggests that common neurobiology may underly all of the impulse control disorders, including intermittent explosive disorder.

Treatment Response

Relatively few clinical trials have investigated the efficacy of medications in the treatment of intermittent explosive disorder. Drugs that block serotonin transport have been reported in case reports as helpful in intermittent explosive disorder (McElroy et al., 1998), which is consistent with findings of serotonin reuptake inhibitor efficacy in treating impulsive aggression. These findings may also suggest similarities to the sometimes favorable use of such drugs in the treatment of other impulse control disorders.

Mood-stabilizing medications, such as lithium and divalproex, have also been reported as helpful in open-label studies of intermittent explosive disorder (McElroy et al., 1998), and again, this is consistent with their use in impulsive aggression. However, in a randomized double-blind placebo-controlled study, 96 subjects with Cluster B personality disorders, 116 subjects with intermittent explosive disorder, and 34 subjects with post-traumatic stress disorder were randomized to divalproex sodium or placebo for 12 weeks of treatment. Using an intent-to-treat analysis, the study found that divalproex had no significant influence on aggression in the subjects with intermittent explosive disorder (Hollander et al., 2003). These findings seem to contradict some promising treatment results of mood-stabilizing medications in the treatment of other impulse control disorders (pathological skin picking, pathological gambling, pyromania).

Additionally, antipsychotic medications, alpha-adrenergic agonists, and beta-adrenergic antagonists have all shown promise in targeting impulsive aggression (Coccaro and Danehy, 2006), but there has been no role yet for these medications in the treatment of other impulse control disorders. These findings suggest that, although the information is quite limited, there may be some similarities in the pharmacological treatments of intermittent explosive disorder and some other impulse control disorders.

Unfortunately, there is limited research in the area of psychotherapy specifically developed for individuals with intermittent explosive disorder, and this may reflect the reluctance of individuals with this disorder to acknowledge a need for or seek treatment. Coccaro and colleagues (2004) reported that only 2 of 28 subjects diagnosed with intermittent explosive disorder pursued help for their aggressive behaviors and only 50% reported distress from their aggressive behaviors. Of those with intermittent explosive disorder that do seek treatment, the motivation is typically some externally related consequence, such as legal problems stemming from aggressive driving or other impulsive behaviors.

Although there are no published controlled psychological studies for intermittent explosive disorder, a nonrandomized pilot study found that adult outpatients who participated in imaginal exposure therapy for anger habituated to anger-provoking scenarios (Grodnitsky and Tafrate, 2000), while another study reported diminished anger for self-identified angry drivers following participation in relaxation training and cognitive therapy (Deffenbacher et al., 2000). In this study, individuals benefited equally from relaxation only and relaxation plus cognitive therapy. Anger and emotional regulation can also be addressed by dialectical behavior therapy (DBT; Linehan et al., 1994). Studies have demonstrated improvements in impulsivity and anger in individuals with borderline personality disorder following participation in DBT (Linehan et al., 1994).

The preliminary treatment findings for individuals with intermittent explosive disorder require further validation with well-controlled studies to assess the use of various treatment combinations (e.g., pharmacological and psychosocial interventions). Cognitive, relaxation, and exposure therapies have demonstrated some benefit in treating individuals with aggressive behaviors. For example, components of programs such as DBT for individuals with borderline personality disorder may prove efficacious for individuals with intermittent explosive disorder. Individuals with intermittent explosive disorder have deficits in the ability to recognize and be mindful of behavioral consequences, necessitating training in self-control in order to inhibit stress responses to benign environmental cues. One additional component of treating anger and the lack of premeditation characteristic of individuals with intermittent explosive disorder is mindfulness training. A case study

TABLE 5.2

Comorbidity of Antisocial Personality Disorder With Impulse Control Disorders

Impulse Control Disorder	Rate of Antisocial Personality Disorder (%)
Intermittent explosive disorder (Coccaro et al., 1998)	38
Compulsive sexual behavior (Black et al., 1997)	19
Compulsive buying (Schlosser et al., 1994)	14
Pathological gambling (Argo and Black, 2004)	15–40
Kleptomania (Grant, 2004)	3.6

(Singh et al., 2003) of an individual with comorbid psychiatric diagnosis and mental retardation demonstrated self-control over anger using a specific mindfulness strategy. A mindfulness strategy may involve learning a meditation technique that requires an individual to shift awareness and attention from the anger-producing situation to a neutral situation or a neutral part of the body (e.g., soles of the feet), as used in Singh and colleagues' pilot investigation. Other areas of research to be explored may include the accuracy of individuals' perception of emotion (Silver et al., 2005) as studied in individuals with schizophrenia and, more specifically, misperception of facial expressions (Eastwood and Smilek, 2005). As noted by Eastwood and Smilek, a rapid physiological response to an "unconsciously perceived" facial expression prepares us to react in an adaptive manner to the presence of a threatening individual. However, this adaptive function as mediated by the amygdala (Davidson and Irwin, 1999) may not function as well in individuals with intermittent explosive disorder in terms of who and what they perceive as threatening.

Antisocial Personality Disorders

Antisocial personality disorder is characterized by a failure to conform to social norms, impulsivity, aggressiveness, disregard for self or others, and indifference to others' feelings (APA, 2000). Antisocial personality disorder has a prevalence in the general population of 3.6% (Grant et al., 2004). Although there appears to be some clinical and biological overlap between intermittent explosive disorder and other impulse control disorders, the findings are complicated by the role of antisocial personality disorder. Intermittent explosive disorder shares impulsivity and aggression with antisocial personality disorder. Pathological gambling, kleptomania, and pyromania share the disregard for social norms and others. The question then arises whether intermittent explosive disorder and some impulse control disorders are related via the same underlying pathophysiology as antisocial personality disorder.

Data indicate that common psychiatric disorders aggregate in two main groups: internalizing and externalizing disorders (i.e., disorders characterized by either withdrawal from society or being at odds with society, respectively; Krueger et al., 1998; Kessler et al., 2005). Intermittent explosive disorder has been categorized as an externalizing disorder (along with antisocial personality disorder and pathological gambling), and the question exists whether externalizing disorders have a pathophysiology distinct from internalizing disorders. The problem is that it is not completely understood where the other impulse control disorders fit within this structure.

The comorbidity data suggest that only certain impulse control disorders (pathological gambling, compulsive sexual behavior, and intermittent explosive disorder) have elevated rates of antisocial personality disorder (Table 5.2). As we learn more about the heterogeneity of impulse control disorders, however, we must ask whether certain individuals with intermittent explosive disorder and antisocial personality disorder may be similar neurobiologically to only certain individuals with other impulse control disorders.

Heterogeneity of Impulse Control Disorders

Although intermittent explosive disorder shares many clinical features with other impulse control disorders, response to serotonergic medications, unlike intermittent explosive disorder, in other impulse disorders has been equivocal, and impulse control disorders may respond to medications (e.g., opioid antagonists) that have not demonstrated benefit for intermittent explosive disorder. One reason for these differences may be that impulse control disorders are more heterogeneous than initially thought. In fact, cluster analysis has demonstrated that kleptomania, compulsive buying, and intermittent explosive disorder may belong to an impulsive subgroup while trichotillomania, pathological gambling and compulsive sexual behavior may belong to a reward deficiency group (Lochner et al., 2005). This cluster analysis raises the question of whether certain impulse control disorders may have a common etiology with intermittent explosive disorder.

Conclusion

The equivocal overlap (in clinical terms, comorbidity data and treatment response) between intermittent explosive disorder and other impulse control disorders demonstrates the need to recognize and further examine the heterogeneity of impulse control disorders. Just as there is evidence that perhaps trichotillomania and pathological skin picking may represent a subgroup of grooming disorders with little in common with some impulse control disorder, so too should we reevaluate the grouping of intermittent explosive disorder with the other impulse control disorders. Features of impulsivity and aggression might represent important treatment targets in both intermittent explosive disorder and certain other impulse control disorders. An examination of whether intermittent explosive disorder shares common pathophysiologies with certain subtypes of impulse control disorders and with antisocial personality disorder—through biochemical, functional neuroimaging, and genetic studies—may further our understanding of the neurobiology of a wide range of impulsive behaviors and improve prevention and treatment strategies.

CHAPTER 6

Etiology of
Impulse Control Disorders

OVER THE CENTURIES, multiple theories have been raised about what causes a psychiatric disorder. Although we have no absolute answers to these questions, a variety of hypotheses have been proposed. In the last two decades, the advent of neuroimaging and genetics, as well as advances in pharmacotherapies, have provided the means by which finding the cause of psychiatric disorders appears possible. Multiple advances have been made toward understanding the etiology of impulse control disorders. Attempts to understand the etiology of these disorders may be complicated by differences between them (Chapter 1) as well as heterogeneity within an impulse control disorder (Chapters 3 and 4). Keeping in mind these complications, this chapter presents what is currently known about both the neurobiological and psychological etiologies for impulse control disorders. Because pathological gambling has garnered the largest amount of attention and research, much of what is discussed here focuses on that particular disorder. How the research regarding pathological gambling generalizes to other impulse control disorders is incompletely understood at this time. Future research into the other disorders will, one hopes, provide answers to those questions.

Neurobiology of Impulse Control Disorders

The neurobiology of impulse control disorders involves multiple areas of inquiry: biochemicals, neuroanatomy, and genetics. These areas are inextricably linked, but this chapter will discuss each as a separate entity.

Biochemistry

Multiple neurochemical systems are involved in any complex behavior. These systems also communicate with each other—that is, one neurochemical may affect the manner in which others are processed. The following presents what is currently known, but research continues to further our knowledge.

SEROTONIN

From a biochemical perspective, serotonin (5-HT) has been a primary focus of inquiry given its role in behavioral inhibition. Pharmacological challenge studies suggest 5-HT dysfunction plays a role in pathological gambling. Eight men and women with pathological gambling and matched controls were given a low dose of clomipramine, a 5-HT and norepinephrine reuptake inhibitor. Compared to control subjects, individuals with pathological gambling displayed at baseline lower prolactin levels and exhibited significantly blunted prolactin responses to clomipramine 1 hour after challenge, suggesting diminished 5-HT transporter availability (Moreno et al., 1991).

Metachlorophenylpiperazine (m-CPP), a metabolite of trazodone that acts as a partial agonist and has high affinity for 5-HT receptors, was administered to 10 men with pathological gambling and 10 healthy male control subjects. Those with pathological gambling reported a high after m-CPP administration. This response is similar to those reported in other disorders in which impulsive or compulsive behaviors are prominent (Moss et al., 1990). Additionally, pathological gambling subjects demonstrated increased prolactin levels compared to controls, with greater responses correlating with increased gambling severity.

Further support for 5-HT dysfunction in pathological gambling comes from analysis of cerebrospinal fluid and blood. Although studies comparing men with pathological gambling to healthy controls have shown no significant differences in 5-HT or its metabolite 5-hydroxyindolacetic acid (5-HIAA; Roy et al., 1988; Bergh et al., 1997), levels of 5-HIAA were found to be lower in those with pathological gambling (Nordin and Eklundh, 1996). These data are consistent with findings of low levels of 5-HIAA in individuals with impulsive characteristics (Linnoila et al., 1983; Coccaro et al., 1989).

Other impulse control disorders may also have underlying serotonergic dysfunction. A study examining the platelet 5-HT transporter in 20 patients with kleptomania found that the number of transporters, evaluated by means of binding to [³H] paroxetine, was lower in the kleptomania subjects compared to healthy control subjects (Marazitti et al., 2000).

Clinical trials in pathological gambling, as well as the other impulse control disorders (compulsive buying, trichotillomania, kleptomania), have shown mixed support regarding the efficacies of drugs that operate through serotonergic mechanisms, and therefore the role of serotonin in impulse control disorders remains unclear (see Chapter 8). Further studies should consider the influences of natural recovery and co-occurring disorders when determining the role of 5-HT modulation in the treatment of impulse control disorders. Additionally, further characterization of a role for 5-HT in the initiation and maintenance of impulse control disorders is warranted, and the specific influences of genetic, gender, and ethnic factors that influence treatment outcome need to be identified.

DOPAMINE

Although much research has focused on serotonin, growing evidence from clinical and preclinical studies suggest that dopamine also plays a role in the pathogenesis of impulse control disorders.

Multiple lines of evidence support the mesocorticolimbic dopamine system in the mediation of reinforcing behaviors (Kalivas and Volkow, 2005). Human studies of individuals with cocaine dependence have shown mesocorticolimbic regional activation after viewing cocaine-related videotapes, and occupancy of the dopamine transporter has been correlated with cocaine's euphorigenic effects (Volkow et al., 1997). Dopamine may also mediate some of the rewarding or reinforcing aspects of gambling. Bergh and colleagues (1997) measured the levels of 3,4-dihydroxyphenylacetic acid (DOPAC) and homovanillic acid (HVA), two dopamine metabolites in cerebrospinal fluid of 10 males with pathological gambling compared to sex-matched controls. The study found decreased levels of dopamine and increased levels of DOPAC and HVA in pathological gambling subjects compared to controls, concluding that these findings were consistent with an increased rate of dopamine neurotransmission.

Drugs with similar mechanisms of action can cross-prime for reinstatement of other drugs within that class through dopamine in the nucleus accumbens (e.g., amphetamine for cocaine; Shalev et al., 2002). Amphetamine increases extracellular catecholamine and serotonin concentrations via vesicular depletion, reuptake inhibition, enhancement of dopamine synthesis, and monoamine oxidase (MAO) inhibition. One study compared problem gamblers with and without problem drinking to controls (gamblers, $n = 10$; gambler/drinkers, $n = 6$; drinkers, $n = 8$; controls, $n = 12$) in a double-blind, placebo-controlled, counterbalanced, between-within design of self-reported motivation for gambling and a modified rapid reading task of relevant and irrelevant semantic domains (Zack and Poulos, 2004). They found that amphetamine increased motivation for gambling in gamblers. These results suggest that amphetamine can cross-prime for gambling behavior, lending further evidence for the involvement of dopaminergic pathways in the pathophysiology of pathological gambling.

Several reports link dopamine agonist use in Parkinson's disease with a wide range of impulse control disorders (pathological gambling, compulsive sexual behavior, compulsive buying; Driver-Dunckley et al., 2003; Dodd et al., 2005; Weintraub et al., 2006). Although the studies are only retrospective, the impulse control behavior appears to resolve within months of discontinuing agonist therapy (Dodd et al., 2005). These findings suggest limbic mechanisms in the association between impulse control disorders and dopamine agonist treatment. A study of 272 patients with Parkinson's disease who were screened and assessed for impulse control disorders did not observe a difference between specific dopamine agonists in their associations with pathological gambling and other impulse control disorders (Weintraub et al., 2006). In a multivariate model, treatment with a dopamine agonist and a history of an impulse control disorder prior to Parkinson's onset predicted current impulse control disorders. Additionally, daily doses of dopamine agonists were higher in patients with an impulse control disorder than in those without. As such, existing data suggest that dopamine agonists, particularly at high dosages and in individuals at risk for impulse control disorders, may be associated with development of an impulse control disorder. Limitations of these studies include possible effects of ascertainment bias and either under- or overreporting. Future prospective studies are needed.

ENDOGENOUS OPIOID SYSTEM

Although dopamine plays a central role in the processing of reward, the endogenous opioid system influences the experiencing of pleasure. Opioids modulate mesolimbic dopamine pathways via disinhibition of gamma-aminobutyric acid input in the ventral tegmental area (Kim, 1998). Gambling or related behaviors have been associated with elevated blood levels of the endogenous opioid beta-endorphin (Shinohara et al., 1999). Given its mechanism of action and its efficacy in the treatment of alcohol and opiate dependence, opioid receptor antagonists have been tested in the treatment of pathological gambling and other impulse control disorders (Chapter 8). Naltrexone showed superiority to placebo in a double-blind single site study of pathological gambling (Kim et al., 2001). More recently, nalmefene, a long-acting opioid antagonist, showed superiority to placebo in a 16-week, randomized, dose-ranging, double-blind, multicentered study of 207 subjects with pathological gambling (Grant et al., 2006b). In addition to their possible utility in treatment, these studies suggest that the opioid system plays an important role in the pathophysiology of these disorders.

NOREPINEPHRINE

Other neurochemical systems have been less studied in the etiology of impulse control disorders. One of these neurochemicals, norepinephrine, has been hypothesized to mediate arousal, attention, and sensation seeking in pathological gambling. To test this hypothesis, cerebrospinal fluid, plasma, and urine were collected for quantitation of norepinephrine and its metabolites and vanillylmandelic acid (Roy et al., 1988). Individuals with pathological gambling were noted to have higher cerebrospinal fluid levels of MHPG (3-methoxy-4-hydroxyphenyl glycol, a metabolite of norepinephrine) and higher urine levels of norepinephrine. Significant positive correlations were found between scores of extraversion on the Eysenck Personality Questionnaire and levels of MHPG in the cerebrospinal fluid and plasma and norepinephrine metabolites (Roy et al., 1989). A different study measured plasma levels of norepinephrine in subjects playing pachinko, a gaming machine that combines elements of pinball and slot machines (Shinohara et al., 1999). They found that plasma levels rose during play, with statistically significant differences in levels in six regular players at the beginning and end of a winning streak.

MONOAMINE OXIDASE

Early research focused on the monoamine oxidase as a proxy for understanding the role of neurochemicals in impulse control disorders. The reason for this was that MAO with its A and B subtypes metabolizes norepinephrine, 5-HT, and dopamine. By drawing blood from a peripheral site (e.g., the arm) researchers hoped to understand the neurochemical workings of the brain. Decreased MAO activity has been associated with high levels of sensation seeking and pathological gambling. Two studies involving men with pathological gambling showed decreases of 26% and 41% of platelet MAO activity compared to matched controls (Carrasco et al., 1994; Blanco et al., 1996). However, in both studies, no correlation between MAO activity and sensation seeking was found.

Stress Pathways

Because many people with impulse control disorders cite stress as a frequent trigger of their behavior, understanding the stress pathways may also shed light on why some individuals develop these disorders.

Cortisol changes have been associated with gambling behaviors. A study of male and female aborigines in Kimberley, Australia whose urine was collected during a 2-day period just after receiving their wages (after which the community members typically partake in or watch gambling) showed significantly higher rates of cortisol and epinephrine excretion than separate volunteers whose urine was collected several days later (Schmitt et al., 1998). A study of salivary cortisol and heart rate recruited 19 volunteers from casinos during blackjack versus card play without monetary stakes. They found statistically significantly elevations in both measures during the blackjack compared to the control condition (Meyer et al., 2000). More recently, in a counterbalanced crossover study of 29 male volunteers recruited from casinos, the same investigators noted statistically significant increases in heart rate and cortisol levels during blackjack gambling compared to a control card-playing condition (Krueger et al., 2005).

Not all studies of the stress response have been consistent. A study of 21 men with pathological gambling found no differences from control subjects in cortisol responsivity on a dexamethasone suppression test (Ramirez et al., 1988). Similarly, no differences were found in cerebrospinal fluid levels of corticotrophin-releasing hormone and corticotrophin between men with pathological gambling and healthy volunteers (Roy et al., 1988).

Although the results are somewhat mixed, these data support the possibility of stress pathway involvement in gambling. Alternatively, gambling may invoke the stress pathway.

To summarize, pharmacological challenges implicate serotonergic systems in the pathophysiology of impulse control disorders, but treatment studies involving serotonergic reuptake inhibition have shown mixed results. Mounting evidence supports the involvement of dopaminergic systems in impulse control disorders, and these data are consistent with the pathophysiology of addictive disorders. Similarly, with the available knowledge on opiate system physiology and large multicenter trials demonstrating benefit from antagonist therapy, substantial evidence exists for opioid system involvement in impulse control disorders.

Neuroimaging

Although neurochemistry provides some evidence as to the etiology of these disorders, other research has focused on how particular areas of the brain process key aspects of these behaviors.

There has been a growing number of neuroimaging studies in the area of impulse control disorders. The ventromedial prefrontal cortex (vmPFC) has been implicated as a critical component of decision-making circuitry in risk-reward assessment in addiction (Kalivas and Volkow, 2005). Decreased activation of vmPFC has been observed in pathological gambling subjects during presentation of gambling cues (Potenza et al., 2003), performance of the Stroop Color-Word Interference Task (Potenza et al., 2003), and simulated gambling (Reuter et al., 2005). In the last study, activation of the vmPFC correlated inversely with gambling severity. Diminished activation of vmPFC has also been found to distinguish individuals with bipolar disorder from control subjects during Stroop performance (Blumberg et al., 2003). Responsiveness of the vmPFC to serotonergic drug challenges (m-CPP, fenfluramine) was blunted in individuals with impulsive aggression, similar to findings in individuals with alcohol dependence (Hommer et al., 1996). These data support a role for vmPFC dysfunction, possibly of a serotonergic nature, in impulse control disorders.

Consistent with the hypofrontality of addictions, a study of cocaine-dependent subjects demonstrated compromised white matter microstructure in inferior frontal regions (Lim et al., 2002). Similar white matter microstructural findings have been demonstrated in individuals with kleptomania (Grant et al., 2006).

Dopamine and its neurocircuitry have also been implicated in impulse control disorders. In a study in which subjects were paid increasing amounts of money based on the skill level reached while playing a video game, positron emission tomography (PET) imaging using ^{11}C-raclopride (a ligand with high affinity for dopamine 2 receptors) showed a 13% decrease in ligand binding compared to control conditions, which the authors suggested indicated a twofold increase in dopamine release in the striatum (Koepp et al., 1998). Decreased binding may reflect increased dopamine release, decreased receptor affinity, or decreased receptor availability. In a simulated gambling task, pathological gambling subjects were distinguished from healthy control subjects by demonstrating diminished ventral striatal activation, and activation of this region correlated inversely with gambling severity (Reuter et al., 2005). In a study of unmedicated subjects with pathological gambling, investigators measured relative metabolic rate using ^{18}F-deoxyglucose in PET imaging, to compare computer blackjack for monetary rewards versus points only (Hollander et al., 2005b). They noted significantly higher relative metabolic rates in the primary visual cortex, cingulate gyrus, putamen, and prefrontal cortex in the monetary condition compared to points only, suggesting heightened sensory and limbic activation with increased valence or risk. Other imaging studies have implicated brain regions involved in attentional processing as distinguishing pathological gambling and control subjects when viewing gambling-related material (Crockford et al., 2005).

The neuroimaging data suggest a complex network of brain regions to be activated during impulse control behaviors. Consistent with its dysfunctional role in other addictive processes and psychiatric conditions (e.g., impulsivity in bipolar disorder), multiple studies using different experimental paradigms provide consistent evidence for the involvement of the vmPFC. Similarly, studies suggest a role for the ventral striatum as well, which is not surprising given the importance of the nucleus accumbens in addictive processes. PET studies provide evidence for the possible involvement of dopamine and 5-HT, although more extensive research is needed to confirm and extend these preliminary studies.

Decision Making

Neurocognitive testing is another way to examine how people with impulse control disorders may have problems with the neurocircuitry underlying these behaviors. The Iowa Gambling Task (IGT) was developed as a tool to investigate decision making, particularly risk-reward assessment. The IGT involves selection from different piles of cards with predetermined patterns of rewards and punishments: two are associated with lower rewards and punishments with ultimate long-term gain, while the other two are associated with higher rewards and punishments, ultimately resulting in loss. Patients with vmPFC lesions performed worse in the IGT than did control subjects. Subjects with substance use disorders similarly displayed impaired performance on the IGT (Bechara, 2003). Individuals with pathological gambling have also demonstrated disadvantageous performance on the IGT (Cavedini et al., 2002). Individuals with pathological gambling, similar to subjects with substance use disorders, more readily chose lower monetary rewards promised immediately over higher monetary rewards promised after delayed intervals (termed *discounted delay* of rewards) compared to control subjects (Petry, 2005). Discounted delay behavior was exacerbated by concurrent substance use disorders in individuals with pathological gambling. These findings give further evidence for the role of frontal cortical regions and the mesocorticolimbic system in pathological gambling and strengthen arguments regarding commonality in brain regions with other addictions.

Genetics

Although neurochemistry and neuroanatomy may illuminate dysfunction in some people with impulse control disorders, it is still not clear why certain people are vulnerable to these dysfunctions. Genetics research has started to examine this question.

With the rapid rate of discovery of genetic contributions to psychiatric disorders, the importance of genetics in understanding the neurobiology of impulse control disorders is becoming increasingly apparent. However, genetics studies are currently lacking for most impulse control disorders other than pathological gambling.

POPULATION GENETICS

Samples of twins allow for the estimation of genetic and environmental contributions to a behavior or disorder of interest. A study examining high-action forms of gambling (lottery, gambling machines, casino cards) showed significantly higher rates of similarities in male monozygotic than dizygotic twins (Winters and Rich, 1998). Using data from the Vietnam Era Twin registry, genetic factors were estimated to account for between 35% and 54% of the liability for *DSM-III-R* pathological gambling symptomatology (Eisen et al., 1998). The degree of heritability is similar to those of other psychiatric disorders. Additional studies of this sample have identified common genetic and environmental contributions to pathological gambling and alcohol dependence, and gambling and antisocial behaviors (Slutske et al., 2000, 2001). A more recent investigation found that shared genetic contributions for pathological gambling were not limited to externalizing disorders, but included major depression (Potenza et al., 2005).

MOLECULAR GENETICS

Investigations into specific genes relating to norepinephrine, serotonin, and dopamine neurotransmitter systems and their contribution to impulse control disorders have been performed. As the *D2A1* allele of the *D2R* has been implicated in compulsive and addictive behavior such as drug abuse, compulsive eating, and smoking, one study found in a sample of 171 non-Hispanic Caucasians with pathological gambling, 51% carried the *D2A1* allele compared to 26% of controls (Comings et al., 1996). Frequency of homozygosity of the *Dde I* allele of the *D1R* is elevated compared to controls in pathological gambling, tobacco smokers, and Tourette's syndrome probands (Comings et al., 1997). Allelic variants of the *D4* receptor (*D4R*) gene, which have been implicated in studies of novelty-seeking behavior, may also have a role in impulse control disorders. A study of 68 pathological gamblers found an association with the longest *D4* variant (7-repeat; Perez de Castro et al., 1997).

An association has also been reported between the short allele and pathological gambling (Perez de Castro et al., 1999). This study suggests that the 5-HT system may also be involved in the pathogenesis of pathological gambling.

Twin studies show a substantial genetic contribution to pathological gambling, and these findings are consistent with genetic contributions to other addictions. Molecular genetic studies have probed components of multiple neurotransmitter systems. Compared to biochemical and neuroimaging studies that implicate dopamine systems in pathological gambling, molecular genetic studies to date have yielded more modest results in dopamine and other neurotransmitter systems. As genetic contributions to all of the impulse control disorders become better understood, their utility in developing and targeting treatment strategies should be examined.

Summary

Biochemical, functional neuroimaging, and genetic studies have implicated multiple neurotransmitter systems in the pathophysiology of impulse control disorders. Biological studies have frequently been hindered by heterogeneity within the subject group being studied, and the identification of intermediary phenotypes or endophenotypes is a strategy for limiting the variability and improving measurements. Endophenotypes have not been adequately investigated in impulse control disorders, and identification of relevant endophenotypes could help improve measurement variances in biological studies.

Psychology of Impulse Control Disorders

In addition to neurobiology, behavioral, cognitive, and dispositional attitudes may also play a role in the etiology of impulse control disorders. Behavioral and social learning theorists have focused on the role of direct and vicarious reinforcement in the development and maintenance of behaviors. Cognitive theorists have focused on information processing biases that inflate subjective estimates of succeeding in various behaviors (e.g., winning in gambling, successfully shoplifting) or that otherwise promote impulse behavior persistence. Dispositional traits such as impulsiveness, sensation seeking, neuroticism, and extraversion as well as antisocial personality traits have also been postulated as significant in the development of impulse control disorders.

Positive Reinforcement Model

Positive reinforcement refers to the introduction of a hedonically positive consequence that strengthens a preceding response. From an operant standpoint, the variable ratio of wins and losses built into gambling, or of success and failure built into shoplifting or compulsive sexual behavior, provide a particularly pathogenic formulation. The quintessential positive reinforcer of many impulse control disorders is acquiring something rewarding (e.g., winning money, stealing or buying an item, acquiring sex). The intermittent reinforcement (i.e., the unpredictably variable ratio of success) of impulse control behaviors describes a schedule of reinforcement that is particularly resistant to extinction, even in the absence of reinforcement over many trials.

A range of reinforcers (other than the item of reward) may be available to people with impulse control disorders that may serve to initiate and perpetuate the behavior (e.g., Ocean and Smith, 1993). These include social reinforcers (e.g., interaction with store employees for the compulsive buyer; Christenson et al., 1994), material reinforcers (e.g., drinks and other goods or services provided for gamblers), ambient reinforcers (e.g., a wide array of visual and auditory stimuli present in many stores for kleptomaniacs; Grant and Kim, 2002a), cognitive reinforcers (e.g., near-misses such as being one card away from a large payout for the pathological gambler), and even physiological arousal itself (e.g., the rush reported by people who set fires; Grant and Kim, in press).

Another idea related to operant conditioning involves the effect of big wins early in one's gambling career or a kleptomaniac getting away with a large theft. Two retrospective studies have found that a disproportionate number of pathological gamblers report experiencing big wins early in their gambling career (Snyder, 1978; Walker, 1992). Studies of individuals with kleptomania have found that rarely have they been caught relative to their frequency of shoplifting, and most were not caught until later in the development of their behavioral addiction (Goldman 1991; McElroy et al., 1991; Grant and Kim, 2002a).

Negative Reinforcement Model

A negative reinforcement theory (i.e., involving the removal of a punishing stimulus) hypothesizes that initiating but not completing a habitual behavior leads to uncomfortable states of arousal (McConaghy, 1980). Applied to kleptomania, this would imply that a frequent shoplifter who has begun shopping but not yet accrued a significant amount of items (i.e., completed the behavior) may continue shoplifting in order to experience relief from aversive arousal. This theory shares features in common with drive-reduction theory and could account for why an impulse control behavior continues despite continuous negative consequences.

Another negative reinforcement–based model argues that addictions in general may allow individuals who are chronically either over- or underaroused to achieve optimal arousal levels (Jacobs, 1986). One study assessing personality traits, arousal patterns, and motivation in 12 problem poker machine gamblers and 13 problem horse racing gamblers found that horse racing gamblers scored higher on boredom proneness and sensation seeking and preferred increased arousal levels (Cocco et al., 1995). The researchers concluded that these gamblers selected horse racing to increase their excitement and arousal levels to more desired levels.

Tension Reduction and Affective Regulation

Another negative reinforcement model is based on the idea of self-medication. A number of studies have found elevated rates of depression and anxiety disorders in individuals with impulse control disorders (Chapter 2). The lifetime prevalence rates for mood and anxiety disorders, depending upon the impulse control disorder, range from 28% to 100% and 33% to 80%, respectively (Christenson et al., 1991; McElroy et al., 1991; Schlosser et al., 1994; Black and Moyer, 1998; Grant and

Kim, in press). Depressed or anxious individuals may engage in the impulsive behavior to distract themselves from life stressors and unpleasant cognitions. Persons who are depressed or anxious may also view gambling winnings, buying or stealing items, or having sex as a means of significant symptom relief and the risks of arrest, debt, or sexually transmitted disease as a relatively minor setback. Ironically, problems resulting directly from impulse control disorders (e.g., financial distress, relationship problems, criminal activity) may, in turn, lead to even more impulsive behaviors as a misguided attempt at symptom management.

How do tension reduction and affective regulation relate to impulse control disorders? Is stress a driving factor that contributes to or precipitates the impulsive behavior? Individuals that struggle with these disorders are preoccupied with the behaviors. When an individual attempts to refrain from or reduce the behavior, he or she may become irritable. In many individuals, impulsive behaviors become a means of escaping from negative moods (e.g., anxiety, depression).

An individual's need for tension reduction has been described as a mediating factor in substance addiction and a possible contributing characteristic of impulse control disorders. For example, individuals that develop pathological gambling appear to have abnormal reactions to stress, which is also characteristic of individuals with comorbid mood and affective disorders (Goudriaan et al., 2004). One study reported greater "negative pre-gambling valence" for problem gamblers, which dramatically decreased if the gambler lost and did not significantly improve after winning (Brown et al., 2004). The gambling behavior is thereby negatively reinforced, in avoidance of negative affect or distress (Clarke, 2004). A study of New Zealand university students found that individuals who suffered from problem gambling were more depressed and impulsive than their non–problem gambling peers (Clarke, 2004). Motivations reported by problem gamblers in this study were tension reduction, guilt, and feeling compelled to prove themselves to others. The need for tension reduction may be better conceptualized, in some individuals with impulse control disorders, as an urge to engage in the problem behavior, which can be reinforcing. Individuals experience a craving or urge to engage in the impulsive behavior and, as in cases of chemical dependency, engaging in the behavior may be considered the only way to alleviate that tension.

In the case of trichotillomania, the impact of heightened levels of stress on psychosocial functioning has also been examined (Diefenbach et al., 2005) by comparing a psychiatric control group to individuals diagnosed with trichotillomania. The study found that those with trichotillomania reported lower life satisfaction, higher levels of distress, and lower levels of self-esteem. The lower levels of self-esteem were related to concerns about appearance, feelings of embarrassment, and frustration with the inability to control the impulse to pull hair. In addition, the majority of the sample (96.4%) reported current problems with negative affect and negative self-evaluations. This affective experience is an important motivator for hair pulling, serving as both a stimulus cue and a reinforcer of the behavior. Hair pulling is associated with decreases in tension, boredom, sadness, and anger.

One hypothesis is that hair pulling develops as a habit to cope with stress and then, ironically, the behavior results in intra- and interpersonal distress. Distress results from having to avoid certain activities due to hair loss, such as public activities, sexual intimacy, and athletic endeavors. Distress also results from the individual's inability to control the hair pulling, resulting in lowered self-esteem. Once this impulse control habit has developed into trichotillomania, the negative self-evaluative thoughts and negative affect can serve to perpetuate this problem by prompting additional pulling episodes.

Vicarious Learning

Social learning theory asserts that individuals have a propensity to imitate behaviors they observe that are followed by reinforcement. Thus, individuals who observe the behavior of friends, family members, or even role models on television who either gamble, shop excessively, or have multiple sexual partners may be more likely to engage in all of these behaviors. For example, the potential for media-based vicarious reinforcement of shopping and sexual behavior (through multiple television shows that glamorize this behavior) is greater than for media-based vicarious punishment. Also, hearing of exciting behaviors by others (e.g., lottery or big casino winners telling their stories; Hollywood stars telling about the acquisition of exciting items) is especially salient, relative to hearing about people losing or not being able to afford items. In short, while deprivation tends to be a private affair, we are bombarded with images of rewarding acquisition that can serve as potent vicarious sources of positive reinforcement of impulse control behavior.

Cognitive Factors

In the case of pathological gambling, studies have demonstrated how thinking errors (or cognitive distortions) are linked directly to gambling behavior. This effort has identified a substantial list of specific thinking errors that are believed to worsen, if not directly cause, problematic gambling: (1) superstitious beliefs (e.g., the belief in good-luck objects or behaviors); (2) interpretative biases (e.g., attributing wins to skill and losses to flukes; wrongly believing that a series of losses increases the chance of a subsequent win); (3) temporal telescoping (e.g., expecting that naturally occurring—that is, probabilistically expected—wins will happen sooner rather than later and for them rather than for others); (4) selective memory (e.g., remembering wins while ignoring losses, or totaling wins without correcting for amounts lost); and (5) illusory correlations (i.e., ascribing causal force to contextual stimuli that are only incidentally associated with a win or loss; Abrams and Kushner, 2004). Cognitive distortions occur in other impulse control disorders as well. The compulsive buyer and kleptomaniac both may believe that the items they acquire will bring them happiness, that they can afford the items or will successfully get away with them, and that they need the items to feel comfortable. Most individuals with impulse control disorders have urges to engage in their behavior of choice. The cognitive distortion that they all have is that only by indulging the urge will it go away.

The *sunk cost effect* has been defined as an increased willingness to engage in behavior one ordinarily might not engage in because of money or time already invested in the process (Arkes and Ayton, 1999). This may be especially true for individuals with pathological gambling or compulsive sexual behaviors. For example, pathological gamblers who lose large sums of money at the front end of a gambling session may imagine that the entire net loss could be recouped with a single large payout. Those who compulsively sit at the computer looking unsuccessfully for the "perfect" sexual image will spend hours awaiting the pornographic picture that will result in the most satisfying sexual outlet. Therefore, gambling and sexual behaviors may continue because of time and money already spent rather than because of a string of independent rational decisions.

Personality

Certain personality characteristics may promote impulse control behaviors. For example, being extremely extroverted, neurotic, or impulsive increases one's risk for addictions in general. One study found that individuals with multiple addictions were more impulsive than those with only one addiction (Vitaro et al., 1998). Individuals with addictions tend to share two common features: (1) being chronically over- or under-aroused, and (2) having experienced events in childhood that led to feelings of inadequacy, rejection, or guilt (Jacobs, 1986). Chronically underaroused individuals may gamble, have sex, steal, set fires or shop to reduce levels of boredom. Adults with impulse control disorders frequently report feelings of inferiority and rejection in childhood (Grant and Kim, 2002, 2002c). Such people may raise their self-esteem by creating feelings of success when they beat the odds, successfully steal something, find someone with whom to have sex, or spend large sums of money.

IMPULSIVENESS

Impulsiveness can be defined as acting with little forethought, self-control, or regard for consequences. Trait impulsiveness may promote impulse control disorders, and research has shown that pathological gamblers and kleptomaniacs score high on measures of impulsiveness (Castanelli and Rugle, 1995; Grant and Kim, 2002c). Among males, impulsivity in early adolescence predicted gambling behavior several years later (Vitaro et al., 1998).

Impulsive individuals may be highly responsive to positive reinforcement but rather insensitive to punishment. Impulsive individuals may have to struggle to imagine negative outcomes. Impulsive individuals may also lack the capacity to divide attention among competing stimuli and thus may be insensitive to internally generated cognitions focusing on restraint (Abrams and Kushner, 2004). Thus, the initiation of an impulse behavior may quickly lead to a loss of control. Studies have found that pathological gamblers and individuals who are compulsively sexual (other impulse control disorders have not been studied on this topic) have a greater incidence of ADHD as children (Specker et al., 1996; Kafka and Hennen, 2002).

SENSATION SEEKING

Individuals high in sensation seeking search for novel, exciting experiences that may entail an element of physical or social risk. High levels of sensation seeking have been associated with pathological gambling (Coventry and Brown, 1993), kleptomania (Grant and Kim, 2002c), compulsive sexual behavior (Raymond et al., 2003), and compulsive buying (Lejoyeux et al., 1997). Individuals high in sensation seeking may seek behaviors that provide excitement and produce high arousal (e.g., casino gambling, illicit sex) but may avoid others that do not.

DISSOCIATION

Dissociation, which has been likened to a trance state, involves the separation of normally connected mental processes. Dissociation has been seen as a possible risk factor for addictive behavior (Jacobs, 1986) and may promote impulse control disorders. Dissociation, particularly amnesia, has been reported in individuals with kleptomania (Grant, 2004b). One study examining dissociative tendencies in various types of gamblers and in individuals with alcoholism found that, while gamblers generally were more prone to dissociation than individuals with alcoholism, video machine gamblers were not (Kofoed et al., 1997). Another study has shown, however, that rates of dissociation may be no higher in pathological gambling subjects than in healthy controls (Grant and Kim, 2003).

Integrating Psychological Theories With Neurobiology

One explanation of why all individuals who engage in various behaviors do not succumb to impulse control disorders may be individual differences in biological constraints surrounding reinforcement sensitivity. For some individuals, negative or positive reinforcement from an impulsive behavior may have a more powerful influence on future behavior. Alternatively, some individuals may be more or less sensitive or responsive to the punishment associated with risks, losses, or social opprobrium related to the behavior. Searching for such individual difference moderating variables may ultimately refine both our psychological and biological understanding of operant processes in the etiology and maintenance of impulse control disorders.

Does disordered thinking cause individuals to make irrational decisions and, based on this, engage pathologically in an impulse control behavior? By contrast, perhaps those who are driven to the behavior pathologically are prone to confabulate ideas and views that are consistent with their behavior. Supporting the causal status of irrational thinking in promoting problematic impulsive behavior are data showing that treatments aimed primarily at changing inaccurate beliefs about the impulse control behavior are effective in reducing the behavior (e.g., Petry, 2005; Mitchell et al., 2006). Basic fear-conditioning research has supported the role of memory in the acquisition and relief of fear responses and has related these processes to brain function involving protein synthesis in the lateral and basal nuclei of the amygdala (Nadir et al., 2000). Similar memory structures integrated with brain systems responsible for stimuli valuation and appetitive behavior (as opposed to those related to fear responding) may provide a starting point in the search for a biologically-grounded formulation of impulse control behavior in which cognition plays a central role.

Some individuals may possess broad traits, characteristics, or response proclivities that leave them vulnerable to pathological involvement with particular classes of stimuli. A common neurobiological process may underlie the urge to engage in a range of appetitive behaviors (Grant et al., 2002). Thus, some of the traits or dispositions purported to predispose individuals to impaired impulse control may reflect an underlying biologically based vulnerability. Evidence for this position includes: (1) neurological data implicating the ventral tegmental area–nucleus accumbens–orbital frontal cortex circuits as a potential source of an appetitive urge-based brain mechanism; (2) psychopharmacological data indicating that impulse control disorders respond to the same medications; and (3) epidemiological data demonstrating that having one impulse control disorder substantially increases one's risk of having other impulse control disorders involving strong appetitive urges. The view that impulse control disorder vulnerability is related to one or more broad psychological traits, which are themselves manifestations of a specific neurobiological status, receives substantial indirect support.

Conclusion

There is growing evidence that particular neurochemical, neuroanatomical, genetic, psychological, and cognitive factors play crucial roles in the genesis and maintenance of impulse control disorders. What we have currently are multiple pieces of a complex puzzle; how they all fit together and whether they will ever all fit together requires further study. We currently speak of these disorders as a group. The examination of pathogenesis may lead us to question whether these behaviors all belong in the same category, and whether all people with a particular disorder should be categorized together. Another question is whether these findings of dysfunction (neurochemically, psychologically, etc.) represent a vulnerability to these behaviors, or a consequence of these behaviors. Longitudinal studies may help answer this important question.

CHAPTER 7

Assessment of Impulse Control Disorders

THE PROCESS OF assessment is an integral and ongoing aspect of the effective treatment of impulse control disorders. Assessment can include establishing the initial diagnosis, comorbid diagnoses, baseline level of symptom severity, associated triggers and reinforcers of the behavior, and treatment-related change.

Assessment should be performed by the clinician, but the patient and the patient's support network play vital roles. The format should include a clinical interview, clinician rating and self-report scales, and self-monitoring. Assessments begin at the initial evaluation but should continue throughout treatment. Assessment may differ based on whether pharmacotherapy or psychotherapy is the primary treatment approach.

This chapter reviews the goals and methods of assessment of impulse control disorders as well as some of the assessment-related difficulties unique to these disorders.

Failure to Diagnose

Although impulse control disorders are quite common in the general population (8.9% with current impulse disorder; Kessler et al., 2006) as well as psychiatric populations (30.9% with current impulse disorder; Grant et al., 2005), they usually go undiagnosed (Grant et al., 2005). Many reasons exist for why these severely distressing behaviors are not diagnosed.

Shame and Secrecy

Shame and secrecy are fundamental to impulse control disorders. Many of the impulse control disorders involve either illegal behaviors (kleptomania, pyromania, intermittent explosive disorder), what might be considered immoral behaviors (pathological gambling, compulsive sexual behavior), financial problems (pathological gambling, compulsive buying), or behaviors related to appearance concerns (trichotillomania, pathological skin picking). Most people are embarrassed by the lack of control that is inherent in impulse control disorders. This embarrassment and shame appear to explain, in part, why so few patients will volunteer information regarding these behaviors unless specifically asked (Grant et al., 2005).

Often related to shame and secrecy is the patient's misunderstanding of what a mental health clinician is required by law to report. Patients suffering from kleptomania and pyromania, in particular, may believe that the clinician is required to report their illegal behaviors. This is also the case when people with pathological gambling and compulsive buying resort to criminal behavior to indulge their impulse control problem or to correct the financial effects of the gambling or buying (Potenza et al., 2000). Clinicians therefore may want to inform patients at the outset of the evaluation what they do and do not have to report.

Patients' Lack of Knowledge

Another possible reason for the failure to diagnose impulse control disorders is that patients often do not know that the behavior they are struggling with is a recognizable disorder with treatment options. Because many of the behaviors associated with impulse control disorders exist along a continuum of severity, and because most people have performed the behaviors at least once in their lives, patients often do not understand when a behavior becomes pathological and deserving attention. For example, our group has completed a study of impulse control disorders among college students. We assessed behaviors as well as the pathological version of the behaviors. We found that a majority of college students pulled their hair at least once, had stolen something, had a sexual experience that they regretted, and so on. It was a considerably smaller percentage of students, however, who met criteria for an actual psychiatric disorder (unpublished data). Using the general criteria for impulse control disorders set forth in *DSM-IV-TR* (APA, 2000), clinicians can inform patients that if a behavior or urge to engage in a behavior preoccupies the person and causes distress or dysfunction, then a more complete discussion of the behavior should occur.

Related to the general lack of knowledge about these disorders is the often erroneous belief that patients can change the behavior on their own. This belief is often related to the shame and secrecy aspect as well. Patients may have gone several months without engaging in the behavior in the past and therefore believe that they can control it on their own. Supporting this idea is the fact that natural recovery, at least in the case of pathological gambling, occurs in approximately one third of cases (Slutske, 2006). Because we have little data regarding the clinical course of these disorders, clinicians should be aware that although some people naturally recover, the majority do not appear to do so. Patients may also be informed that although natural recovery is possible, treatment may speed the process and make the recovery less burdensome.

Clinicians' Lack of Knowledge

Few health care professionals have education or training in impulse control disorders. Even those clinicians who are aware of related disorders (e.g., obsessive-compulsive disorder) may have no knowledge of impulse behaviors. In addition, clinicians may have many of the same biases about these behaviors that patients do. For example, clinicians may see themselves as potential victims of the illegal behaviors associated with impulse control disorders—that is, clinicians pay more for items due to shoplifting; insurance premiums are higher because of fire-setting risks—and therefore may not feel the behavior is an illness and deserving of treatment. In both instances, continuing education in the area of impulse control disorders and their neurobiological underpinnings may help alleviate some of the ignorance and judgment that possibly impede proper diagnosis.

Misdiagnosis

Impulse control disorders bear phenomenological similarities to many other psychiatric disorders (Grant and Potenza, 2004a). This overlap in clinical presentation makes diagnosis difficult. When combined with lack of knowledge regarding the clinical characteristics of impulse control disorders, the likelihood of misdiagnosis is considerable. Some of the more common misdiagnoses are discussed in this section.

Mood Disorder

Bipolar manic episodes are characterized by impulsive behaviors (APA, 2000). These manic behaviors may include many of the behaviors seen in impulse control disorders: impulsive sexual behavior, excessive spending, gambling, and stealing. In addition, individuals with impulse control disorders have high rates of co-occurring bipolar disorder: 9–60% in kleptomania (McElroy et al., 1991; Grant and Kim, 2002a); 10–35% in compulsive buying (McElroy et al., 1994; Lejoyeux et al., 1997); 24% in pathological gambling (Linden et al., 1986); and 14% in compulsive sexual behavior (Black et al., 1997).

During a manic episode, however, people often exhibit multiple symptoms of mood dysregulation—excess energy, distractibility, elevation, or irritability (APA, 2000)—whereas the behavior of an impulse control disorder may have none of those associated symptoms. In addition, the behaviors during a manic episode may last only a few days or a couple of weeks, whereas the behaviors associated with impulse control disorders tend to be more consistent. The *DSM-IV-TR* excludes a diagnosis of an impulse control disorder when the behavior occurs exclusively during a manic episode (APA, 2000). Individuals with impulse control disorders may also suffer from bipolar disorder, and then it is important for the clinician to determine if the behaviors exist only during mania or possible simply worsen during a manic episode.

Many patients may report engaging in their behavior only when feeling depressed (Steel and Blaszczynski, 1996). Rates of depression are elevated in individuals with impulse control disorders (50–100% depending upon the particular disorder; McElroy et al., 1991; Christenson and Mansueto, 1999; Argo and Black, 2004). These patients, therefore, may also be given a diagnosis of bipolar disorder, mixed state, or unipolar depression. In fact, there may be a subtype of impulse control patient who finds mood elevation from the behavior and therefore self-medicates with the impulse behavior (Fishbain, 1987). In cases where the behavior is secondary to mood, the underlying mood should be treated, but the impulsive behavior may need additional treatment as well. Although the behavior may have been started to self-medicate the mood, the behavior may be maintained by a different neurobiological mechanism (Grant, et al., 2002).

Obsessive-Compulsive Disorder

As mentioned in Chapter 3, there is often significant clinical overlap between obsessive-compulsive disorder and impulse control disorders (Grant and Potenza, 2006). Patients may even refer to themselves as obsessive or engaged in a behavior compulsively. Although patients with impulse control disorders, like those with obsessive-compulsive disorder, may engage in a behavior repetitively and be preoccupied with thoughts of the behavior, the key difference is that people with impulse control disorders feel pleasure from the behavior (Grant and Potenza, 2006c). Obsessive-compulsive behaviors are generally done to alleviate anxiety.

Grooming disorders, in particular, may be confused with obsessive-compulsive disorder. Many individuals with trichotillomania and pathological skin picking exhibit significant clinical similarities to obsessive-compulsive disorder and body dysmorphic disorder (Grant et al., 2007). Is the person pulling or picking because of contamination fears or symmetry issues? If so, a diagnosis of obsessive-compulsive disorder may be appropriate. Is the person pulling or picking to improve appearance? If so, body dysmorphic disorder may be the proper diagnosis (Phillips and Taub, 1995). In these cases, it is important for the clinician to assess whether the person finds pleasure in pulling or picking and whether the person has urges to pull or pick, as they may distinguish an impulse control disorder. These disorders may also co-occur (Phillips and Taub, 1995; Stewart et al., 2005) and, in that case, should be treated as independent issues. Because treatment approaches between obsessive-compulsive disorder and these grooming disorders differ, accurate diagnosis is important.

Substance Use Disorders

Substance use disorders frequently co-occur in individuals with impulse control disorders: pathological gambling, 36–63% (Argo and Black, 2004); compulsive buying, 21–36% (Black 2006); kleptomania, 20–45% (McElroy et al., 1991; Bayle et al., 2003); pyromania, 33% (Grant and Kim, in press); and compulsive sexual behavior, 22% (Black et al., 1997). It is important for clinicians to determine: (1) Does the substance use problem result in the impulsive behavior perhaps through disinhibition (e.g., shoplifting only when intoxicated) or modulation of particular brain pathways (e.g., methamphetamine may result in uncontrollable picking); (2) Does the impulsive behavior, and the shame and the desire to escape, cause the substance use (e.g., shame over sexual behavior leads to frequent drinking); or (3) are they two related but independent problems?

Personality Disorders

Although rates of personality disorders in individuals with impulse control disorders have been less rigorously examined, some studies suggest that personality disorders may be present at higher rates than seen in the community: pathological gambling (most commonly borderline, obsessive-compulsive, and antisocial personality disorders; Argo and Black, 2004); trichotillomania (most commonly histrionic and avoidant personality disorders; Christenson and Mansueto, 1999); kleptomania (most commonly paranoid and borderline personality disorders; Grant, 2004a); compulsive sexual behavior (most commonly histrionic and paranoid personality disorders; Black et al., 1997); and compulsive buying (most commonly obsessive compulsive and borderline personality disorders; Schlosser et al., 1994).

The clinician must therefore determine if the impulsive behavior is an independent disorder, or secondary to a personality disorder. This may be particularly difficult in the case of borderline personality and antisocial personality disorders, which are characterized by impulsivity (APA, 2000). Several clues may help the clinician. For example, people with antisocial personality disorder exhibit a wide range of behaviors that are contrary to social norms. In the case of individuals with kleptomania, pyromania, or pathological gambling, the impulse control behavior is often their only behavior that violates social norms. Borderline personality disorder may also be associated with impulsive behaviors such as stealing, sex, and fire setting. Unlike many individuals with impulse control disorders, those with borderline personality disorder most likely will exhibit a history of unstable interpersonal relationships. The clinician should be aware that the impulse disorders often co-occur with personality disorders, and clear separation of the behaviors may not be possible at first assessment. Continued assessments may be necessary to determine to what extent these various disorders interact in a patient.

Initial Assessment

Because of the risk of missed or inaccurate diagnoses, the clinician should conduct a thorough psychiatric evaluation that encompasses a description of the presenting problem, a complete mental status examination, comprehensive psychosocial and family histories, and history of psychiatric treatment. Clinicians should also assess relevant triggers and reinforcers associated with the impulse control behavior to focus both psychosocial and pharmacological treatment efforts.

Prior to starting treatment, the clinician should establish a baseline level of severity of the impulse control disorder, which will provide for subsequent comparison with severity levels during treatment. This assessment can be performed using clinician-based scale and patient self-report forms.

The following is a systematic description of an assessment method. Where possible, the various measures are described. For some disorders, there are no validated measures to assess change in treatment response. In these cases, the chapter provides reasonable means of assessment.

Clinician Interview

The initial clinical interview for impulse control disorders should be similar to that used for assessment of any psychiatric disorder. Given the significant comorbidity of psychiatric disorders (particularly mood and substance use disorders) with impulse control disorders, the interview should be broad in focus.

To help overcome the patient's reluctance to answer questions regarding impulse control disorders, the clinician can use a simple screening instrument, the Minnesota Impulse Disorders Interview (MIDI; see Appendix A). This can be performed by the nurse or clinic staff before the patient sees the clinician so as to target certain behaviors of concern. The MIDI is a semistructured clinical interview widely used to screen for pathological gambling, trichotillomania, kleptomania, pyromania, intermittent explosive disorder, compulsive buying, and compulsive sexual behavior. It has demonstrated very good reliability and validity in both adolescents and adults (Grant et al., 2005, in press). The MIDI consists of probe questions for each disorder, with additional follow-up questions reflecting *DSM* criteria. Questions for compulsive buying and compulsive sexual behavior reflect the impulse control disorder criteria of increasing tension followed by relief, personal distress, and impairment. The MIDI takes no more than 20 minutes to administer and can be quickly scored (see the scoring sheet in Appendix A).

Given the shame and embarrassment associated with the impulse control disorders, questions arise concerning the involvement of significant others in the interview. On the one hand, accurate information may not be forthcoming from the patient alone, largely due to the patient's denial over the behavior and its repercussions. For example, pathological gamblers may not reveal the extent of their financial difficulties due to gambling. On the other hand, patients often have not told significant others about their behaviors due to shame (Grant and Kim, 2002a); therefore, they may not want a significant other present for the interview. Clinicians need to balance the privacy wishes of the patient with the need for accurate information. For example, the clinician may therefore conduct the initial interview with the patient alone and over time discuss the need for collateral information.

The clinician should conduct a functional analysis of the problematic behavior. This will help identify relevant cues or triggers that precede the impulse control behavior and the reinforcers that maintain the behavior (Petry, 2005). The triggers that prompt the urges can be emotional, situational, behavioral, or cognitive (Christenson et al., 1991;

Grant and Kim, 2002a). Identifying the stimulus for the behavior is crucial to better prepare the patient to cope with high-risk situations in the future.

The clinician should also enquire about the impact of the behavior on the patient's emotional, social, and occupational functioning. Commonly reported negative consequences of impulse control disorders include decrease in self-esteem, problems within relationships, legal difficulties, health problems, and thoughts of suicide (McElroy et al., 1991; Christenson and Mansueto, 1999; Desai et al., 2004; Ledgerwood and Petry, 2004). Identification of these consequences can be a motivational tool and can target areas of functioning affected by the impulse control disorder that can also be monitored during treatment.

Making the Diagnosis

Several instruments are used to standardize the diagnosis of certain impulse control disorders:

- *Trichotillomania.* Clinicians may wish to use the Trichotillomania Diagnostic Interview (Rothbaum and Ninan, 1994). This instrument was modeled after the Structured Clinical Interview for *DSM* (First et al., 1995).
- *Pathological gambling.* The Structured Clinical Interview for Pathological Gambling is a valid and reliable clinician-administered instrument for diagnosing pathological gambling (Grant et al., 2004).
- *Kleptomania.* Clinicians should use the valid and reliable Structured Clinical Interview for Kleptomania (Grant et al., 2006).

The other impulse control disorders currently included in *DSM-IV-TR* (pyromania and intermittent explosive disorder) lack published structured clinical interviews. For those disorders, the clinician can make the diagnosis by simply following the inclusion and exclusion criteria for the disorders.

The impulse control disorders that have been proposed for inclusion in the *DSM* (compulsive sexual behavior, compulsive buying, pathological skin picking, and Internet addiction) lack agreed-upon diagnostic criteria. Diagnosis of these disorders is best made by using criteria that have been proposed and used in multiple phenomenological and treatment studies.

COMPULSIVE BUYING

The diagnostic criteria for this disorder are the following (McElroy et al., 1994):

1. Maladaptive preoccupation with buying or shopping, or maladaptive buying or shopping urges or behavior as indicated by either preoccupations with buying or urges to buy that are irresistible, intrusive, or senseless or frequent buying of more than can be afforded, buying unneeded items, or shopping for longer periods of time than intended.
2. Preoccupations, urges, or behavior causes marked distress or interferes with functioning or results in financial problems.
3. The shopping or buying does not exclusively occur during hypomania or mania.

PATHOLOGICAL SKIN PICKING

The following criteria help to diagnose this disorder (Arnold et al., 2001):

1. Recurrent picking at or otherwise manipulating the skin that results in noticeable damage to the skin.
2. Increasing sense of tension, or an unpleasant emotional or physical state, immediately before picking the skin, or when trying to resist picking.
3. Pleasure, gratification, or relief at the time of picking.
4. Disturbance causes clinically significant distress or impairment in social, occupational, or other important areas of function.
5. Skin picking is not due to a substance (e.g., cocaine, amphetamine) or a general medical condition (e.g., eczema, psoriasis, diabetes, liver or kidney disease, Hodgkin's disease, polycythemia vera, systemic lupus).
6. Skin picking is not better accounted for by another mental disorder

(e.g., body dysmorphic disorder, obsessive-compulsive disorder, delusional disorder, substance use disorder).

INTERNET ADDICTION

These criteria have been used to diagnose this disorder (Shapira et al., 2003):

1. Maladaptive preoccupation with Internet use defined by either pre-occupations that are irresistible or excessive use of the Internet for periods longer than intended.
2. Use of the Internet causes marked distress or impairment.
3. Excessive use does not occur exclusively during hypomania or mania.

COMPULSIVE SEXUAL BEHAVIOR

The criteria used for this disorder mirror those used for the other impulse control disorders:

1. Maladaptive preoccupation with sexual behavior defined by urges or thoughts about sex that are irresistible or excessive sexual behavior that is uncontrollable.
2. Sexual urges, thoughts, or behavior that cause marked distress or impairment.
3. Sexual urges, thoughts, or behavior do not occur exclusively during hypomania or mania.

Symptom Severity Scales

In addition to diagnosing the problem, the clinician should assess the severity of the disorder. Scales help to assess severity and, when performed over time, allow the clinician to see if improvement occurs.

CLINICIAN-RATED SCALES

Several clinician-administered scales are currently available that can be used to rate the severity of baseline symptoms and measure treatment-related improvement, and so the following list is not exhaustive. Below are examples of scales for the various disorders. One scale that was originally designed for the assessment of obsessive-compulsive disorder has been modified for multiple impulse control disorders.

The Yale-Brown Obsessive Compulsive Scale (Y-BOCS) is a 10-item scale originally designed to assess the severity of obsessions and compulsions in obsessive-compulsive disorder. The scale has shown good content and construct validity and is sensitive to change in response to treatment.

The Y-BOCS has been adapted for multiple impulse control disorders. The Y-BOCS has been modified for pathological gambling (PG-YBOCS; Pallanti et al., 2005), pathological skin picking (also called neurotic excoriation; NE-YBOCS; Arnold et al., 1999), kleptomania (Koran et al., 2007a), compulsive buying (Koran et al., 2007b), compulsive sexual behavior (Wainberg et al., 2006), and trichotillomania (Stanley et al., 1993). In each of these instances, the Y-BOCS comprises two subscales, one that rates urges and thoughts and one that rates behavior. The PG-YBOCS and the trichotillomania version have shown good preliminary psychometrics. The other versions do not have published validity or reliability results.

In addition to the various versions of the Y-BOCS, trichotillomania has another clinician-administered scale, the National Institute of Mental Health Trichotillomania Symptom Severity and Impairment Scale (Swedo et al., 1989). The symptom severity subscale includes 6 items assessing hair-pulling frequency, urge intensity and ability to resist, distress, and interference. The impairment subscale is an 11-point test of impairment severity.

PATIENT-RATED SCALES

Sometimes patients are embarrassed about their behaviors. Allowing them to complete forms can tell the clinician how the patient is doing without embarrassing the patient with direct questions and answers.

Trichotillomania. Only one self-report instrument exists for the assessment of repetitive hair pulling. The Massachusetts General Hospital Hairpulling Scale (Keuthen et al., 1995) is a 7-item scale examining frequency and intensity of urges to pull, ability to control urges, frequency of behavior, resistance to pulling, and distress.

Pathological skin picking. The Skin Picking Impact Scale (Keuthen et al., 2001) is a 10-item self-report scale examining duration of daily picking, satisfaction during picking, and shame subsequent to picking. The scale has demonstrated good reliability and validity.

Pathological gambling. There are actually several scales for the patient to report the severity of pathological gambling symptoms. A few examples follow:

The Time-Line Follow-Back modified for gambling (Grant and Potenza, 2004b) assesses the number of days and the amount of money spent gambling over the past month. This modified scale has demonstrated excellent psychometric properties.

The Gambling Treatment Outcome Monitoring System (GAM-TOMS) is a multidimensional assessment that has demonstrated good validity and reliability (Grant and Potenza, 2004b).

The Gambling Symptom Assessment Scale (G-SAS; Kim et al., 2001) is a 12-item, reliable and valid, self-rated scale assessing gambling urges, thoughts, and behaviors during the previous 7 days. Each item is rated 0 to 4 with a possible total score of 48. Higher scores reflect greater severity of pathological gambling symptoms.

The G-SAS has been modified for many of the other impulse control disorders: the Kleptomania Symptom Assessment Scale (Grant and Kim, 2002b), Sexual Symptom Assessment Scale (Raymond et al., 2007), the Skin Picking Symptom Assessment Scale (Grant et al., in press), and the Pyromania Symptom Assessment Scale (available from the author).

Ongoing Symptom Monitoring

Ongoing assessment is important for the evaluation and documentation of treatment outcome. In the case of behavioral treatment, it is important to assess the circumstances under which the behavior continues to occur during treatment. Doing so will underscore those situations in which the patient needs to use previously learned coping skills more consistently or learn new strategies.

The measures previously mentioned can be used throughout treatment to document changes. In addition, clinicians can use the Clinical Global Improvement (CGI) Scale (Guy, 1976) to rate progress. The CGI consists of two reliable and valid 7-item Likert scales used to assess severity and change in clinical symptoms. The improvement scale ranges from 1 = very much improved to 7 = very much worse. Both clinician- and subject-rated improvement scores can be performed at each visit. The CGI severity scale ranges from 1 = not ill at all to 7 = among the most extremely ill. The CGI has been used extensively in pharmacological treatment studies. This scale can be extremely valuable for those impulse control disorders—intermittent explosive disorder and pyromania—that currently lack either clinician-administered or self-report scales.

Clinicians should also consider using a measure of psychosocial functioning (e.g., Sheehan Disability Scale; Sheehan, 1983) and quality of life (e.g., Quality of Life Inventory; Frisch et al., 1993). Research indicates that overall functioning is often severely impaired in individuals suffering impulse control disorders (Grant et al., 2006b) and that these individuals suffer from poor quality of life (Grant and Kim, 2005). Assessing the change in these domains may not only let the clinician know if treatment effects extend beyond the symptoms of the disorder but may also play a role in predicting who continues in treatment. (If someone's functioning or quality of life does not improve, would we expect that person to continue to take medication or come for therapy?)

Only a few studies have attempted to measure the acceptability of treatment procedures. Noncompliance is more likely when the patient has negative views about the treatment. Clinicians should consider assessing the acceptability of their treatment approach at various junctures throughout treatment.

Problems in Assessing Impulse Control Disorders

Several issues complicate the process of assessment in impulse control disorders. Among these are shame and embarrassment (as discussed for diagnostic purposes), symptom denial, fluctuating symptoms, and multiple impulsive behaviors with switching between behaviors.

Patients with impulse control disorders can be highly secretive about their symptoms, which can lead to avoidance of symptom disclosure or denial of symptom severity.

Additionally, the severity of these disorders can fluctuate widely in terms of frequency and intensity of behavior. Severity may worsen when the patient is under additional life stress or, conversely, improve during times of low stress. Triggers for behavior can also vary depending on circumstances in a patient's life. Therefore, it is imperative that baseline monitoring be of sufficient duration so that treatment is not started when the symptoms are naturally decreasing.

Furthermore, given the comorbidity of multiple impulse control disorders in the same patient, the assessment might examine only one behavior, and overlook that the patient has switched to another impulsive behavior. For example, the pathological gambler is able to stop gambling for a period of time, but becomes compulsive about Internet pornography. If the assessment is only examining gambling symptoms, the patient may appear vastly improved. Assessments should therefore include reassessment of other impulsive behaviors, even if these behaviors were not of concern at the time of initial evaluation. Also, because mood or anxiety may worsen when someone limits impulsive behavior, the assessment should include a thorough mental health examination.

Because the behaviors of impulse control disorders are difficult to assess in an objective manner, changes in behavior may not be detected or may be considered better than they actually are. When self-report of behavior is the way improvement is assessed, the clinician and patient will need to find solutions that will allow for objective data collection without significant interference in the patient's life or violation of the patient's privacy. Daily self-monitoring of urges and behavior may be a more accurate assessment than retrospectively recalling the past week or two. Credit card receipts and bank statements can be used to better assess compulsive buying and pathological gambling. In addition, information from a significant other may improve examination of behavior if the person has adequate contact to assess this.

Duration of the Assessment

Because of the lack of adequate longitudinal studies, there is no definitive answer to the question of how long impulse control disorders persist. Given the waxing and waning course of these disorders, it is important that the patient and clinician do not prematurely terminate treatment.

When assessing improvement, it is important to determine if the person desires the behavior even when not engaging in the behavior.

Many patients can have long abstinence from the behavior but will be preoccupied with related thoughts or urges. As pointed out earlier, many patients may also simply switch behaviors and not mention this to the clinician.

In general, if a patient has at least 1 year of abstinence without any urges to engage in the behavior and not switch to another behavior, then the clinician should consider starting to reduce the frequency and intensity of treatment.

Conclusion

The issue of assessment presents particular challenges in the field of impulse control disorders. At present, there is no standard for the perfect assessment of these disorders. Different researchers may employ varying assessment techniques. These differences have made comparison of treatment interventions difficult. Also, different assessment techniques may depend upon whether the assessment is for consultation only or for continuing treatment.

Given these limitations, the clinician should consider multiple assessment measures to produce the most reliable and valid assessment. Confirmation of clinician-administered and self-report measures with significant others should be considered.

CHAPTER 8

How to Treat Impulse Control Disorders

DESPITE HIGH PREVALENCE rates in the general population (Kessler, Berglund et al., 2005) and in psychiatric cohorts (Grant et al., 2005), the treatment of impulse control disorders has been relatively under-studied. Controlled treatment trials do not exist for many of the impulse control disorders. Arguably the most-well researched—pathological gambling—has only recently been systematically investigated with respect to empirically supported behavioral and pharmacological treatments. Because rigorous research is particularly limited for several of the impulse control disorders (e.g., pyromania and Internet addiction), this chapter reviews the available research on the treatment of pathological gambling, trichotillomania, compulsive buying, compulsive sexual behavior, pathological skin picking, intermittent explosive disorder, and kleptomania.

Pathological Gambling

Pharmacological Treatment

Several medications have been investigated as treatments for pathological gambling. These medications have included antidepressants (particularly serotonin reuptake inhibitors, SRIs), mood stabilizers, and opioid antagonists. Seven open-label studies using various medications (citalopram, carbamazepine, nefazodone, bupropion, valproate, and naltrexone) for short periods of time (8–14 weeks) have demonstrated efficacy in 73% of pathological gambling subjects. Also, 12 double-blind, placebo-controlled pharmacotherapy studies have been performed in pathological gambling, but the results of these studies have demonstrated mixed efficacy and tolerability.

ANTIDEPRESSANTS

Hypotheses underlying the examination of antidepressant medications for pathological gambling are based on the neurobiology of impulse control disorders. Low levels of the serotonin metabolite 5-hydroxyindolacetic acid (5-HIAA) and blunted serotonergic response within the ventromedial prefrontal cortex (vmPFC) have been associated with impulsive behaviors (Linnoila et al., 1993; Mehlman et al., 1995; Virkkunen et al., 1995; Coccaro, 1996; Rogers et al., 1999). Individuals with pathological gambling demonstrate diminished activation of the vmPFC when viewing gambling-related videotapes or during prepotent response inhibition when performing the Stroop color-word interference task (Potenza, Leung, et al., 2003; Potenza, Steinberg, et al., 2004). Individuals with pathological gambling also show relatively diminished activation of the vmPFC during a simulated gambling task, and severity of gambling problems correlated inversely with signal intensity within this brain region (Reuter et al., 2005). Together, the findings suggest that decreased serotonin function within vmPFC may engender disinhibition and contribute to pathological gambling. Thus, drugs targeting serotonin neurotransmission have been examined in the treatment of pathological gambling.

Of the 12 double-blind, placebo-controlled pharmacological studies in pathological gambling, 7 have examined SRIs. Clomipramine, an SRI that also inhibits norepinephrine reuptake, was the first SRI tested in a controlled fashion. After receiving placebo for 10 weeks without response, the single subject reported a 90% improvement in gambling symptoms after being treated with 125 mg per day of clomipramine (Hollander et al., 1992). There have been no further controlled studies of clomipramine, however, to confirm the limited results of this initial study. In addition to its more common side effects (dry mouth, constipation, blurred vision, sexual dysfunction, weight gain, fine tremor, muscle twitching), clomipramine may also cause cardiac conduction problems and has significant drug-drug interactions.

In a double-blind, placebo-controlled study using sertraline, 60 subjects with pathological gambling were treated for 6 months (mean dose = 95 mg per day; Saiz-Ruiz et al., 2005). At the end of the study, 23 sertraline-treated subjects (74%) and 21 placebo-treated subjects (72%) were rated as responders based on the primary outcome measure (Criteria for Control of Pathological Gambling Questionnaire), which assessed urges to gamble and gambling behavior. Sertraline did not demonstrate superiority to placebo. Sertraline was generally well tolerated, but sertraline may cause sedation, constipation, weight gain, headache, sexual dysfunction, and dry mouth.

Only two SRIs have been examined in at least two randomized, placebo-controlled trials of pathological gambling. A double-blind, 16-week crossover study of fluvoxamine in 15 subjects demonstrated a statistically significant difference compared to placebo (Hollander et al., 2000). Interpretation of the study is complicated, however, by a phase order treatment interaction (i.e., the medication did not separate from placebo during the first phase but did in the second phase). A 6-month double-blind placebo-controlled trial of fluvoxamine in 32 gamblers failed to show statistical significance compared to placebo. The results of the latter study, however, are complicated by high rates of treatment discontinuation (only 3 subjects on medication completed the study) and a high placebo response rate (59%; Blanco et al., 2002). Differences in the results may be attributable to the temporal duration of each study as well as the differences in outcome measures. Although fluvoxamine is generally well tolerated, it may result in gastrointestinal distress, sedation, mild anxiety, headache, increased urinary frequency, and sexual dysfunction. Fluvoxamine is a potent P450 1A2 inhibitor, and drug-drug interactions should be considered before it is prescribed.

As with fluvoxamine, studies of paroxetine have failed to demonstrate consistent efficacy in treating pathological gambling. An initial double-blind, placebo-controlled study of paroxetine indicated its potential efficacy. Significant improvement was seen in subjects randomized to 8 weeks of treatment with paroxetine compared to those assigned to placebo (Kim et al., 2002). A larger multicenter double-blind placebo-controlled trial, however, failed to reproduce the results (Grant et al., 2003). In this second study, a high placebo response rate was observed: at study end, 48% of those assigned to placebo and 59% of those taking paroxetine were considered responders. Further study appears warranted to determine whether specific subgroups of individuals with pathological gambling (e.g., those with specific genetic characteristics) will respond preferentially to treatment with paroxetine or other SRIs.

In an attempt to target one subtype of pathological gamblers (those with significant anxiety driving their gambling behavior), a study examined escitalopram in an open-label 12-week trial with an 8-week double-blind discontinuation period for responders (Grant and Potenza, 2006). Of 13 subjects treated with a mean dose of 25.4 mg per day, 62% were considered responders in terms of both pathological gambling and anxiety symptoms. Four of six subjects who completed the study and were responders were entered into an 8-week double-blind discontinuation. Of the three assigned to escitalopram, improvement continued for the next 8 weeks, whereas both gambling symptoms and anxiety returned within 4 weeks for the subject assigned to placebo.

In the only controlled study of a non-SRI antidepressant, Black and colleagues (2007) examined the efficacy of bupropion in a 12-week double-blind design, in which 39 subjects were randomized to bupropion or placebo. Although both groups showed response, the treatment groups did not differ significantly.

MOOD STABILIZERS
Early case reports suggested that alternate classes of drugs, such as mood stabilizers, might be helpful for specific individuals with pathological gambling (Haller and Hinterhuber, 1994; Pallanti, Quercioli et al., 2002). Although carbamazepine and valproate appeared efficacious in open-label examinations of pathological gambling, there has been only one randomized, placebo-controlled trial of a mood stabilizer in pathological gambling.

In a double-blind, placebo-controlled study of 40 pathological gambling subjects with bipolar spectrum disorders (bipolar type II, bipolar not otherwise specified, or cyclothymia), sustained-release lithium carbonate (mean lithium level 0.87 meq/L) was shown to be superior to placebo in reducing pathological gambling symptoms during 10 weeks of treatment (Hollander et al., 2005a). Although a majority (83%) of subjects in the treatment group displayed significant decreases in gambling urges, thoughts, and behaviors, no differences were found in amount of money lost, episodes of gambling per week, or time spent per gambling episode. Subjects in this study tolerated lithium without difficulty, but lithium may cause fine tremor, nausea, diarrhea, and nephrotoxicity when used chronically.

OPIOID ANTAGONISTS

Mu-opioid receptor antagonists inhibit dopamine release in the nucleus accumbens and ventral pallidum through the disinhibition of gamma-aminobutyric acid (GABA) input to the dopamine neurons in the ventral tegmental area (Broekkamp and Phillips, 1979; Phillips and LePiane, 1980; van Wolfswinkel and van Ree, 1985). Mu-opioid antagonists are thought to decrease dopamine neurotransmission in the nucleus accumbens and linked motivational neurocircuitry, thus dampening gambling-related excitement and cravings (Kim, 1998). As compared with control comparison subjects, individuals with pathological gambling show differences in nucleus accumbens activation during a simulated gambling task (Reuter et al., 2005). Although modulation of drive and subsequent behavioral output by dopamine, endorphin, and GABA have been investigated, the specific mechanisms underlying mu-opioid receptor antagonism in specific patient groups such as those with pathological gambling remain incompletely understood (Koob, 1992; Kalivas and Barnes, 1993).

Following a promising open-label study (Kim and Grant, 2001c), a 12-week double-blind placebo-controlled trial of naltrexone demonstrated superiority to placebo in 45 subjects with pathological gambling (Kim et al., 2002). Naltrexone (mean dose 188 mg per day) reduced the frequency and intensity of gambling urges and gambling behavior. A separate analysis of those subjects with at least moderate urges to gamble revealed that naltrexone was more effective in gamblers with more severe urges. Naltrexone's clinical use, however, is limited by significant side effects as well as the occurrence of liver enzyme elevations, especially in patients taking nonsteroidal anti-inflammatory drugs (Kim et al., 2001a). Over 20% of subjects receiving active naltrexone developed abnormal liver function tests during the 12-week study (Kim et al., 2001b).

A multicenter study further demonstrated the efficacy of another opioid antagonist, nalmefene (25 mg per day), in the treatment of pathological gambling. In a sample of 207 subjects, nalmefene demonstrated statistically significant improvement in gambling symptoms compared to placebo in a 16-week double-blind trial (Grant et al., 2006). This study, however, suffered from high rates of treatment discontinuation (63%) due to side effects. Common side effects of opioid antagonists include nausea, dizziness, insomnia, headaches, and loose stool. Nalmefene in tablet form is not approved for use in the United States.

GLUTAMATERGIC AGENTS

Dopaminergic systems, which influence rewarding and reinforcing behaviors, have been implicated in impulse control disorders. Research hypothesizes that agents that can improve glutamatergic tone within the nucleus accumbens may reduce reward-seeking behavior in addictions (Kalivas et al., 2006). Studies examining cocaine addiction in rats demonstrate that N-acetylcysteine, an amino acid and cysteine pro-drug, appears to increase extracellular levels of glutamate, stimulate inhibitory metabotropic glutamate receptors, and thereby reduce synaptic release of glutamate. Restoring extracellular glutamate concentration in the nucleus accumbens appears to block reinstitution of compulsive behaviors and decrease cravings (Baker et al., 2003).

In the first study to examine a glutamatergic agent in pathological gambling, we examined the efficacy of N-acetylcysteine. Some 27 subjects with pathological gambling were treated in an 8-week open-label trial of N-acetylcysteine with responders randomized to 6 weeks of double-blind drug or placebo. During the open-label phase, gambling symptoms were significantly reduced, with 59% of subjects meeting responder criteria. Of those who entered the double-blind phase and were assigned to N-acetylcysteine, 83.3% still met responder criteria at the end of the double-blind phase, compared to only 28.6% of those assigned to placebo (Grant et al., 2007).

Psychological Treatments

The majority of the psychosocial treatment literature for pathological gambling has focused on cognitive and behavioral therapy techniques. The cognitive aspect includes psychoeducation, increased awareness of irrational cognitions, and cognitive restructuring. The behavioral techniques include identification of gambling triggers and the development of nongambling sources to compete with the reinforcers associated with gambling. There have been nine published randomized trials of cognitive behavioral therapy (CBT) as treatment for pathological gambling. Motivational enhancement therapy in combination with CBT has been examined in a single randomized study. In addition, Gamblers Anonymous and self-exclusion programs have been examined, but not in controlled studies.

COGNITIVE BEHAVIORAL THERAPY

In one study of 40 subjects, individual cognitive therapy plus relapse prevention resulted in reduced gambling frequency and increased perceived self-control over gambling at 12 months when compared with a wait-list control group (Sylvain et al., 1997). Another study of cognitive therapy plus relapse prevention in 88 subjects also produced improvement in gambling symptoms when compared to a wait-list group at 3 months, which was maintained for 12 months (Ladouceur et al., 2001). Treatment discontinuation was high in both studies (37% and 47%, respectively), and the outcome analyses included only those subjects who completed the studies.

A randomized study of CBT in pathological gambling compared four groups: (1) individual stimulus control and in vivo exposure with response prevention, (2) group cognitive restructuring, (3) a combination of 1 and 2, and (4) a wait-list control (Echeburua et al., 1996). At 12 months, rates of abstinence or minimal gambling were higher in the individual treatment (69%) compared with group cognitive restructuring (38%) and the combined treatment (38%). The same investigators further assessed individual and group relapse prevention for completers of a 6-week individual treatment program. At 12 months, 86% of those receiving individual relapse prevention and 78% of those in group relapse prevention had not relapsed, compared to 52% with no follow-up.

In a large eight-session manualized form of CBT, 231 subjects were randomized to weekly sessions with an individual counselor, therapy in the form of a workbook, or referral to Gamblers Anonymous (Petry, 2005). Using an intent-to-treat analysis, the individual therapy and workbook reduced gambling behaviors to a greater degree than referral to Gamblers Anonymous. At 12-month follow-up, however, the three groups did not differ significantly in terms of rates of abstinence. Long-term benefit from CBT relative to Gamblers Anonymous cannot therefore be supported.

Group cognitive therapy was tested against a wait-list control condition in 71 subjects with pathological gambling (Ladouceur et al., 2003). Groups met weekly for 10 weeks and each session was 2 hours. After 10 sessions, 65% of those in group CBT no longer met criteria for pathological gambling, compared to 20% in the wait-list condition. At 24-month follow-up, 33% of the original sample still did not meet criteria for pathological gambling.

In one study of brief interventions, Dickerson et al. (1990) randomly assigned 29 subjects to either workbook or workbook plus a single in-depth interview. The workbook included cognitive-behavioral and motivational enhancement techniques. Both groups reported significant reductions in gambling at 6 months. A separate study assigned gamblers to a CBT workbook, a workbook plus a telephone motivational enhancement intervention, or a wait list. Rates of abstinence at 6 months did not differ between groups, although the frequency of gambling and money lost gambling were lower in the motivational intervention group (Hodgins et al., 2001). Compared to the workbook alone, those gamblers assigned to the motivational intervention and workbook reduced gambling throughout a 2-year follow-up period (Hodgins et al., 2004).

Imaginal desensitization has been used in conjunction with CBT in the treatment of pathological gambling. Subjects are taught relaxation and then instructed to imagine experiencing and resisting triggers to gamble. Imaginal desensitization resulted in significantly greater reduction in gambling symptoms compared to traditional aversion therapy in the randomized treatment of 20 compulsive gamblers (McConaghy et al., 1983). In a larger study of 120 subjects randomly assigned to aversion therapy, imaginal desensitization, in vivo desensitization, or imaginal relaxation, subjects assigned to imaginal desensitization reported better outcomes at 1 month and up to 9 years later (McConaghy et al., 1991).

Trichotillomania

Pharmacological Treatments

Several controlled pharmacological trials have been performed for trichotillomania. Four of the six double-blind pharmacological studies published to date have examined antidepressants, particularly SRIs. One study examined clomipramine compared to desipramine in a 10-week double-blind crossover (5 weeks for each agent) design (following 2 weeks of single-blind placebo lead-in; Swedo et al., 1989); 12 of 13 subjects had significant improvement on clomipramine.

Fluoxetine has been studied in three randomized trials with conflicting results. In one study, fluoxetine was compared with placebo in a 6-week double-blind crossover study (with a 5-week washout period between treatment arms; Christenson, Mackenzie, Mitchell, and Callies, 1991). No significant differences were found between fluoxetine and placebo on measures of hair-pulling urges, frequency, or severity. In a study comparing fluoxetine with clomipramine, a 2-week placebo lead-in was followed by a double-blind, randomized 20-week crossover design (10 weeks on each agent). Both clomipramine and fluoxetine demonstrated a similar positive treatment effect (O'Sullivan et al., 1999). A third controlled study used a double-blind, placebo-controlled crossover design with 16 subjects treated with each agent for 12 weeks separated by a 5-week washout period (Streichenwein and Thornby, 1995). Fluoxetine failed to show significant improvement compared to placebo.

In one of only two studies not examining an antidepressant, Christenson performed a placebo-controlled, 6-week, randomized, double-blind parallel arm study of the opioid antagonist naltrexone (O'Sullivan et al., 1999). Of 17 subjects completing the study, 10 received placebo and 7 received 50 mg per day of naltrexone. Significant improvement was noted for the naltrexone group on one measure of trichotillomania symptoms. However, although two other measures of symptom improvement showed change in the anticipated direction for the naltrexone group, they failed to reach statistical significance.

A study examined the efficacy of using an atypical antipsychotic (olanzapine) in the treatment of trichotillomania. Based on the hypothesis that antipsychotics are beneficial for motor tics, the study examined olanzapine in a double-blind fashion for 12 weeks in 25 subjects. The results were that 85% of those assigned to olanzapine compared to 17% of those on placebo improved during the trial. The mean effective dose of olanzapine was 10.8 mg per day (van Ameringen et al., 2006).

Psychological Treatments

Few controlled psychological treatment studies for trichotillomania have been published to date. Azrin and colleagues (1980) randomized 34 subjects to either habit reversal therapy or negative practice (where subjects were instructed to stand in front of a mirror and act out motions of hair pulling without actually pulling). Habit reversal reduced hair pulling by more than 90% for 4 months, compared to a 52–68% reduction for negative practice at 3 months. No control group was included and therefore time and therapist attention could not be adequately assessed.

Another recent study examined 25 subjects randomized to 12 weeks (10 sessions) of either acceptance and commitment therapy (with habit reversal) or wait list (Woods et al., 2005). Subjects assigned to the therapy experienced significant reductions in hair-pulling severity and impairment compared to those assigned to the wait list, and improvement was maintained at 3-month follow-up.

Comparison Studies

Two studies have used controlled designs to compare treatment interventions. Ninan and colleagues used a placebo-controlled, randomized, parallel treatment design to compare CBT and clomipramine (Ninan, Rothbaum, et al., 2000). A total of 23 subjects entered the 9-week study. The CBT was a modified manualized treatment based on the habit reversal therapy tested in a controlled study by Azrin and colleagues. CBT was significantly more effective in reducing the symptoms of trichotillomania than either clomipramine or placebo. Although clomipramine resulted in greater symptom reduction than placebo, the difference was not statistically significant.

In a second comparison study, behavioral therapy was compared to fluoxetine in a 12-week randomized trial using a wait-list control (van Minnen et al., 2003). A total of 43 subjects were enrolled and 40 completed the trial (14 in behavioral therapy, 11 in the fluoxetine group, and 15 on the wait list). Behavioral therapy resulted in statistically significant reductions in trichotillomania symptoms compared to either fluoxetine or wait list.

Compulsive Buying

Pharmacological Treatments

The effectiveness of pharmacotherapy in treating compulsive buying has been examined in four double-blind randomized, placebo-controlled trials. In the first of two double-blind fluvoxamine studies, 37 subjects were treated for 13 weeks. Only 9 of 20 patients assigned to medication were responders (mean dose 215 mg per day), and this rate did not differ significantly from that in the placebo group (8 of 17 were responders) (Ninan, McElroy et al., 2000). In the second double-blind study, Black and colleagues (2000) treated 23 patients for 9 weeks following a 1-week placebo lead-in phase. Using a mean dose of 200 mg per day, no differences in response rates were observed between the groups treated with active drug or placebo.

The third controlled study was a 7-week open-label study of citalopram that randomized the responders to 9 weeks of double-blind medication or placebo (Koran et al., 2003). Subjects taking active citalopram demonstrated statistically significant decreases in the frequency of shopping and the intensity of thoughts and urges concerning shopping.

Although citalopram showed promise in treating compulsive buying, escitalopram failed to demonstrate efficacy. In a 7-week open-label study, 19 of 26 subjects (73%) responded and 17 were then randomized to 9 weeks of double-blind discontinuation. Of the 8 subjects assigned to escitalopram during the double-blind phase, 5 (62.5%) relapsed, compared to 6 out of 9 (66.7%) of those assigned to placebo (Koran et al., 2007b).

Psychological Treatments

Although CBT has been discussed in uncontrolled reports, only one study has examined CBT in compulsive buying. Mitchell and colleagues (2006) studied 39 subjects with compulsive buying (28 assigned to group CBT and 11 assigned to wait list for 10 weeks or 12 sessions; Mitchell et al., 2006). Those assigned to group CBT were able to significantly reduce buying episodes and amount spent. In addition, the benefits were maintained for the 6 months of follow-up.

Pathological Skin Picking

Pharmacological Treatment

Two double-blind studies of fluoxetine have been conducted for the treatment of pathological skin picking. In the first trial, 21 subjects received 10 weeks of either placebo or active medication. The fluoxetine group improved significantly more than the placebo group on only one of three measures used to rate improvement at a mean dosage of 55 mg per day (Simeon et al., 1997).

The second study consisted of an open-label component for 6 weeks followed by a double-blind discontinuation for 6 weeks for responders. Of the eight subjects who responded to open-label treatment, the four that were randomized to the fluoxetine group maintained their improvement while the placebo group returned to their baseline symptom severity level (Bloch et al., 2001).

Psychological Treatments

There has been only one formal study of psychotherapy for pathological skin picking. In a study examining habit reversal compared to wait list, 19 subjects with pathological skin picking were randomly assigned (Teng et al., 2006). Habit reversal consisted of standard self-monitoring and competing responses. Those assigned to habit reversal were able to significantly reduce picking behavior compared to wait list and maintain those gains for 3 months.

Kleptomania

Pharmacological Treatments

There has been only one randomized placebo-controlled study of medication in the treatment of kleptomania. Unlike a typical double-blind design, this study involved 7 weeks of open-label escitalopram treatment followed by having the responders randomized to either continue on escitalopram or be switched to placebo for an additional 16 weeks (Koran et al., 2007a). When the responders were randomized, 43% of those on escitalopram relapsed, compared to 50% on placebo, thereby showing no drug effect in terms of response.

Psychological Treatments

No controlled studies of psychological treatments exist for kleptomania. Case reports suggest that cognitive and behavioral therapies may be effective in treating kleptomania. Undergoing seven sessions of covert sensitization combined with exposure and response prevention over a 4-month period, a young man was able to reduce his stealing frequency (Guidry, 1969). In addition, the man went to stores and was asked to imagine that the store manager was observing him. The young man reduced his stealing behavior although his urges to steal went unchanged.

In a case of covert sensitization, a young woman underwent five weekly sessions wherein she was instructed to practice covert sensitization whenever she had urges to steal. She was then able to go 14 months with only a single lapse in behavior and with no reported urges to steal (Gauthier and Pellerin, 1982). Similarly, another woman was instructed to have increasing nausea when tempted to steal with imagery of vomiting associated with actual stealing (Glover, 1985). After four sessions over 8 weeks, the woman was able to go with only a single lapse in behavior over the next 19 months. Aversive breath-holding in combination with diary keeping of urges to steal and six weekly sessions of therapy resulted in significantly reduced stealing frequency in a single case (Keutzer, 1972).

Imaginal desensitization in fourteen 15-minute sessions over 5 days resulted in complete remission of symptoms for a 2-year period for two subjects (McConaghy and Blaszczynski, 1988). One case involved a woman treated weekly for 5 months to assist her in finding alternative sources of excitement, pleasure, and self-fulfillment. She was able to report a 2-year period of remitted symptoms (Gudjonsson, 1987).

Compulsive Sexual Behavior

Pharmacological Treatments

In the only double-blind study of compulsive sexual behavior, 28 gay men were assigned to 12 weeks of either citalopram or placebo. Those assigned to citalopram demonstrated significant reductions in sexual desire, frequency of masturbation, and use of pornography. High-risk sexual behavior did not differ between groups. Mean effective citalopram dose was 43.4 mg per day (Wainberg et al., 2006).

Psychological Treatments

Although case reports have discussed the possible benefits of CBT for compulsive sexual behavior, only one study has been published. The uncontrolled study examined the efficacy of group CBT for gay and bisexual men with compulsive sexual behavior (Quadland, 1985). The group therapy was effective in reducing targeted sexual behaviors.

Intermittent Explosive Disorder

Pharmacological Treatments

Pharmacological treatment data for intermittent explosive disorder are limited. Although pharmacotherapies have been studied in the treatment of aggression, impulsivity, and violent behavior, there is only one controlled study specific to intermittent explosive disorder. In a randomized, double-blind, placebo-controlled study, 96 subjects with Cluster B personality disorders, 116 subjects with intermittent explosive disorder, and 34 subjects with post-traumatic stress disorder were randomized to divalproex sodium or placebo for 12 weeks of treatment. Using an intent-to-treat analysis, the study found that divalproex had no significant influence on aggression in the subjects with intermittent explosive disorder (Hollander et al., 2003).

Psychological Treatments

Although case reports suggest that insight-oriented psychotherapy and behavioral therapy may be beneficial, there are no controlled psychological treatment studies in intermittent explosive disorder (McElroy et al., 1998).

Recommendations Based on Treatment Outcome Literature

In the area of impulse control disorders, the systematic study of treatment efficacy and tolerability is in its infancy. With few studies published, it is not possible to make treatment recommendations with a substantial degree of confidence (Tables 8.1, 8.2). No drugs are currently approved by the Food and Drug Administration for the treatment of any of the formal impulse control disorders. Nonetheless, specific drug and behavioral therapies offer promise for the effective treatment of pathological gambling. Opioid antagonists and lithium currently appear to be the most promising pharmacological treatments for pathological gambling. CBT and imaginal desensitization both appear beneficial for pathological gambling using a psychotherapeutic approach.

For other impulse control disorders, fewer data are available to generate empirically supported treatment recommendations. For trichotillomania, habit reversal therapy may be beneficial, but the evidence is based on only three studies with small samples, each using a different variation of habit reversal therapy and, in two studies, lacking a control group. Various forms of CBT generally appear promising for a wide array of impulse control disorders. In terms of medication treatment, opioid antagonists also have support for their use in these disorders. Serotonergic medications, on the other hand, do not appear particularly promising for most of the impulse control disorders.

Clinicians should be aware of the limitations of our treatment knowledge. Most published studies have employed relatively small sample sizes, are of limited duration, and involve possibly nonrepresentative clinical groups (e.g., those without co-occurring psychiatric disorders). In addition, response measures have varied across studies, in part because the definition of response in many of these disorders remains debated. Heterogeneity of treatment samples may also complicate identification of effective treatments. At present, issues such as which medication to use and for whom, or the duration of pharmacotherapy or CBT, cannot be sufficiently addressed with the available data. Two consistent findings across treatment studies are the high placebo response and discontinuation rates, and identification of factors related to placebo response and treatment discontinuation would help inform future studies and advance treatment strategies for the disorder.

TABLE 8.1

Double-Blind, Placebo-Controlled Pharmacotherapy Trials for Impulse Control Disorders

Impulse Control Disorder	Medication	Design and Duration
Pathological Gambling		
Hollander et al., 1992	Clomipramine (Anafranil)	Parallel design 10 weeks
Hollander et al., 2000	Fluvoxamine (Luvox)	Crossover 16 weeks with a 1-week placebo lead-in
Blanco et al., 2002	Fluvoxamine (Luvox)	Parallel design 6 months
Kim et al., 2002	Paroxetine (Paxil)	Parallel design 8 weeks with 1-week placebo lead-in
Grant et al., 2003	Paroxetine (Paxil)	Parallel design 16 weeks
Saiz-Ruiz et al., 2005	Sertraline (Zoloft)	Parallel design 6 months
Grant and Potenza, 2006	Escitalopram (Lexapro)	12 week open-label followed by 8-week double-blind discontinuation
Black et al., 2007	Bupropion (Wellbutrin)	Parallel design 12 weeks
Hollander, Pallanti, Allen et al., 2005	Lithium carbonate SR (Lithobid SR)	Parallel design 10 weeks
Kim et al., 2001	Naltrexone (ReVia)	Parallel design 12 weeks with 1-week placebo lead-in
Grant, Potenza, et al., 2006	Nalmefene	Parallel design 16 weeks
Grant et al., 2007	N-Acetyl Cysteine	8 week open-label followed by 6-week double-blind discontinuation

Subjects	Mean Daily Dose ($\pm SD$)	Outcome
1 enrolled 1 completer	125 mg	90% improvement in gambling symptoms on medication
15 enrolled 10 completers	195 mg ($\pm$50)	Fluvoxamine superior to placebo
32 enrolled 13 completers	200 mg	Fluvoxamine not statistically significant versus placebo
53 enrolled 41 completers	51.7 mg ($\pm$13.1)	Paroxetine group significantly improved compared to placebo
76 enrolled 45 completers	50 mg ($\pm$8.3)	Paroxetine and placebo groups with comparable improvement
60 enrolled 44 completers	95 mg	Similar improvement in both groups
13 pathological gamblers with anxiety; 4 completed double-blind phase	25.4 mg	Of the 4 randomized, all 3 on escitalopram maintained improvement; 1 on placebo lost improvement
39 enrolled 22 completed	324 mg	No difference between groups on any measure
40 bipolar spectrum patients enrolled 29 completers	1,170 mg ($\pm$221)	Lithium group significantly improved compared with placebo
89 enrolled 45 completers	188 mg ($\pm$96)	Naltrexone group significantly improved compared with placebo
207 enrolled 73 completers	Fixed-dose study	Nalmefene 25 mg and 50 mg significantly improved compared to placebo
27 enrolled in open-label; 13 randomized to double-blind; 13 completed double-blind phase	1,476.9 $\pm$ 311.3 mg	83.3% of those assigned to *N*-acetylcysteine were still responders at end of the double-blind phase, compared to 28.6% assigned to placebo

TABLE 8.1 (*continued*)
Double-Blind, Placebo-Controlled Pharmacotherapy Trials
for Impulse Control Disorders

Impulse Control Disorder	Medication	Design and Duration
Compulsive Buying		
Black et al., 2000	Fluvoxamine (Luvox)	Parallel design 9 weeks with 1-week placebo lead-in
Ninan, McElroy, et al., 2000	Fluvoxamine (Luvox)	Parallel design 13 weeks
Koran et al., 2003	Citalopram (Celexa)	7 weeks open-label followed by 9 weeks randomized
Koran et al., 2007b	Escitalopram (Lexapro)	7-week open-label followed by 9-week double-blind discontinuation
Trichotillomania		
Swedo et al., 1989	CMI versus DMI	Crossover 5 weeks each agent
Christenson, Mackenzie, Mitchell, and Callies, 1991	Fluoxetine (Prozac)	Crossover 6 weeks fluoxetine and then placebo
O'Sullivan et al., 1999	CMI versus fluoxetine	Crossover 10 weeks each agent
Streichenwein and Thornby, 1995	Fluoxetine (Prozac)	Crossover 6 weeks on fluoxetine and placebo
Christenson et al., 1994	Naltrexone (ReVia)	Parallel design 6 weeks
Van Ameringen et al., 2006	Olanzapine (Zyprexa)	Parallel design 12 weeks

Subjects	Mean Daily Dose (±*SD*)	Outcome
23 enrolled 18 completers	220 mg	Fluvoxamine and placebo groups with comparable improvement
37 enrolled 23 completers	215 mg (±76.5)	Fluvoxamine and placebo groups with comparable improvement
24 enrolled 15 completers	42.1 mg (±15.3)	Citalopram group significantly improved compared to placebo
26 enrolled; no data on number who completed	10–20 mg	During double-blind phase, no difference in rates of relapse with elevated rates in both groups
13 enrolled 13 completers	CMI: 180 mg (±56); DMI: 173 mg (±33)	CMI significantly greater improvement
21 enrolled 15 completers	Fixed titration to 80 mg	Fluoxetine not significantly different from placebo
12 enrolled; no data on number of completers	CMI: 200 mg (±15); fluoxetine: 75 mg (±5)	Similar significant improvement on both agents
23 enrolled 16 completers	70 mg	No differences between groups
No data on number enrolled 17 completers	50 mg	Naltrexone significant improvement on one measure
25 enrolled 23 completers	10.8 mg	Olanzapine significant improvement

TABLE 8.1 (*continued*)
Double-Blind, Placebo-Controlled Pharmacotherapy Trials for Impulse Control Disorders

Impulse Control Disorder	Medication	Design and Duration
Kleptomania		
Koran et al., 2007a	Escitalopram (Lexapro)	7 week open-label followed by 16- week double-blind discontinuation
Compulsive Sexual Behavior		
Wainberg et al., 2006	Citalopram (Celexa)	Parallel design 12 weeks
Intermittent Explosive Disorder		
Hollander et al., 2003	Divalproex (Depakote)	Parallel design 12 weeks

Note. CMI = clomipramine; DMI = desipramine.

Subjects	Mean Daily Dose ($\pm SD$)	Outcome
24 enrolled 12 completers	18.6 mg	No differences beteen escitalopram and placebo in terms of relapse rates
28 enrolled 26 completers	43.4 mg	Significant reductions in sexual urge and masturbation frequency
109 subjects; no data on number of subjects who completed	1,567 mg	Similar improvement on divalproex and placebo

TABLE 8.2

Controlled Psychological Treatment Trials for Impulse Control Disorders

Impulse Control Disorder	Design and Duration
Pathological Gambling	
Echeburua et al., 1996	Stimulus control, in vivo exposure, relapse prevention versus cognitive restructuring versus combined treatment versus wait list / 6 weeks with 12-month follow-up
Sylvain et al., 1997	Cognitive therapy with relapse prevention compared to wait list / 30 sessions with 6-month follow-up
Ladouceur et al., 2001	Cognitive therapy plus relapse prevention compared to wait list / 20 sessions with 12-month follow-up
Ladouceur et al., 2003	Group cognitive therapy plus relapse prevention compared to wait list / 10 weeks with 2-year follow-up
Petry et al., 2005	Manualized CBT in individual counseling versus CBT workbook versus Gamblers Anonymous referral / 8 sessions with 1-year follow-up
Dickerson et al., 1990	CBT workbook versus workbook plus a single in-depth interview
Hodgins et al., 2001	CBT workbook versus workbook plus motivational enhancement intervention via telephone versus wait list
McConaghy et al., 1983	Aversion therapy compared to imaginal desensitization
McConaghy et al., 1991	Aversion therapy versus imaginal desensitization versus in vivo desensitization versus imaginal relaxation

Subjects	Outcome
64 enrolled 50 completers	At 12 months, 69% abstinence or much reduced in the first condition compared to 38% for cognitive restructuring or combined treatment
40 enrolled 14/22 in treatment group completed	36% improved on five variables compared to 6% on wait list
88 enrolled 35/59 in treatment group completed	32% improved on four variables compared to 7% on wait list
71 enrolled 34/46 in treatment group completed	65% no longer met pathological gambling criteria compared to 20% for wait-list group
231 enrolled 181 completers	CBT was more effective than Gamblers Anonymous and individual counseling more effective than workbook; at 12 months, groups did not differ in rates of abstinence
29 enrolled	Both groups showed improvement at 6 months
102 enrolled 85 available at 12 months	74% with motivational enhancement improved according to CGI compared to 61% with workbook and 44% on wait list
20 enrolled 20 completers	Improvement in both groups over 12 months
120 enrolled 63 available 2 and 9 years later	Imaginal desensitization improved at 1 month and at 9 years

TABLE 8.2 *(continued)*

Controlled Psychological Treatment Trials for Impulse Control Disorders

Impulse Control Disorder	Design and Duration
Trichotillomania	
Azrin et al., 1980	Habit reversal therapy compared to negative practice
Woods et al., 2005	Acceptance and commitment therapy/habit reversal compared to wait list
Ninan, Rothbaum, et al., 2000	CBT compared to clomipramine compared to placebo
van Minnen et al., 2003	Behavior therapy compared to fluoxetine compared to wait list
Pathological Skin Picking	
Teng et al., 2006	CBT compared to wait list
Compulsive Buying	
Mitchell et al., 2006	Group CBT compared to wait list

Note. CBT = cognitive behavior therapy.

Subjects	Outcome
34 enrolled 34 completers	Habit reversal reduced hair pulling by more than 90% for 4 months, compared to 52–68% reduction for negative practice at 3 months
28 enrolled 25 completers	Improvement for acceptance and commitment therapy/habit reversal maintained at 3 months
23 enrolled 16 completers	CBT was significantly more effective in reducing the symptoms of trichotillomania than either clomipramine or placebo
43 enrolled 40 completers	Behavior therapy resulted in statistically significant reductions in trichotillomania symptoms compared to either fluoxetine or wait list
19 enrolled	Habit reversal significantly more effective than wait list for up to 3 months
39 enrolled 17 completed 6- month follow-up	CBT resulted in significant improvement compared to wait list and gains were maintained for 6 months

Factors That Influence Treatment Decisions

Even knowing the evidence for various treatment options for impulse control disorders, multiple other factors may influence which treatment is chosen for a particular patient.

First, many clinicians are simply unaware of these disorders. Therefore, if a clinician is referring a patient for either medication management or psychotherapy, it may simply be difficult to find people who know how to treat the behavior. This problem can be minimized by having a list of providers who know about these disorders and can provide treatment. For example, if no one is available who does CBT for these disorders, then perhaps medication management should be maximized.

Second, there are no clear recommendations of treatment for the clinician to follow. For example, it is unclear how many sessions of CBT are most helpful for a particular impulse control disorder. The exact dose of medication or duration of medication trial for optimal treatment is also unknown. These gaps in knowledge make it difficult to inform patients about what their care may entail and what expectations they may have.

Third, patients with impulse control disorders exhibit high rates of placebo response in treatment studies. Clinicians need to understand that for many patients with these behaviors, just talking about their problems will help substantially at first. This initial robust response, however, may cause clinicians to believe that their treatment approach is successful. Clinicians should carefully monitor patients for several months and not assume they will continue to do well.

Fourth, impulsive patients often do not follow recommendations or follow up with treatment. The data show that dropout rates are high for most of the impulse control disorders. This may be due to two factors: (1) Patients often believe they are doing better than they really are, and therefore they see treatment as unnecessary; (2) they do not have an instantaneous response and therefore do not stay with treatment. Both of these concerns can be minimized by simply providing psychoeducation about the illness, the expectations of treatment, and the need to stay in treatment.

CHAPTER 9

The Role of the Family

IMPULSE CONTROL DISORDERS affect not only an individual but also his or her family. In fact, family members of people with impulse control disorders may be more likely to seek assistance than the person with the disorder. Although there is very little data regarding these family members, behaviors such as pathological gambling, kleptomania, compulsive buying, and compulsive sexual behavior all greatly affect loved ones in terms of trust (because of lying and deception), finances (e.g., pathological gambling and compulsive buying), legal repercussions (e.g., pathological gambling and kleptomania) and health (e.g., sexually transmitted disease associated with compulsive sexual behavior). This chapter reviews what is known about the influence of impulse control disorders on family members and offers advice for family members.

> Sheila is a 35-year-old married woman who works in a physician's office as a receptionist. Approximately 2 years ago, her husband of 15 years informed her of his gambling problem and the financial situation of the family. Apparently he had used all of their savings ($25,000) to gamble and recently had taken out a second mortgage to pay off some gambling debts. Still $60,000 in debt, he has been unable to make payments on credit cards and pay their son's parochial school tuition.
>
> During the past 2 years, Sheila has refused to see friends, claiming that going out would cost too much. Shame and embarrassment prevent her from telling family members and so she calls her parents infrequently and talks only briefly. Isolated and depressed, Sheila reports problems sleeping

131

and weight loss of 20 pounds over the past year. She has no sexual relationship with her husband and actually lives in some fear of him, given his
anger outbursts regarding her spending on groceries and for her son.

Myths About Impulse Control Disorders

When scientific information is lacking, myths develop. Such is the case
with impulse control disorders. Family members need to be disabused
of these myths and instead educated about the truths of these
disorders.

> Myth: Impulse control disorders are just bad habits, can be con-
>   trolled, and have no serious consequences.

The impulse control disorders are severely disabling behaviors that
patients attempt repeatedly and unsuccessfully to control (Black et al.,
1997; Grant and Kim, 2002a; Petry, 2005; Flessner and Woods, 2006;
Woods et al., 2006). In addition, these behaviors lead to significant
social and occupational dysfunction (Goldman, 1991; Grant and Kim,
2001; Flessner and Woods, 2006; Woods et al., 2006). Kleptomania
and pyromania often result in prison terms (Goldman, 1991; Grant and
Kim, in press); trichotillomania may lead to gastric complications and
death (Christenson and Mansueto, 1999); pathological skin picking
may result in skin grafts and septicemia (Grant et al., in press); pathological gambling and compulsive buying are associated with significant
financial distress (Grant and Kim, 2001); and intermittent explosive disorder may result in severe harm or death (McElroy et al., 1998).

> Myth: Impulse control disorders are a sign of a disturbed
>   childhood.

It has been suggested that early life events, such as sexual or physical abuse, can lead to impulse control disorders later in life. There is,
however, little empirical evidence that any consistent pattern of adverse
childhood events exists among individuals with impulse control
disorders.

There is a suggestion in the literature that some individuals (albeit a minority) with compulsive sexual behavior (Kafka and Hennen, 2002) and those with pathological gambling (Taber et al., 1987) have histories of physical or sexual abuse. As in the case of pyromania, it is not clear that abuse always precedes an impulse control disorder (Grant and Kim, in press). We also have no basis to think that abuse is the cause of the impulse behavior.

> Myth: Impulse control disorders are bad behaviors performed by bad people.

While many of the impulse control disorders are defined by behaviors that violate social norms (e.g., assault, stealing, fire setting, excessive sexual behavior), there is little evidence that individuals suffering from these disorders are antisocial. In fact, rates of antisocial personality disorder are quite low in people with kleptomania (Grant, 2004a) and pyromania (Grant and Kim, in press). Even in the case of pathological gambling, where some evidence suggests elevated rates of antisocial personality disorder (17–29%; Black and Moyer, 1998; Blaszczynski and Steel, 1998), it is unclear whether the gambling behavior preceded the development of the personality disorder. In fact, many gamblers develop a reactive psychopathy—that is, doing illegal activities to fund their gambling or repay their debts (Grant and Kim, 2001).

Influence of Impulse Control Disorders on Families

Children, parents, siblings, and significant others can be affected by an impulse control disorder. In general, the people closest to the patient are the most often adversely affected. It has been estimated that in the case of pathological gambling, a gambler directly affects the lives of at least 8 to 10 other people (Petry, 2005). The ways in which family members are affected vary considerably, and are usually intertwined.

Finances

Financial problems are most commonly seen in cases of pathological gambling and compulsive buying. Although gambling may result in a range of financial difficulties, on average, someone with pathological gambling loses about one half of their gross income to gambling during a calendar year (Grant and Kim, 2001). Compulsive buyers report similar financial problems. In fact, one study showed that compulsive buyers use approximately 46% of their take-home pay to pay off credit card debts resulting from spending (O'Guinn and Faber, 1989). This financial toll can result in unpaid bills, loans from family members, disconnected utilities, repossession of property, eviction or loss of one's home, and illegal activities (National Council of Welfare, 1996).

Financial difficulties can also result in stress within relationships. If the significant other is financially independent and can leave the relationship, then the patient often ends up alone. If the significant other is financially dependent, then the relationship may survive but will be under significant stress (Hodgins et al., 2007).

Communication and Trust

Communication and trust between family members is often severely affected by impulse control disorders, which are secretive behaviors. It is common for people with these disorders to lie to family members about their behaviors or at least the extent of their behaviors (McCarthy, 1994; Grant and Kim, 2002). For example, approximately one half of individuals with kleptomania had never told their spouse about their shoplifting even though they stole frequently and had done so for many years (Grant and Kim, 2002). There is also evidence that the more severe the impulse control disorder, the worse the interpersonal relationships (Hodgins, Shead, et al., 2007). Alternatively, in some relationships the impulse control disorder may be a response to poor communication and trust issues.

Financial difficulties often result in communication problems. The embarrassment of financial stress results in chronic lying to hide the extent of the problem. Also, because many people with impulse control disorders are in denial about their problem or the extent of their problem, they instead blame the spouse, the economy, their job, or bad luck. Either for these reasons or because they believe the spouse is making an issue out of nothing, marital discord is common. For example, studies of pathological gambling have demonstrated that marital problems commonly result from the behavior (Grant and Kim, 2001; Petry, 2005).

Even when a patient's behavior improves, trust may continue to be an issue in the family. Conflict often results because the person expects to regain the family's trust immediately upon ceasing the behavior. The family, however, is sometimes unable to trust again for years after the person has abstained from the impulsive behavior. A study of children living with a gambler parent showed that the loss of trust had a significant emotional effect on the children (Darbyshire et al., 2001).

Physical and Psychological Abuse

An increase in domestic violence has been associated with a proliferation of casinos (Gerstein et al., 1999). Other studies further support an association between pathological gambling and domestic violence. In two studies of pathological gambling, 23–50% of spouses had experienced physical or verbal abuse from their partner who had a problem with gambling (Lorenz and Shuttlesworth, 1983; Bland et al., 1993). A study of 413 children in Thailand found that children with a parent who had a gambling problem were more likely to be victims of parental aggression (Isaranurug et al., 2001), and another study supports the finding that gambling parents are more likely to throw things and become violent (Lesieur and Rothschild, 1989). Of course, violence associated with pathological gambling is complicated by alcoholism and antisocial personality disorder (Petry, 2005), and so how much is due only to gambling remains unclear.

Physical and Emotional Health

There is evidence that certain impulse control disorders (pathological gambling, compulsive sexual behavior, pathological skin picking) are associated with a variety of health-related concerns. For example, individuals with pathological gambling suffer from greater rates of angina and cirrhosis (Morasco et al., 2006), individuals with compulsive sexual behavior suffer from greater rates of sexually transmitted disease

(Dodge et al., 2004), and infections are common among pathological skin pickers (Grant, Odlaug, and Kim, in press).

In addition, family members of individuals with impulse control disorders are also at greater health risk. Studies of spouses of pathological gamblers have noted that headaches, gastrointestinal complaints, and depression are frequently endorsed (Lorenz and Yaffee, 1988). Spouses also report decreased satisfaction in intimacy (Lorenz and Yaffee, 1988). Partners of those with compulsive sexual behavior are at increased risk of acquiring a sexually transmitted disease (Benotsch et al., 1999). Similarly, due to family debt, spouses of a compulsive buyer often have increased rates of anxiety, low self-esteem, and depression.

Children who have a parent with a gambling problem are more likely to abuse drugs or have a problem with overeating. In addition, these children describe their childhood as unhappy (Jacobs, 1989). A study of children of parents in Gamblers Anonymous reported poor sleep and feelings of insecurity and inadequacy (Lesieur and Rothschild, 1989).

Isolation, Frustration, and Resentment

When impulse control disorders become known to others, they can often lead to social and emotional isolation for the spouse of the afflicted individual. Violence, financial concerns, and health issues may all result in the spouse cutting ties with friends and outside family members. Enabling is also common and may lead to the spouse covering up financial problems, providing financial bailouts, and making his or her needs secondary to the spouse with the impulse problem.

Because the impulse control disorders are underrecognized, some family members feel a sense of stigma because the loved one has a psychiatric illness. If family members do confide in others, their stories are often met with disbelief or their concerns may be hard to understand. Reactions such as these may intensify feelings of isolation.

Even a family member who knows something about the impulse control disorder may experience frustration over the loved one's minimization of the problem, repeated declarations of control, and refusal to seek treatment. Given that the loved one has the problem, family members may minimize their own frustration, feel that their frustration is not legitimate, or feel resentment that no one is listening or caring about their concerns. Also, family members may alternately feel sympathy one minute, hostility and resentment the next, which may also lead to feeling anxious, angry, and hopeless. It is not uncommon for family members to resort to various unhealthy means of coping (e.g., drinking, avoidance of the home, extramarital affairs).

Interventions for Family Members

Sheila sought treatment for herself and began to address several issues. First, given her husband's anger outbursts, it was important for her to determine if living in the house was safe or whether she and her son should live with relatives or a friend. She decided to stay, but for those who leave, guilt over abandoning someone may need to be addressed. Second, Sheila began weekly therapy and medication to help with her feelings of stress and depression. Third, when she began feeling more emotionally stable, Sheila started the process of changing her credit cards to her name only to help salvage her credit score. Because assignment of debt within couples can vary from state to state, Sheila sought counseling at a legal aid clinic associated with the state university law school. This provided free help so that Sheila could determine what she was responsible for in terms of debt. Finally, Sheila began attending GamAnon where she found support for family members of pathological gamblers.

Spouses and family members should be aware that multiple treatment options are available for themselves as well as the person suffering from an impulse control disorder. In the case of pathological gambling, family members should know about Gam-Anon. Although not available everywhere, the meetings educate family members about pathological gambling and how to cope with and interact with a family member who suffers from it. Some research suggests that participation in Gam-Anon may be associated with greater rates of abstinence in the loved one who suffers from pathological gambling (Zion et al., 1991; Johnson and Nora, 1992). There are Sex-Anon groups in some cities, although these are less common than Gam-Anon. Also, there are no published studies regarding the effects of Sex-Anon attendance. The other impulse control disorders lack specific groups for the partners of the loved one.

Many partners of individuals with impulse control disorders experience anxiety and depression of a significant magnitude and may need individual counseling. The goal of therapy may be multifaceted: helping partners cope with anxiety, frustration, and depression, teaching them to better recognize the consequences of the impulse control behavior, assisting them in helping the loved one reduce the impulse control behavior, and assisting them in getting the loved one into treatment. This type of therapy has been examined in the case of partners of pathological gamblers and has been shown to result in modest benefits (Makarchuk et al., 2002). Self-help workbooks have demonstrated benefits in reducing the loved one's gambling behavior when used with the significant others of problem gamblers (Hodgins et al., 2007). Couples group therapy may also be an option for the person with an impulse control disorder and the partner (Tepperman, 1985). Family and marital therapy have shown benefit when used with the significant others of individuals with compulsive sexual behavior (Bird, 2006).

Advice for Family Members

Sheila continued her therapy with good success. Unbeknownst to Sheila, her husband was not attending Gamblers Anonymous or individual counseling. The previous debts mounted—credit card interest accrued and financial stress increased in the family. Sheila's mother had recently passed away and left her a small inheritance. Sheila told her husband about the money and informed him that she would put it in savings for their son. Three months later, Sheila's husband asked Sheila for the money to "get out of the hole," promising her that he would use it to pay bills and not gamble with the money. Sheila gave him $15,000, believing he was doing well in therapy. Sheila's husband received the money on Monday and by Friday had lost it all playing blackjack.

Coping strategies are easier to describe than to implement. In fact, some coping strategies can be frustrating and difficult. Family members need to realize that their response to a problem is about choosing a healthier approach, not a perfect approach. These coping strategies are additional approaches that should enhance effective treatments for impulse control disorders, make the behavior easier for the family to live with, and help counteract the family's feelings of helplessness. Although family members may feel powerless in dealing with impulse control behaviors, there are many things they can do to help.

Ignorance About the Disorders

There is significant misinformation and ignorance about impulse control disorders in the general public and in the medical community. As a result, family members and the loved one often do not take the disorder seriously. Lack of information may result in the behavior continuing for many years and gradually worsening before anyone in the family intervenes. Although these disorders respond to treatment, most respond more robustly when they are caught earlier. Thus, ignorance may inadvertently lead to having a more severe problem at the time of seeking treatment.

COPING STRATEGY

Family members should educate themselves about impulse control disorders. Due to possible denial by the person suffering from the behavior, family members cannot count on the loved one to teach them about the disorder. Unfortunately, although professional interest in these disorders has increased, family members often cannot rely on providers to supply much information.

Enabling the Behavior

Impulse control disorders can be especially difficult because family members may be drawn into the behaviors through feelings of guilt or a need to help. The ways in which they are asked to help by the loved one, however, are usually counterproductive. For example, family members of a pathological gambler or compulsive buyer are usually asked to assist financially with the debt. Similarly, legal problems are often at issue for individuals with kleptomania, and they may ask family members to lie for them so that they can avoid jail. Given the severity of the consequences of impulse control disorders, the family member often fears that the person may commit suicide unless the problems are resolved. Although suicide attempts are elevated in many impulse control disorders (Feigelman et al., 2006), individuals with impulse control disorders can use this fear to extort money, lie, and further support their behavior.

COPING STRATEGY

Do not enable the loved one's behavior. Family members should avoid being complicitous in impulse control behaviors. Their participation may help keep the behaviors going and may even make them possible. Family members' involvement also drains their time and energy and worsens feelings of frustration and hopelessness. Family members often participate in the hope that they are helping the loved one. They hope that something good will result and that "this time it will be different." Often they are not sure if they have contributed to the problem and helping may relieve some guilt. Enabling has never cured an impulse control disorder, and in fact, it may make it worse by reinforcing the behaviors.

On a practical level, what this means is that the family should not give money to the gambler or the compulsive buyer. They should not lie for the individual with pyromania, kleptomania, or compulsive sexual behavior. They should not allow the loved one to pull his or her hair or pick his or her skin. Consistency is crucial so that the loved one learns that the behaviors are not acceptable or helpful. Not participating in these behaviors is not easy for family members. The person with the impulse behavior may become angry or distraught when turned down. Therefore, family members need to inform the loved one that they are not participating in the behavior because it is not in the loved one's best interests to do so. Family members should tell the person that they know the person is in pain but their participation simply extends and possibly worsens that pain. Explain that the requested help would only provide temporary relief, not long-term benefit. All family members need to agree on this.

Becoming a Therapist

Some family members make a considerable effort to talk with the loved one and help control the impulse behavior. The family members may believe that a compelling argument or heartfelt attempt to convince the person to stop is all that is needed. Although understandable, it often leaves the family member frustrated when it fails.

COPING STRATEGY

People with insight into their behaviors may benefit somewhat from being reminded that their behavior is not typical, that serious consequences may be associated with their impulse behavior, and that they have little control over their behavior. Although these reality checks can be helpful for some individuals, family members should use them as part of ongoing therapy for the loved one or in consultation with a professional to determine whether and how they should use this approach. In general, family members are advised to get their loved one into professional treatment rather than attempt to fix them on their own.

Functional Difficulties

Another consequence of impulse control disorders that affects family members is the loved one's inability to function well. Many people with impulse control disorders have problems being on time for work or school, keeping a job, or socializing (Delfabbro et al., 2006; Flessner and Woods, 2006; Woods et al., 2006). Family members may spend considerable time and money supporting the loved one and urging better functioning. This can result in a significant strain on financial and emotional resources.

COPING STRATEGY

While being mindful of the limitations of functioning, family members should encourage better functioning. This should be done in conjunction with professional therapy and the family members can develop an approach with the therapist. The goal should be self-support, but the time frame to achieve that goal may differ considerably from person to person. As idleness can often foster urges to engage in an impulse control behavior, the loved one should be encouraged to keep busy. Unstructured time, and the boredom that often goes with it, can be potential triggers to impulse behaviors. A stepwise approach from jobs around the house, to volunteer positions, to part-time and then full-time work has been helpful for many patients. Family members can provide useful encouragement during these periods.

Family members should keep in mind that improvement in symptoms often comes about much sooner than improvement in functioning. For example, someone can stop gambling and have no urges to gamble, but still cannot find a job, no longer has friends because of the gambling, and has no financial resources. These functional consequences take time to correct. Patients and their families need to be aware of this and be patient.

Family members who observe that a loved one is impaired should take the steps necessary to have the person receive psychiatric treatment. Simply insisting that the person function better is generally fruitless.

Reluctance to Seek Treatment

Impulse control disorders are pleasurable. That does not mean that the person is unaware and untroubled by the negative consequences of the behavior, but the act of gambling, sex, stealing, and so on, produces a rewarding feeling of euphoria or calm. This means that many people with impulse control disorders are often reluctant to seek treatment. Most want the consequences of the behavior to end but do not necessarily want to stop the actual behavior. Family members can become quite frustrated and helpless due to this reluctance.

COPING STRATEGY

Family members may want to provide the loved one with information about treatment and about the possible benefits of treatment. For example, they can inform the person that this is a real psychiatric disorder, that treatment is often beneficial, that it may lead to greater control over the behavior, that treatment is not necessarily for life, and that it may help diminish the shame associated with the behavior. Family members may also inform the loved one that they are willing to help with treatment. They might provide transportation, meet with the psychiatrist, and get advice concerning what they can provide outside of treatment. Family members can be helpful in encouraging compliance with treatment, reminding the loved one to take medication and attend appointments. Maintaining hope for the loved one is crucial, particularly if improvement is slower than the patient expects.

Suicidal Thoughts

Many individuals with impulse control disorders contemplate suicide (Hodgins et al., 2006; Grant et al., in press). Nothing is more likely to precipitate a family crisis than suicidal thinking or behavior. Family members often respond to suicidal thoughts or behavior by feeling fearful, guilty and powerless.

COPING STRATEGY

Family members should have a very low threshold for suicidal thinking. They need to understand that the desperation that often results from impulse control behaviors can lead someone who has never thought of suicide not only to think about it but also to act on those thoughts. Suicidal thoughts are a serious warning sign that a person is suffering. Given the general impulsivity of these patients, thoughts of suicide can result in action very quickly.

Many family members deny or minimize suicidal thinking in a loved one. Many family members are so frightened by these thoughts that they hope by ignoring them that they will go away. Ignoring such thoughts is a serious mistake. If a loved one looks depressed, a family member should consider asking if the person has thought of suicide or causing self-harm. Many family members worry that by asking they may plant thoughts of suicide. Studies have shown that is not the case.

Suicide should also be inquired about if the person has underlying psychiatric issues (e.g., panic disorder, major depressive disorder, personality disorders, bipolar disorder, substance use disorders), other than the impulse control disorder, as these have been shown to be risk factors for suicide attempts (Warshaw et al., 1995; Sokero et al., 2003; Yen et al., 2003). Because suicide is not reliably predictable, however, family members should ask about it when the person is depressed, when big changes have occurred or when there are incidents involving significant stress in the loved one's life.

When family members know of or suspect suicidal thoughts or plans, they should insist that the loved one obtain psychiatric treatment, which can often effectively treat suicidal thinking as well as the impulse control disorder. If the loved one refuses psychiatric treatment after voicing suicidal thoughts, a family member should contact emergency services (e.g., take the person to an emergency room, or call 911 or the police).

Blaming Themselves

There is now substantial evidence that there might be a genetic variable in the etiology of some impulse control disorders. For example, early evidence suggests that rare variations in a certain gene (*SLITRK1*) may account for some cases of trichotillomania (Zuchner et al., 2006). Similarly, genetic influences have been found to account for a substantial part of the development of pathological gambling (Lobo and Kennedy, 2006). Although this genetic information is valuable in determining causes of these disorders, family members can use this information to blame themselves—for example, "It's because of me that my son is a gambler." This blame may not only lead to the enabling discussed above ("I caused this problem in my son and therefore I should correct his mistakes by helping him"), but can also result in significant distress for the family member.

COPING STRATEGY
Instead of looking back and blaming themselves, family members should focus on the present and the future. There is no benefit from blame. Family members should do what they can now to help the loved one overcome the disorder.

Family members should also educate themselves about the behavior in question. This will not only relieve some of their distress—largely because they will learn that genetics is only one piece of a very complex puzzle—but also provide greater support for the loved one suffering from the behavior.

Guidelines for Response

There is no universal set of guidelines on how a family member should respond to someone with an impulse control disorder. Every person with an impulse control disorder is unique and therefore will need or prefer to receive different assistance from family members. It is only through discussion with the loved one that a family member will understand how he or she can provide support and assistance. Family members should therefore realize that the best way to help is by listening to the person suffering from the disorder. It is ultimately the responsibility of that person to address the problem. Family members can play a major role in providing support, increasing awareness, and reinforcing healthy choices.

The following are general guidelines on how a family member should interact with the person suffering from the impulse control disorder.

Offer support. People with impulse control disorders experience significant shame due to their behaviors and are reluctant to disclose their difficulties. Blaming the person serves no purpose. Family members, however, can support the person without supporting or condoning the behavior. Family members can recognize that the behavior is inappropriate but should convey to the loved one that he or she is not a bad person.

Because controlling these behaviors may take time and the person may experience lapses along the way, family members should be aware of the waxing and waning course of these disorders, offer reinforcement for small, steady steps toward progress, and see lapses as learning experiences.

Ask about the disorder and how you can support the person. Ask the loved one about the struggle, the disorder, and what he or she is going through. Family members should never assume they understand the behavior or its emotional effects. In addition, family members should express a desire to help and ask how they can help the loved one achieve his or her goals.

Sheila felt empowered by attending Gam-Anon and started to understand that she was not to blame for her husband's gambling. Because of the continued difficulties with trust, Sheila separated from her husband, telling him that she would work with him in marital counseling and would be a source of support for him if he wanted to stop gambling. After several months of marital counseling, Sheila's husband entered a treatment program for pathological gamblers. Sheila provided emotional support during his treatment but did not help him financially. Sheila continued to do well on her own and she and her husband were reunited after he was able to stay abstinent for 1 year. Although trust continues to be a problem at times, Sheila and her husband are currently out of debt and continuing to build a strong relationship.

CHAPTER 10

Legal Issues with Impulse Control Disorders

IMPULSE CONTROL DISORDERS present unique legal issues for both the patient and the clinician. Not only do these disorders often result in illegal behaviors, but the behaviors in turn raise complex forensic issues. This chapter discusses the illegal behaviors associated with certain impulse control disorders and then examines how impulsivity and impulsive behaviors have a complicated status under the law.

Kleptomania

No other psychiatric disorder (except drug use disorders) has the status of kleptomania. That is, the disorder itself is defined by an illegal activity. Whereas someone can be diagnosed with pedophilia simply by having urges or thoughts of children (without ever having acted on the behavior), someone can only be diagnosed with kleptomania if they in fact steal.

The diagnostic criteria for kleptomania are: (1) recurrent failure to resist impulses to steal objects that are not needed for personal use or for their monetary value; (2) increasing sense of tension immediately before committing the theft; (3) pleasure, gratification, or relief at the time of committing the theft; (4) the stealing is not committed to express anger or vengeance and is not in response to a delusion or a hallucination; (5) the stealing is not better accounted for by conduct disorder, a manic episode, or antisocial personality disorder (APA, 2000).

Not all shoplifters meet diagnostic criteria for kleptomania. The exact prevalence of shoplifting is unknown (as many who steal are never caught), but one study found that 10% of randomly chosen customers followed while shopping were observed stealing (Astor, 1969). In fact, it is estimated that more than $10 billion worth of goods are stolen from retailers each year, which translates into more than $25 million per day according to a shoplifting prevention organization. The majority of shoplifters are described as amateurs with sporadic activity, with no known history of other criminal activity, and who steal for their own consumption rather than for resale (Cox et al., 1990). One author suggested that because shoplifting is so widespread, it may be a basic element of human nature (Meyers, 1970).

Studies of apprehended, legally referred shoplifters indicate that shoplifting may be more common in women (ranging from 52–100%) than in men. But as with kleptomania, these rates may be falsely elevated because women may be more likely to be referred for psychiatric evaluation than men. Male shoplifters are more likely to be apprehended during adolescence and early adulthood, whereas women are more likely to be apprehended during puberty, early adulthood, and around the age of menopause (McElroy et al., 1991). Some of these same studies also revealed that shoplifting was not related to lower socioeconomic level and that most stole for personal gain (McElroy et al., 1991).

Rates of kleptomania among people who are arrested for shoplifting have ranged from 0% to 8% (McElroy et al., 1991). According to the *DSM-IV-TR*, fewer than 5% of shoplifters are identified as kleptomaniacs (APA, 2000). These rates may be falsely low due to incomplete psychiatric evaluations, lack of strict diagnostic criteria for kleptomania, and selection bias in these samples (McElroy et al., 1991).

A study that compared kleptomaniacs to shoplifters interviewed directly after apprehension found that 58% of the shoplifters were male compared to only 32.4% of kleptomania patients (Sarasalo et al., 1997). The mean age among shoplifters was 27 years and among the kleptomaniacs, 41 years. Although none of the shoplifters met *DSM* criteria for kleptomania, approximately one fifth had not stolen for personal use and had eventually discarded the object (Sarasalo et al., 1997). The study also found that both groups reported the same degree of impulsivity and "a feeling of not being oneself." On the other hand, kleptomaniacs reported a relatively greater number of previous thefts compared to shoplifters, which supports the compulsive aspect of kleptomania. The course of shoplifting is not exactly known, but it appears that it can be chronic, as there are reports of middle-aged and elderly people who continue to steal. Overall, this study found that many shoplifters, although they do not meet criteria for kleptomania, share characteristics with kleptomania and therefore may benefit from treatment (Sarasalo et al., 1997).

Given that both typical shoplifting and kleptomania may start at a relatively early age, it is important to briefly examine childhood and adolescent stealing. A young child generally has little, if any, concept of stealing—for him or her, desiring or wanting means possession of the object. By the age of 6 or 7, children begin to realize they are doing something wrong when they take something that does not belong to them. Children may steal because they are unhappy, lonesome, jealous, fearful, or craving attention. For older children and adolescents, stealing can be used to gain acceptance from a group but is also a strong predictor of future delinquency and a marker for families lacking in warmth and personal stimulation. A strong attachment to parents decreases involvement in shoplifting.

Overall, studies have shown that roughly 40% of apprehended shoplifters are adolescents. A study involving almost 1,700 adolescents found that 37% reported shoplifting at least once in the prior 12 months (Cox et al., 1990). The percentage of respondents peaked around the 10th grade and then declined, which is consistent with official crime statistics. So why are so many adolescents stealing? The researchers hypothesized that this could be a function of immaturity during a stressful transition to adulthood, an inability to purchase certain items, and increased opportunity (the steepest gain of independence occurs around age 16 when most adolescents are allowed to drive and work). On the other hand, the adolescents stated they shoplifted because of the novelty and risk involved, social reasons, and desire for the product. The majority of shoplifters in this study were male, which contrasts the popular view that shoplifting is a female crime, but supports U.S. government statistics that thievery is strongly male dominated during the teenage years. Additionally, no relationship was found between family occupational status and adolescent shoplifting. How many of these adolescent shoplifters currently suffer from or will develop a problem with kleptomania is not clear. Longitudinal studies of this nature, to help clinicians better assess who should receive treatment, are needed.

A study of 22 kleptomaniacs revealed that they stole, on average, 2.3 times a week and had urges 3.7 days per week (Grant and Kim, 2002a). Studies have reported that 64–87% of kleptomania subjects have a history of being apprehended (McElroy et al., 1991; Sarasalo et al., 1996). Individuals with kleptomania report a mean number of lifetime apprehensions of approximately three per subject (Grant and Kim, 2002). Although most apprehensions do not result in jail time, early evidence suggests that 15–23% of kleptomania patients have been jailed for shoplifting (McElroy et al., 1991; Grant and Kim, 2002). Of those that were apprehended, 79% reported that urges to steal were virtually abolished, but only for an average of 3.5 days. Therefore, apprehension does not appear to be a treatment for the urge.

Subjects reported that they stole mainly from stores (department, grocery, clothing, housewares), friends, relatives, and work (Grant and Kim, 2002). All stated they could afford what they stole, but did not understand why they stole. Most reported that the value of stolen items increased over time and that most items were kept (or hoarded), although many were given away, returned, or discarded (McElroy et al., 1991). Examples of commonly stolen objects include sweets, newspapers, food, books, jewelry, and clothes.

Kleptomania has been thought to be merely a symptom of an antisocial or borderline personality disorder. One study consisting of 28 individuals with kleptomania found that 10.7% met criteria for borderline personality disorder, while only 3.5% had antisocial personality disorder. Interestingly, the most frequently co-occurring disorder was paranoid personality disorder (17.9%), which is characterized by long-standing suspiciousness and mistrust of people. The results of this study suggest that kleptomania occurs independently of any particular personality disorder (Grant, 2004a).

Kleptomania is a severe disorder that results in illegal behavior. People who suffer from this behavior are often apprehended and not infrequently face jail time. Suicidal thoughts are common in kleptomania particularly when there are legal repercussions. Clinicians are advised to have their patients seek legal advice when apprehended.

Pyromania

Although pyromania, like kleptomania, often results in illegal behaviors (e.g., arson), little is known about this impulse control disorder. The diagnostic criteria for pyromania are: (1) deliberate and purposeful fire setting on more than one occasion; (2) tension or affective arousal before the act; (3) fascination with, interest in, curiosity about, or attraction to fire and its situational contexts; (4) pleasure, gratification, or relief when setting fires or when witnessing or participating in their aftermath; and (5) the fire setting is not done for monetary gain, criminal purposes, out of anger, or due to other psychiatric or mental conditions (APA, 2000).

Research involving pyromania has largely focused on criminal populations of convicted arsonists (Robbins and Robbins, 1967; Ritchie and Huff, 1999) with little attention given to clinical samples of individuals who meet *DSM* criteria for pyromania. Not everyone who suffers from pyromania is an arsonist. Although state statutes may differ on the explicit language, arson is generally defined as a crime of maliciously, voluntarily, and willfully setting fire to a building or other property of another person or burning one's own property for an improper purpose (e.g., insurance fraud). Arson therefore is defined by the object burned and the intent, whereas pyromania is defined by the thoughts and feelings associated with fire setting. A person meeting *DSM-IV* criteria for pyromania may also meet the legal definition of arson, but the *DSM-IV* criteria for pyromania do not require that a person ever set fire to another person's property.

A study of 21 people who suffer from pyromania found that subjects reported setting one fire in 1-2 months (Grant et al., in press). The majority of subjects (57.1%) reported that they set what they considered controlled fires in dumpsters, their bathrooms, backyards, or vacant lots. A minority (42.9%) reported setting fire primarily to empty buildings (e.g, sheds, garages, doghouses, barns) or empty fields. These subjects would most likely face arson charges. Of the nine subjects who set fires to buildings, all reported being able to resist the urge long enough to check for the safety of people and animals before setting the fires. If someone were to die in a fire, the person with pyromania would likely face murder charges. Only 2 (9.5%) had been arrested for setting fires, and one of the two voluntarily turned himself in as a means of stopping his behavior. No subject suffered from antisocial personality disorder.

Pathological Gambling

Although some forms of gambling are legal, people meeting criteria for pathological gambling are more likely to have legal issues. In fact, one of the *DSM-IV-TR* criteria for pathological gambling includes illegal behaviors: "has committed illegal acts such as forgery, fraud, theft, or embezzlement to finance gambling" (APA, 2000).

Pathological gambling has long been associated with crime (Rosenthal and Lorenz, 1992). Prevalence of criminal activity among pathological gamblers has been estimated as ranging from 20% to 80% (Brown, 1987; Blaszczynski et al., 1989). In one study involving 109 problem gamblers, 55% reported having committed a crime related to gambling and 21% had been charged with a crime (Blaszczynski et al., 1989). Illegal activities of problem gamblers often include writing bad checks, embezzlement, robbery, blackmail, tax fraud, and prostitution.

The question of whether there is a causal relationship between criminal behavior and problem gambling remains unclear. Some gamblers resort to illegal activities to fund their gambling or pay debts. As losses increase, the pressure to offend increases. In two surveys of Gamblers Anonymous attendants, 46–56% reported that they had stolen something to gamble, and 39% reported having been arrested (Pallanti et al., 2006).

Bankruptcy was declared by 18–28% of men and 8% of women due to gambling problems (Pallanti et al., 2006). In fact, bankruptcy rates in counties with at least one gambling establishment are 18% higher than for counties without gambling. Of gamblers filing for bankruptcy, the mean unsecured debt was approximately $40,000 and each gambler had, on average, six credit cards.

Alternatively, both crime and gambling may simply be behaviors associated with antisocial personality disorder. Approximately 15–40% of individuals with pathological gambling suffer from comorbid antisocial personality disorder (Argo and Black, 2004) compared to rates of 1–3% in the general population. Similarly, approximately

26% of prison inmates suffer from pathological gambling (Templer et al., 1993). In a study of gamblers calling a helpline, those who reported gambling-related illegal behaviors were more likely to have a severe gambling problem, owe debts to acquaintances, have received mental health treatment, have a substance use disorder, and have features of antisocial personality disorder (Potenza et al., 2000).

Among adolescents, groups with serious gambling-related problems are twice as likely to report involvement in illegal activities (Jacobs, 2004). Illegal activities for adolescent gamblers include stealing from families or from others. In fact, illegal activities may be more prevalent among young gamblers due to their limited abilities to generate funds and due to peer pressure.

Legal Issues of Impulse Control Disorders

Insanity Defense

The law has recently grappled with the concept of criminal responsibility in cases involving impulse control disorders. Mental disease alone does not exculpate a defendant from criminal responsibility. The mental disease must bear a relationship to the criminal behavior such that the defendant is morally not culpable. How to determine that relationship has been debated for decades in the law. In response to this difficult question, the law has established tests of criminal responsibility, often referred to as insanity defenses, and each state has adopted different tests with different names.

Although the insanity defense has existed since the 12th century, it was initially not considered an argument for the defendant to be found not guilty, but instead a way for a defendant to mitigate a sentence. The seminal case on insanity occurred in England and is now called the M'Naghten rule. In 1843, Daniel M'Naghten, an Englishman who was apparently a paranoid schizophrenic under the delusion he was being persecuted, shot and killed Edward Drummond, secretary to British Prime Minister Sir Robert Peel. M'Naghten believed that Drummond was Peel. M'Naghten was found not guilty on the grounds that he was insane at the time of his act. The case in turn led to a standard regarding the defense of insanity. The M'Naghten rule states: "To establish a defense on the ground of insanity, it must be clearly proved that, at the time of the committing of the act, the party accused was laboring under such a defect of reason, from disease of mind, as not to know the nature and quality of the act he was doing; or if he did know it, that he did not know he was doing what was wrong" (8 Eng. Rep. 718, 1843). The test to determine if defendants can distinguish right from wrong is based on the idea that they must know the difference in order to be convicted of a crime.

The *irresistible impulse defense* is another test of criminal responsibility designed to address defendants who know their acts are against the law but who cannot control their impulses to commit them. This test is often combined with M'Naghten in many jurisdictions. It suggests that the defendant is not liable if, by reason of mental illness, he is unable to exert control over his actions (Weil, 1989). Generally this is construed to apply only to impulses that arise suddenly and are acted upon without reflection. How can one differentiate an uncontrolled act from an uncontrollable act? Also, courts have been loath to believe that most mental illnesses impair the will to such an extent that the person is a mere robot giving in to his impulses.

A slightly different standard was devised by the American Law Institute and is currently used in 18 states: "a person is not responsible for criminal conduct if at the time of such conduct as a result of mental disease or defect he lacks substantial capacity either to appreciate the wrongfulness of his conduct or to conform his conduct to the requirements of law." (American Law Institute Model Penal Code Section 4.02) This standard asks whether defendants have a substantial incapacity to appreciate the criminality of their conduct or to conform their conduct to the law (Bromberg, 1992).

The Federal Insanity Defense Reform Act holds: "It is an affirmative defense to a prosecution under any Federal statute that, at the time of the commission of the acts constituting the offense, the defendant, as a result of a severe mental disease or defect, was unable to appreciate the nature and quality or the wrongfulness of his acts. Mental disease or defect does not otherwise constitute a defense" (18 U.S.C. § 17(a)). The federal statue therefore does not use the irresistible impulse test, and it is the defendant who must prove his inability to appreciate the nature and quality of the crime.

Robert is a 36-year-old investment banker. As part of his profession, Robert handles millions of dollars of other people's money. Robert also has a severe gambling problem. Over the last 6 years, he has lost his home and his savings, and has accumulated credit card debt of $60,000. Approximately 2 years ago, Robert began embezzling from his clients' accounts. It started with small sums and he was able to prevent clients from being aware of his actions by stealing primarily from long-term accounts (where clients were less observant) and creating false account statements. Over the past 2 years, Robert was able to embezzle approximately $2 million, all of which he lost gambling. Robert was tried and convicted of embezzlement. He offers his pathological gambling disorder as a mitigating factor in his sentencing hearing.

Julie is a 30-year-old family practice physician who makes a good liviing. Julie also suffers from kleptomania and shoplifts clothing items every time she enters a store. Many of the items are the same, and she hoards them. She could easily afford the items. One day as she was shopping, she stole a scarf. She reports that she had a strong urge to steal it and felt unable to resist the urge. She was caught by security and turned over to the police. She uses her diagnosis of kleptomania as her defense.

Are these cases the same and should they be treated the same by the courts? Are both people unable to resist their impulses? Both have legitimate psychiatric disorders. Should the disorders be used to mitigate the offenses? When presented with impulse control behaviors, courts have generally considered the insanity defense only as a possible mitigating factor in sentencing. Although gambling addiction has been raised in multiple court cases, the following represent some of the more recent cases and thereby indicate the direction courts may lean when deciding cases of impulse control disorders.

In *United States v. Iaconetti* (59 F. Supp. 2d 139; Dist. Ct. Mass, 1999), the defendant pled guilty to the charge of possession of cocaine with intent to distribute. His defense at sentencing was that he suffered from pathological gambling, had enormous debts from gambling, and sold cocaine to assist with those debts. The defendant did not have a history of criminal behavior prior to his gambling addiction. The court found that departure from federal sentencing guidelines was appropriate given that the criminal behavior was "causally connected" to the gambling.

In *United States v. Grillo* (2004 U.S. App. Lexis 19087 2nd Cir. N.Y.) gambling was again raised as a reason to reduce sentence for the defendant, who was found guilty of mail theft and fraud. The defense claimed that when the defendant had money to gamble, he did not steal. He stole only when he had no funds for gambling. The court determined that a reduction in sentence was allowed only if the conduct provoked by the mental disorder constituted the crime itself, but not where the mental disorder had either just a direct causal connection to the crime or provided motive for the crime.

The Grillo case is important as it shows the courts do not want to support a defense that might be abused. The court stated that many crimes could be committed for a variety of motives and that the courts should not allow all those motives to affect sentencing. In addition, the court aligned itself with the 7th Circuit, which has held that the mental disorder must significantly impair the defendant's capacity to control his conduct at the time of the offense (*United States v. Roach*, 296 F.3d 565, 7th Cir. 2002. The courts also explicitly stated that this defense would preclude sentencing mitigation in the case of a compulsive shopper would stole because of running out of money.

These cases demonstrate that although Robert (in the case above) may have been allowed a reduced sentence due to his gambling in some jurisdictions, currently this is significantly less likely. Robert's crimes were motivated by his gambling, but gambling did not, arguably, result in impaired capacity at the time of his embezzlement. Julie, however, represents a different problem.

In *United States v. McBroom* (991 F. Supp 445, 1998 U.S. Dist NJ) the defendant was charged with possession of child pornography. At sentencing, the defendant showed that he suffered from compulsive sexual behavior, that he was obsessed with Internet pornography, and that his compulsivity changed his mental state and led to the commission of the offense. The court found that his compulsive sexual behavior reduced his ability to control his behavior and was integrally linked with his crime.

Given the courts' holdings, Julie (in the case above) might avail herself of sentence mitigation due to kleptomania. Like the case of compulsive sexual behavior, the mental disorder of kleptomania is defined by the criminal act (i.e., stealing). One could argue that klepto-mania is a sign of her impaired mental state and that the impairment is directly linked to the criminal behavior. Kleptomania, however, has not been brought before the courts as a defense since these rulings.

Interpretation of legal precedent and statute are often as likely to be based on sound judicial reasoning as personal bias of the judge. Therefore, what could or should be the outcome might not in fact be the result. In Robert's case, the court felt that the embezzlement was not causally connected to the gambling addiction and did not allow the gambling behavior to mitigate his sentence. Although the court tried to understand pathological gambling, the court felt that allowing the sentence mitigation would result in any number of people trying to excuse their illegal behaviors with a psychiatric diagnosis. This ruling was consistent with sentencing in several cases presented with a pathological gambling defense at the time of sentencing. Whether all jurisdictions will follow this reasoning is unclear at this time. Also, whether further neurobiological advances in impulse control disorders (e.g., neuroimaging, genetics) will change the way courts understand and adjudicate these cases remains to be seen.

Lawsuits Against Casinos

Although pathological gambling may have limited utility as a defense against criminal charges, the courts have also examined if someone with pathological gambling has any cause of action under the law.

In *Broan v. Argosy Gaming Company* (384 F.3d 413, 7th Cir. 2004), the plaintiff brought suit against the Argosy Casino claiming that he had a gambling addiction and that Argosy was negligent in failing to exercise reasonable care after being notified by the plaintiff's wife that the plaintiff was a pathological gambler and ruining the family finances. In fact, the plaintiff's gambling had led to inability to make mortgage payments, disconnection of telephone and water, and loss of insurance. The court held that not only does a gambler not have a cause of action against a casino, but a family member (i.e. spouse) also fails to have a cause of action.

In *Williams v. Aztar Casino* (351 F3d 290; 7th Cir. 2003), David Williams began gambling at a casino and soon developed a pathological gambling problem. When his problem became unmanageable ($160,000 in debt), his girlfriend informed the casino that Williams had compulsively gambled himself into financial debt and depression and that he was contemplating suicide. In response to her pleadings, two members of the casino's Responsible Gaming Committee approached Williams in the casino to discuss his gambling habits. Later that night, he checked into a local mental health facility, where he was subsequently committed. The casino then sent Williams a "cease admissions" letter barring him from the casino. Williams, however, returned to the casino without difficulty. He then sued the casino claiming breach of the duty of care. Although the court's decision was largely about jurisdictional issues, it reinforced the idea that casino operators are not under a duty of care (under common law) to protect gambling addicts from their own addictive and injurious behavior. Therefore, if states wish to allow for such suits, they will have to provide a statutory means for plaintiffs to sue casinos.

Pathological Gambling and Tax Laws

Although most countries do not include gambling gains and losses in the tax system, the United States does. In fact, all gambling gains are taxable. Losses are deductible only as an offset of gambling gains during the same year.

Arguably one of the most famous cases dealing with gambling and taxes is *Zarin v. Commissioner*, 92 T.C. 1084 (1989), rev'd, 916 F.2d 110 (3d Cir. 1990). Mr. Zarin suffered from pathological gambling. He gambled 12–16 hours a day, 7 days a week, betting up to $15,000 on each roll of the dice. In 2 years, he lost $2.5 million of his own funds and $3.5 million in chips furnished by the casino on credit. He settled his debt for $0.5 million and then was assessed taxes on the entire amount of his cancelled debt. The tax court saw cancelled debt as equivalent to gambling gains. Although the case was reversed on appeal due to an interpretation that the debts were unenforceable and therefore could not generate income, not all states have made gambling debts unenforceable. Therefore, pathological gamblers who work to reduce their gambling debts may still be taxed on those "gains" if the state where they incurred the debts make such debts enforceable. In fact, many states makes gambling debts unenforceable and the issues of the legal status of gambling debts paid for via credit cards continues to be an unsettled area of the law.

Conclusion

Individuals with certain impulse control disorders have significant legal problems. Clinicians should therefore refer patients with these issues for legal counseling. The legal issues not only may result in significant depression, anxiety, and low self-esteem, but they might also interfere with treatment and trigger relapse.

Impulse control disorders raise unique and unsettled questions of law. What does it mean legally to be unable to control one's impulses? The courts have started to grapple with this issue in terms of criminal liability, but it is far from settled. The courts have even hinted at the heterogeneity within impulse control disorders (see Chapter 3). Perhaps individuals whose impulse disorder is actually linked to criminal behavior (e.g., kleptomania patients, some compulsive sexual patients) should be treated differently under the law than those whose criminal behavior is merely an extension of having a mental disorder (e.g., the pathological gambler who embezzles).

Furthermore, as neuroscience advances, what role will this information play in legal arenas? For example, if one could show that there was an objective abnormality in brain functioning at the time of the criminal behavior, would and should that affect sentencing? There have been cases where neuroimaging (e.g., SPECT scan showing perfusion deficits) has been used to reduce the sentences of individuals with impulse control disorders. Will this in turn be an opportunity for the law to further revise criminal statutes in keeping with biological knowledge?

References

Abelson ES. *When Ladies Go A-thieving: Middle-Class Shoplifters in the Victorian Department Store*. New York, NY: Oxford University Press; 1989:173–196.

Abrams K, Kushner MG. Behavioral Understanding. In: *Pathological Gambling: A Clinical Guide to Treatment*. In: Grant JE, Potenza MN, eds. American Psychiatric Publishing; 2004:113–126.

American Psychiatric Association. *Diagnostic and Statistical Manual of Mental Disorders*. 4th ed., text revision (DSM-IV-TR). Washington, DC: American Psychiatric Publishing; 2000.

Anton RF, Moak DH, Waid LR, Latham PK, Malcolm RJ, Dias JK. Naltrexone and cognitive behavioral therapy for the treatment of outpatient alcoholics: results of a placebo-controlled trial. *Am J Psychiatry* 1999;156:1758–1764.

Argo TR, Black DW. Clinical characteristics. In: Grant JE, Potenza MN, eds. *Pathological Gambling: A Clinical Guide to Treatment*. Washington, DC: American Psychiatric Publishing; 2004:39–53.

Arkes HR, Ayton P. The sunk cost and Concorde effects: are humans less rational than lower animals? *Psychol Bull* 1999;125:591–600.

Arnold LM, Mutasim DF, Dwight MM, et al. An open clinical trial of fluvoxamine treatment of psychogenic excoriation. *J Clin Psychopharmacol* 1999;19:15–18.

Arnold LM, Auchenbach MB, McElroy SL. Psychogenic excoriation: clinical features, proposed diagnostic criteria, epidemiology and approaches to treatment. *CNS Drugs* 2001;15(5):351–359.

Arzeno Ferrao Y, Almeida VP, Bedin NR, et al. Impulsivity and compulsivity in patients with trichotillomania or skin picking compared with patients with obsessive compulsive disorder. *Compr Psychiatry* 2006;47:282–288.

Astor SD. Shoplifting: far greater than we know? *Security World* 1969;6:12–13.

Azrin NH, Nunn RG, Frantz SE. Treatment of hairpulling (trichotillomania): a comparative study of habit reversal and negative practice training. *J Behav Ther Exper Psychiatry* 1980;11:13–20.

Baker DA, McFarland K, Lake RW, et al. N-acetylcysteine-induced blockade of cocaine-induced reinstatement. *Ann NY Acad Sci* 2003;1003:349–351.

Barth RJ, Kinder BN. The mislabeling of sexual impulsivity. *J Sex Marital Ther* 1987:21:262–268.

Bayle FJ, Caci H, Millet B, Richa S, Olie J. Psychopathology and comorbidity of psychiatric disorders in patients with kleptomania. *Am J Psychiatry* 2003;160:1509–1513.

Bechara A. Risky business: emotion, decision-making, and addiction. *J Gambl Stud* 2003;19:23–51.

Benotsch EG, Kalichman SC, Kelly JA. Sexual compulsivity and substance use in HIV-seropositive men who have sex with men: prevalence and predictors of high-risk behaviors. *Addict Behav* 1999;24(6):857–868.

Bergh C, Eklund T, Sodersten P, Nordin C. Altered dopamine function in pathological gambling. *Psychol Med* 1997;27(2):473–475.

Biederman J, Wilens T, Mick E, Milberger S, Spencer TJ, Faraone SV. Psychoactive substance use disorders in adults with attention deficit hyperactivity disorder (ADHD): effects of ADHD and psychiatric comorbidity. *Am J Psychiatry* 1995;152:1652–1658.

Bienvenu OJ, Samuels JF, Riddle MA, et al. The relationship of obsessive-compulsive disorder to possible spectrum disorders: results from a family study. *Biol Psychiatry* 2000;48:287–93.

Bird MH. Sexual addiction and marriage and family therapy: facilitating individual and relationship healing through couple therapy. *J Marital Fam Ther* 2006;32(3):297–311.

Black DW. Compulsive buying: a review. *J Clin Psychiatry* 1996;57(8, suppl):50–54.

Black, DW. An open-label trial of bupropion in the treatment of pathologic gambling [letter]. *J Clin Psychpharmacol* 2004;24:108–110.

Black DW. Compulsive shopping. In: *Clinical Manual of Impulse Control Disorders* (Hollander E, Stein DJ, eds). Washington, DC: American Psychiatric Publishing; 2006:203–228.

Black DW, Arndt S, Coryell WH, et al. Bupropion in the treatment of pathological gambling: a randomized, double-blind, placebo-controlled, flexible-dose study. *J Clin Psychopharmacol* 2007;27(2):143–150.

Black DW, Belsare G, Schlosser S. Clinical features, psychiatric comorbidity, and health-related quality of life in persons reporting compulsive computer use behavior. *J Clin Psychiatry* 1999;60:839–844.

Black DW, Repertinger S, Gaffney GR, et al. Family history and psychiatric comorbidity in persons with compulsive buying: preliminary findings. *Am J Psychiatry* 1998;155:960–963.

Black DW, Gabel J, Hansen J, Schlosser S. A double-blind comparison of fluvoxamine versus placebo in the treatment of compulsive buying disorder. *Ann Clin Psychiatry* 2000;12:205–211.

Black DW, Kehrberg LL, Flumerfelt DL, Schlosser SS. Characteristics of 36 subjects reporting compulsive sexual behavior. *Am J Psychiatry* 1997; 154(2): 243–249.

Black DW, Monahan PO, Temkit M, Shaw M. A family study of pathological gambling. *Psychiatry Res* 2006;141:295–303.

Black DW, Moyer T. Clinical features and psychiatric comorbidity of subjects with pathological gambling behavior. *Psychiatr Serv* 1998;49:1434–1439.

Black DW, Moyer T, Schlosser S. Quality of life and family history in pathological gambling. *J Nerv Ment Dis* 2003;191:124–126.

Blanco C, Grant J, Potenza MN, et al. Impulsivity and compulsivity in pathological gambling [abstact]. Paper presented at: College on Problems of Drug Dependence; June 2004; San Juan, PR.

Blanco C, Moreyra P, Nunes EV, Saiz-Ruiz J, Ibanez A. Pathological gambling: Addiction or compulsion? *Sem Clin Neuropsychiatry* 2001;6:167–176.

Blanco C, Orensanz-Munoz L, Blanco-Jerez C, Saiz-Ruiz J. Pathological gambling and platelet MAO activity: a psychobiological study. *Am J Psychiatry* 1996;153(1):119–121.

Blanco C, Petkova E, Ibanez A, Saiz-Ruiz J. A pilot placebo-controlled study of fluvoxamine for pathological gambling. *Ann Clin Psychiatry* 2002;14(1):9–15.

Blanco C, Potenza MN, Kim SW, et al. A preliminary investigation of impulsivity and compulsivity in pathological gambling. *Psychiatry Res.* In press.

Bland RC, Newman SC, Orn H, Stebelsky G. Epidemiology of pathological gambling in Edmonton. *Can J Psychiatry* 1993;38:108–112.

Blaszczynski A. Pathological gambling and obsessive compulsive spectrum disorders. *Psychol Rep* 1999;84:107–113.

Blaszczynski A, McConaghy N, Frankova A. Crime, antisocial personality, and pathological gambling. *J Gambl Behav* 1989;5:137–152.

Blaszczynski A, Steel Z. Personality disorders among pathological gamblers. *J Gambl Stud* 1998;14:51–71.

Bloch MR, Elliott M, Thompson H, Koran LM. Fluoxetine in pathologic skin-picking: open-label and double-blind results. *Psychosomatics* 2001;42(4): 314–319.

Blumberg HP, Leung HC, Skudlarski P, et al. A functional magnetic resonance imaging study of bipolar disorder: state- and trait-related dysfunction in ventral prefrontal cortices. *Arch Gen Psychiatry* 2003;60(6):601–609.

Brady KT, Randall CL. Gender differences in substance use disorders. *Psychiatr Clin North Am* 1999;22(2):241–252.

Broekkamp CL, Phillips AG. Facilitation of self-stimulation behavior following intracerebral microinjections of opioids into the ventral tegmental area. *Pharmacol Biochem Behav* 1979;11:289–295.

Bromberg W. Diminished capacity as an alternative to McNaghten in California law. *Bull Am Acad Psychiatry Law* 1992;20(2):179–183.

Brown RIF. Pathological gambling and associated patterns of crime: comparisons with alcohol and other drug addictions. *J Gambl Behav* 1987;3:98–114.

Brown SL, Rodda S, Phillips JG. Differences between problem and non-problem gamblers in subjective arousal and affective valence amongst electronic gaming machine players. *Addict Behav* 2004; 29:1863–1867.

Calamari JE, Wiegartz PS, Janeck AS. Obsessive-compulsive disorder subgroups: a symptom-based clustering approach. *Behav Res Ther* 1999;37:113–125.

Carrasco JL, Saiz-Ruiz J, Hollander E, Cesar J, Lopez-Ibor JJ. Low platelet monoamine oxidase activity in pathological gambling. *Acta Psychiatr Scand* 1994;90(6):427–431.

Castellani B, Rugle L. A comparison of pathological gamblers to alcoholics and cocaine misusers on impulsivity, sensation seeking, and craving. *Int J Addict* 1995;30:275–289.

Cavedini P, Riboldi G, Keller R, D'Annucci A, Bellodi L. Frontal lobe dysfunction in pathological gambling. *Biol Psychiatry* 2002;51:334–341.

Chamberlain SR, Fineberg NA, Blackwell AD, Robbins TW, Sahakian BJ. Motor inhibition and cognitive flexibility in obsessive-compulsive disorder and trichotillomania. *Am J Psychiatry* 2006;163(7):1282–1284.

Chamberlain SR, Sahakian BJ. The neuropsychiatry of impulsivity. *Curr Opin Psychiatry* 2007;20:255–261.

Chambers RA, Potenza MN. Neurodevelopment, impulsivity, and adolescent gambling. *J Gambl Stud* 2003;19:53–84.

Chambers RA, Taylor JR, Potenza MN. Developmental neurocircuitry of motivation in adolescence: a critical period of addiction vulnerability. *Am J Psychiatry* 2003;160:1041–1052.

Christenson GA, Faber RJ, de Zwaan M, et al. Compulsive buying: descriptive characteristics and psychiatric comorbidity. *J Clin Psychiatry* 1994;55:5–11.

Christenson GA, Mackenzie TB, Mitchell JE. Characteristics of 60 adult chronic hair pullers. *Am J Psychiatry* 1991a;148:365–370.

Christenson GA, Mackenzie TB, Mitchell JE, Callies AL. A placebo-controlled, double-blind crossover trial of fluoxetine in trichotillomania. *Am J Psychiatry* 1991;148(11):1566–1571.

Christenson GA, Mansueto CS. Trichotillomania: descriptive characteristics and phenomenology. In: Stein DJ, Christenson GA, Hollander E, eds. *Trichotillomania*, Washington, DC: American Psychiatric Publishing; 1999:1–42.

Christenson GA, Popkin MK, Mackenzie TB, Realmuto GM. Lithium treatment of chronic hair pulling. *J Clin Psychiatry* 1991;52:116–120.

Christenson GA, Pyle RL, Mitchell JE. Estimated prevalence of trichotillomania in college students. *J Clin Psychiatry* 1991;52:415–417.

Clarke D. Impulsiveness, locus of control, motivation, and problem gambling. *J Gambl Stud* 2004;20:319–345.

Coccaro EF. Neurotransmitter correlates of impulsive aggression in humans. *Ann NY Acad Science* 1996;794:82–89.

Coccaro EF. Impulsive aggression: a behavior in search of clinical definition. *Harv Rev Psychiatry* 1998;5:336–339.

Coccaro EF, Danehy M. Intermittent explosive disorder. In: Hollander E, Stein DJ, eds. *Clinical Manual of Impulse Control Disorders*. American Psychiatric Publishing; 2006:19–37.

Coccaro EF, Kavoussi RJ, Sheline YI, Lish JD, Csernansky JG. Impulsive aggression in personality disorder correlates with tritiated paroxetine binding in the platelet. *Arch Gen Psychiatry* 1996;53(6):531–536.

Coccaro EF, Kavoussi RJ, Berman ME, et al. Intermittent explosive disorder revised: development, reliability and validity of research criteria. *Compr Psychiatry* 1998;39:368–376.

Coccaro EF, Posternak M, Zimmerman M. Prevalence and features of intermittent explosive disorder in a clinical setting. *J Clin Psychiatry* 2005;66:1121–1227.

Coccaro EF, Schmidt CA, Samuels JF, Nestadt G. Lifetime and 1-month prevalence rates of intermittent explosive disorder in a community sample. *J Clin Psychiatry* 2004;65:820–824.

Coccaro EF, Siever LJ. Pathophysiology and treatment of aggression. In: Charney D, Davis KL, Coyle JT, eds. *Neuropsychopharmacology: The 5th Generation of Progress*. Philadelphia, PA: Williams and Wilkins; 2002:1709–1723.

Coccaro EF, Siever LJ, Klar HM, et al. Serotonergic studies in patients with affective and personality disorders. Correlates with suicidal and impulsive aggressive behavior. *Arch Gen Psychiatry* 1989;46(7):587–599.

Cocco N, Sharpe L, Blaszczynski AP. Differences in preferred level of arousal in two sub-groups of problem gamblers: a preliminary report. *J Gambl Stud* 1995;11:221–229.

Coleman E. Is your patient suffering from compulsive sexual behavior? *Psychiatry Ann* 1992;22:320–325.

Collins RL, Ellickson PL, McCaffrey D, Hambarsoomians K. Early adolescent exposure to alcohol advertising and its relationship to underage drinking. *J Adolesc Health* 2007 Jun;40(6):527–534.

Comings DE. The molecular genetics of pathological gambling. *CNS Spectr* 1998;3:20–37.

Comings DE, Gade R, Wu S, et al. Studies of the potential role of the dopamine D1 receptor gene in addictive behaviors. *Mol Psychiatry* 1997;2(1):44–56.

Comings DE, Rosenthal RJ, Lesieur HR, et al. A study of the dopamine D2 receptor gene in pathological gambling. *Pharmacogenetics* 1996;6(3):223–234.

Corrigan PW, Yudofsky SC, Silver JM. Pharmacological and behavioral treatments for aggressive psychiatric inpatients. *Hosp Community Psychiatry* 1993;44:125–133.

Coventry KR, Brown RIF. Sensation seeking, gambling, and gambling addictions. *Addiction* 1993;88:541–554.

Cox D, Cox A, Moschis G. When consumer behavior goes bad: an investigation of adolescent shoplifting. *J Consum Res* 1990;17:149–159.

Crockford DN, el-Guebaly N. Psychiatric comorbidity in pathological gambling: a critical review. *Can J Psychiatry* 1998;43:43–50.

Crockford DN, Goodyear B, Edwards J, Quickfall J, el-Guebaly N. Cue-induced brain activity in pathological gamblers. *Biol Psychiatry* 2005;58(10):787–795.

Cullen BA, Samuels JF, Bienvenu OJ, et al. The relationship of pathological skin picking to obsessive-compulsive disorder. *J Nerv Ment Dis* 2001;189:193–195.

Cunningham-Williams RM, Cottler LB. The epidemiology of pathological gambling. *Sem Clin Neuropsychiatry* 2001;6:155–166.

Cunningham-Williams RM, Cottler LB, Compton III WM, Spitznagel EL. Taking chances: problem gamblers and mental health disorders—results from the St. Louis Epidemiologic Catchment Area study. *Am J Pub Health* 1998;88:1093–1096.

Dahl RE. The development of affect regulation: bringing together basic and clinical perspectives. *Ann N Y Acad Sci* 2003;1008:183–188.

Dannon PN. Topiramate for the treatment of kleptomania: a case series and review of the literature. *Clin Neuropharmacol* 2003;26:1–4.

Dannon P, Iancu I, Grunhaus L. Naltrexone treatment in kleptomanic patients. *Hum Psychopharmacol* 1999;14:583–585.

Dannon PN, Lowengrub K, Gonopolski Y, Musin E, Kotler M. Topiramate versus fluvoxamine in the treatment of pathological gambling: a randomized, blind-rater comparison study. *Clin Neuropharmacol* 2005;28:6–10.

Dannon PN, Lowengrub K, Shalgi B, et al. Dual psychiatric diagnosis and substance abuse in pathological gamblers: a preliminary gender comparison study. *J Addict Dis* 2006;25:49–54.

Darbyshire P, Oster C, Carrig H. The experience of pervasive loss: children and young people living in a family where parental gambling is a problem. *J Gambl Stud* 2001;17:23–45.

Davanzo P, Yue K, Thomas MA, et al. Proton magnetic resonance spectroscopy of bipolar disorder versus intermittent explosive disorder in children and adolescents. *Am J Psychiatry* 2003;160:1442–1452.

Davidson RJ, Irwin W. The functional neuroanatomy of emotion and affective style. *Trends Cogn Sci* 1999; 3:11–21.

Dawson DA, Grant BF, Ruan WJ. The association between stress and drinking: modifying effects of gender and vulnerability. *Alcohol* 2005; 40(5):453–460.

De Castro V, Fong T, Rosenthal RJ, Tavares H. A comparison of craving and emotional states between pathological gamblers and alcoholics. *Addict Behav* 2007;32:1555–1564.

Deffenbacher JL, Filetti LB, Lynch RS, et al. Cognitive-behavioral treatment of high-anger drivers. *Behav Res Ther* 2002;40:895–910.

Delfabbro P, Lahn J, Grabosky P. Psychosocial correlates of problem gambling in Australian students. *Aust N Z J Psychiatry* 2006;40(6–7):587–595.

Desai RA, Maciejewski PK, Dausey DJ, Caldarone BJ, Potenza MN. Health correlates of recreational gambling in older adults. *Am J Psychiatry* 2004;161(9):1672–1679.

Dickerson M, Hinchy J, England SL. Minimal treatments and problem gamblers: a preliminary investigation. *J Gambl Stud* 1990;6:87–102.

Diefenbach GJ, Tolin DF, Hannan S, Crocetto J, Worhunsky P. Trichotillomania: impact on psychological functioning and quality of life. *Behav Res Ther* 2005;43:869–884.

Dingemans AE, Bruna MJ, van Furth EF. Binge eating disorder: a review. *Int J Obes Reat Metab Disorder* 2002;26:299–307.

Dodd ML, Klos KJ, Bower JH, Geda YE, Josephs KA, Ahlskog JE. Pathological gambling caused by drugs used to treat parkinson disease. *Arch Neurol* 2005;62(9):1377–1381.

Dodge B, Reece M, Cole SL, Sandfort TGM. Sexual compulsivity among heterosexual college students. *J Sex Res* 2004;41(4):343–350.

Dougherty RS, Rauch SL, Deckersbach T, et al. Ventromedial prefrontal cortex and amygdala dysfunction during an anger induction positron emission tomography study in patients with major depressive disorder with anger attacks. *Arch Gen Psychiatry* 2004;61(8):795–804.

Driver-Dunckley E, Samanta J, Stacy M. Pathological gambling associated with dopamine agonist therapy in Parkinson's disease. *Neurology* 2003;61(3):422–423.

Duhig AM, Maciejewski PK, Desai RA, Krishnan-Sarin, Potenza MN. Characteristics of adolescent past-year gamblers and non-gamblers in relation to alcohol drinking. *Addict Behav* 2007;32:80–89.

Du Toit PL, van Kradenburg J, Niehaus D, Stein DJ. Comparison of obsessive-compulsive disorder in patients with and without comorbid putative obsessive-compulsive spectrum disorders using a structured clinical interview. *Compr Psychiatry* 2001;42:291–300.

Eastwood JD, Smilek D. Functional consequences of perceiving facial expressions of emotion without awareness. *Conscious Cogn* 2005;14:565–584.

Echeburua E, Baez C, Fernandez-Montalvo J. Comparative effectiveness of three therapeutic modalities in psychological treatment of pathological gambling: long term outcome. *Behav Cog Psychotherapy* 1996;24:51–72.

Eisen SA, Lin N, Lyons MJ, et al. Familial influences on gambling behavior: an analysis of 3359 twin pairs. *Addiction* 1998;93(9):1375–1384.

El-Guebaly N, Patten SB, Currie S, et al. Epidemiological associations between gambling behavior, substance use and mood and anxiety disorders. *J Gambl Stud* 2006;22:275–287.

Esquirol E. (Hunt EK, trans). Mental Malades: a treatise on insanity. Philadelphia: Lea and Blanchard, 1845.

Ettelt S, Ruhrmann S, Barnow S, et al. Impulsiveness in obsessive-compulsive disorder: results from a family study. *Acta Psychiatr Scand* 2007;115:41–47.

Favaro A, Ferrara S, Santonastaso P. Self-injurious behavior in a community sample of young women: relationship with childhood abuse and other types of self-damaging behaviors. *J Clin Psychiatry* 2007;68:122–131.

Feigelman W, Gorman BS, Lesieur HR. Examining the relationship between at-risk gambling and suicidality in a national representative sample of young adults. *Suicide Life Threat Behav* 2006;36:396–408.

First M, Spitzer R, Gibbon M, Williams J. *Structured Clinical Interview for DSM-IV Axis I Disorders, Clinician Version*. Washington, DC: American Psychiatric Publishing; 1995.

Fishbain DA. Kleptomania as risk-taking behavior in response to depression. *Am J Psychother* 1987;41(4):598–603.

Flessner CA, Woods DW. Phenomenological characteristics, social problems, and the economic impact associated with chronic skin picking. *Behav Modif* 2006;30(6):944–963.

Fontenelle LF, Mendlowicz MV, Versiani M. Impulse control disorders in patients with obsessive-compulsive disorder. *Psychiatr Clin Neuroscience* 2005;59: 30–37.

Frisch MB, Cornell J, Villaneuva M. Clinical validation of the Quality of Life Inventory: a measure of life satisfaction for use in treatment planning and outcome assessment. *Psychology Assess* 1993;4:92–101.

Frost RO, Kim HJ, Morris C, et al. Hoarding, compulsive buying and reasons for saving. *Behav Res Ther* 1998;36:657–664.

Frost RO, Meagher BM, Riskind JH. Obsessive-compulsive features in pathological lottery and scratch-ticket gamblers. *J Gambl Stud* 2001;17:5–19.

Galovski T, Blanchard EB, Veazey C. Intermittent explosive disorder and other psychiatric comorbidity among court-referred and self-referred aggressive drivers. *Behav Res Ther* 2002;40:641–651.

Gauthier J, Pellerin D. Management of compulsive shoplifting through covert sensitization. *J Behav Ther Exp Psychiatry* 1982;13:73–75.

Gerstein DR, Volberg RA, Toce MT, et al. *Gambling Impact and Behavior Study: Report to the National Gambling Impact Study Commission.* Chicago: National Opinion Research Center; 1999.

Glover JH. A case of kleptomania treated by covert sensitization. *Br J Clin Psychology* 1985;24:213–214.

Goldman MJ. Kleptomania: making sense of the nonsensical. *Am J Psychiatry* 1991;148:986–996.

Goldstein RZ, Volkow ND. Drug addiction and its underlying neurobiological basis: Neuroimaging evidence for the involvement of the frontal cortex. *Am J Psychiatry* 2002;159:1642–1652.

Goudriaan AE, Oosterlaan J, de Beurs E, van den Brink W. Pathological gambling: a comprehensive review of biobehavioral findings. *Neurosci Biobehav Rev* 2004; 28:123–141.

Goudriaan AE, Oosterlaan J, de Beurs E, van den Brink W. Neurocognitive functions in pathological gambling: a comparison with alcohol dependence, Tourette sundrome and normal controls. *Addiction* 2006;101:534–547.

Grant BF, Hasin DS, Stinson FS, et al. Prevalence, correlates, and disability of personality disorders in the United States: results from the national epidemiologic survey on alcohol and related conditions. *J Clin Psychiatry* 2004;65:948–958.

Grant JE. Family history and psychiatric comorbidity in persons with kleptomania. *Compr Psychiatry* 2003a;44:437–441.

Grant JE. Three cases of compulsive buying treated with naltrexone. *Int J Psychiatr Clin Pract* 2003b;7:223–225.

Grant JE. Co-occurrence of personality disorders in persons with kleptomania: a preliminary investigation. *J Am Acad Psychiatry Law* 2004a;34:395–398.

Grant JE. Dissociative symptoms in kleptomania. *Psychol Rep* 2004b;94:77–82.

Grant JE. Kleptomania. In: Hollander E, Stein DJ, eds. *A Clinical Manual of Impulse Control Disorders.* Washington, DC: American Psychiatric Publishing; 2006:175–201.

Grant JE. Outcome study of kleptomania patients treated with naltrexone: a chart review. *Clin Neuropharmacol* 2005b;28:11–14.

Grant JE, Kim SW. Pyromania: clinical characteristics and psychiatric comorbidity. *J Clin Psychiatry.* In press.

Grant JE, Correia S, Brennan-Krohn T. White matter integrity in kleptomania: a pilot study. *Psychiatry Res* 2006;147:223–237.

Grant JE, Kim SW. Demographic and clinical features of 131 adult pathological gamblers. *J Clin Psychiatry* 2001;62(12):957–962.

Grant JE, Kim SW. Clinical characteristics and associated psychopathology of 22 patients with kleptomania. *Compr Psychiatry* 2002a;43:378–384.

Grant JE, Kim SW. An open label study of naltrexone in the treatment of kleptomania. *J Clin Psychiatry* 2002b;63:349–356.

Grant JE, Kim SW. Temperament and early environmental influences in kleptomania. *Compr Psychiatry* 2002c;43:223–229.

Grant JE, Kim SW. Comorbidity of impulse control disorders among pathological
gamblers. *Acta Psychiatr Scand* 2003;108:207–213.

Grant JE, Kim SW. Quality of life in kleptomania and pathological gambling.
Compr Psychiatry 2005;46:34–37.

Grant JE, Kim SW, McCabe J. A Structured Clinical Interview for Kleptomania
(SCI-K): preliminary validity and reliability testing. *Int J Meth Psychiatr Res*
2006;15:83–94.

Grant JE, Kim SW, Odlaug BL. N-acetylcysteine, a glutamate modulating agent, in
the treatment of pathological gambling: a pilot study. *Biol Psychiatry*. In
press.

Grant JE, Kim SW, Potenza MN, et al. Paroxetine treatment of pathological gambling: a multi-centre randomized controlled trial. *Int Clin Psychopharmacol*
2003;18(4):243–249.

Grant JE, Kushner MG, Kim SW. Pathological gambling and alcohol use disorder.
Alcohol Res Health 2002;26:143–150.

Grant JE, Levine L, Kim D, Potenza MN. Impulse control disorders in adult psychiatric inpatients. *Am J Psychiatry* 2005;162(11):2184–2188.

Grant JE, Mancebo MC, Pinto A, Eisen JL, Rasmussen SA. Impulse control disorders in adults with obsessive-compulsive disorder. *J Psychiatr Res* 2006;
40:494–501.

Grant JE, Odlaug BL, Potenza MN. Addicted to hair pulling?—How an alternate
model of trichotillomania may improve treatment outcome. *Harv Rev Psychiatry* 2007;15:80–85.

Grant JE, Odlaug BL, Kim SW. Lamotrigine-treatment of pathologic skin picking:
an open-label study. *J Clin Psychiatry* (in press).

Grant JE, Potenza MN. Impulse control disorders: clinical characteristics and
pharmacological management. *Ann Clin Psychiatry* 2004a;16:27–34.

Grant JE, Potenza MN. *Pathological Gambling: A Clinical Guide to Treatment.*
Washington, DC: American Psychiatric Publishing; 2004b.

Grant JE, Potenza MN. Tobacco use and pathological gambling. *Ann Clin Psychiatry* 2005a;17:237–241.

Grant JE, Potenza MN. Pathological gambling and other "behavioral addictions."
In: *Clinical Textbook of Addictive Disorders*, 3rd Ed. (Frances RJ, Miller SI,
Mack AH, eds.). New York: Guilford Press, 2005b: 303–320.

Grant JE, Potenza MN. Escitalopram treatment of pathological gambling with co-
occurring anxiety: an open-label pilot study with double-blind discontinuation. *Int Clin Psychopharmacol* 2006a;21(4):203–209.

Grant JE, Potenza MN, Hollander E, Cunningham-Williams R, Nurminen T, Kallio A. Multicenter investigation of the opioid antagonist nalmefene in the treatment of pathological gambling. *Am J Psychiatry* 2006b;163(2):303–312.

Grant JE, Potenza MN. Compulsive aspects of impulse control disorders. *Psychiatr Clin North Am* 2006c;29:539–551.

Grant JE, Steinberg M, Kim SW, Rounsaville B, Potenza MN. Preliminary validity and reliability testing of a Structured Clinical Interview for Pathological Gambling (SCI-PG). *Psychiatr Res* 2004;128:79–88.

Grant JE, Williams KA, Potenza MN. Impulse control disorders in adolescent psychiatric inpatients:co-occurring disorders and sex differences. *J Clin Psychiatry* (in press).

Griesemer RD. Emotionally triggered disease in a dermatologic practice. *Psychiatr Ann* 1978;8:407–412.

Grisham JR, Brown TA, Savage CR, et al. Neuropsychological impairment associated with compulsive hoarding. *Behav Res Ther* 2007;45:1471-1483.

Grodnitsky GR, Tafrate RC. Imaginal exposure for anger reduction in adult outpatients:a pilot study. *J Behav Ther Exp Psychiatry* 2000;31:259–279.

Gudjonsson GH. The significance of depression in the mechanism of "compulsive" shoplifting. *Med Sci Law* 1987;27:171–176.

Guidry LS. Use of a covert punishing contingency in compulsive stealing. *J Behav Ther Exper Psychiatry* 1969;6:169.

Gupta MA, Gupta AK, Haberman HF. The self-inflicted dermatoses: a critical review. *Gen Hosp Psychiatry* 1987;9:45–52.

Guy W. ECDEU-Assessment Manual for Psychopharmacology. *National Institute of Mental Health*. 1976.

Haller R, Hinterhuber H. Treatment of pathological gambling with carbamazepine [letter]. *Pharmacopsychiatry* 1994;27:129.

Halperin JM, Schulz KP, McKay KE, Sharma V, Newcorn JH. Familial correlates central serotonin function in children with disruptive behavior disorders. *Psychiatry Res* 2003;119:205–216.

Hodgins DC, Currie SR, el-Guebaly N. Motivational enhancement and self-help treatments for problem gambling. *J Consult Clin Psychol* 2001;69:50–57.

Hodgins DC, Currie SR, el-Guebaly N. Brief motivational treatment for problem gambling: a 24-month follow-up. *Psychol Addict Behav* 2004;18:293–296.

Hodgins DC, Mansley C, Thygesen K. Risk factors for suicide ideation and attempts among pathological gamblers. *Am J Addict* 2006;15(4):303–310.

Hodgins DC, Petry NM. Cognitive and behavioral treatments. In: Grant JE, Potenza MN, eds. *Pathological gambling: a clinical guide to treatment*. Washington, DC: American Psychiatric Publishing; 2004:169–187.

Hodgins DC, Shead NW, Makarchuk K. Relationship satisfaction and psychological distress among concerned significant others of pathological gamblers. *J Nerv Ment Dis* 2007;195:65–71.

Hodgins DC, Toneatto T, Makarchuk K, Skinner W, Vincent S. Minimal treatment approaches for concerned significant others of problem gamblers: a randomized controlled trial. *J Gambl Stud* 2007;23:215–230.

Holden C. Behavioral addictions: do they exist? *Science* 2001;294:980–982.

Hollander E. Obsessive-compulsive spectrum disorders: an overview. *Psychiatr Ann* 1993;23:355–358.

Hollander E, DeCaria CM, Finkell JN, Begaz T, Wong CM, Cartwright C. A randomized double-blind fluvoxamine/placebo crossover trial in pathologic gambling. *Biol Psychiatry* 2000;47(9):813–817.

Hollander E, DeCaria CM, Mari E, et al. Short-term single-blind fluvoxamine treatment of pathological gambling. *Am J Psychiatry* 1998;155:1781–1783.

Hollander E, Frenkel M, Decaria C, Trungold S, Stein DJ. Treatment of pathological gambling with clomipramine. *Am J Psychiatry* 1992;149(5):710–711.

Hollander E, Pallanti S, Allen A, Sood E, Rossi NB. Does sustained-release lithium reduce impulsive gambling and affective instability versus placebo in pathological gamblers with bipolar spectrum disorders? *Am J Psychiatry* 2005a;162(1):137–145.

Hollander E, Pallanti S, Baldini Rossi N, Sood E, Baker BR, Buchsbaum MS. Imaging monetary reward in pathological gamblers. *World J Biol Psychiatry* 2005b;6(2):113–120.

Hollander E, Stein DJ, Kwon JH, et al. Psychosocial function and economic costs of obsessive-compulsive disorder. *CNS Spectr* 1997;2:16–25.

Hollander E, Tracy KA, Swann AC, et al. Divalproex in the treatment of impulsive aggression: efficacy in cluster B personality disorders. *Neuropsychopharmacol* 2003;28:1186–1197.

Hommer D, Andreasen P, Rio D, et al. Effects of m-chlorophenylpiperazine on regional brain glucose utilization: a positron emission tomographic comparison of alcoholic and control subjects. *J Neurosci* 1996;17(8):2796–2806.

Ibanez A, Blanco C, Moreryra P, Saiz-Ruiz J. Gender differences in pathological gambling. *J Clin Psychiatry* 2003;64:295–301.

Isaranurug S, Notirat P, Chauytong P, Wongarsa C. Factors relating to the aggressive behavior of primary caregivers toward a child. *J Med Assoc Thailand* 2001;84:1481–1489.

Jacobs DF. A general theory of addictions: a new theoretical model. *J Gambl Behav* 1986;2:15–31.

Jacobs DF. Illegal and undocumented: a review of teenage gambling and the plight of children of problem gamblers in America. In: Shaffer H, ed. *Compulsive Gambling: Theory, Research and Practice*. Toronto, Ontario: Lexington Books; 1989:249–292.

Jacobs DF. Youth gambling in North America: long-term trends and future prospects. In: Derevensky JL, Gupta R, eds. *Gambling Problems in Youth: Theoretical and Applied Perspectives.* New York, NY: Kluwer Academic/ Plenum; 2004:1–24.

Jaisoorya TS, Reddy YCJ, Srinath S. The relationship of obsessive-compulsive disorder to putative spectrum disorders:results from an Indian study. *Compr Psychiatry* 2003;44:317–323.

Johnson BA. Topiramate-induced neuromodulation of cortico-mesolimbic dopamine function: a new vista for the treatment of comorbid alcohol and nicotine dependence? *Addict Behav* 2004;29:1465–1479.

Johnson EE, Nora RM. Does spousal participation in Gamblers Anonymous benefit compulsive gamblers? *Psychol Reports* 1992;71:914.

Kabel DI, Petty F. A placebo controlled double-blind study of fluoxetine in severe alcohol dependence: adjunctive pharmacotherapy during and after inpatient treatment. *Alcohol Clin Exp Res* 1996;20:780–784.

Kafka MP, Hennen J. A DSM-IV Axis I comorbidity study of males (n = 120) with paraphilias and paraphilia-related disorders. *Sex Abuse* 2002;14: 3349–3366.

Kafka MP, Prentky RA. Preliminary observations of DSM-III-R axis I comorbidity in men with paraphilias and paraphilia-related disorders. *J Clin Psychiatry* 1994;55:481–487.

Kalivas PW, Barnes CD. *Limbic Motor Circuits and Neuropsychiatry.* Boca Raton, FL: CRC Press; 1993.

Kalivas PW, Peters J, Knackstedt L. Animal models and brain circuits in drug addiction. *Mol Interv* 2006;6(6):339–344.

Kalivas PW, Volkow ND. The neural basis of addiction: a pathology of motivation and choice. *Am J Psychiatry* 2005;162(8):1403–1413.

Kelly TH, Robbins C, Martin CA, et al. Individual differences in drug abuse vulnerability: d-amphetamine and sensation-seeking status. *Psychopharmacology (Berl)* 2006;189(1):17–25.

Kessler RC, Berglund P, Demler O, Jin R, Merikangas KR, Walters EE. Lifetime prevalence and age-of-onset distributions of DSM-IV disorders in the National Comorbidity Survey Replication. *Arch Gen Psychiatry* 2005;62: 593–602.

Kessler RC, Chiu WT, Demler O, Merikangas KR, Walters EE. Prevalence, severity, and comorbidity of 12-month DSM-IV disorders in the National Comorbidity Survey Replication. *Arch Gen Psychiatry* 2005;62(6):617–627.

Kessler RC, Coccaro EF, Fava M, Jaeger S, Jin R, Walters E. The prevalence and correlates of DSM-IV intermittent explosive disorder in the National Comorbidity Survey Replication. *Arch Gen Psychiatry* 2006;63:669–678.

Kessler RC, McGonagle KA, Zhao S, et al. Lifetime and 12-month prevalence of

DSM-III-R psychiatric disorders in the United States. Results from the National Comorbidity Survey. *Arch Gen Psychiatry* 2004;51:8–19.

Keuthen NJ, Deckersbach T, Wilhelm S, et al. Repetitive skin-picking in a student population and comparison with a sample of self-injurious skin-pickers. *Psychosomatics* 2000;41(3):210–215.

Keuthen NJ, Deckersbach T, Wilhelm S, et al. The Skin Picking Impact Scale (SPIS): scale development and psychometric analyses. *Psychosomatics* 2001;42(5):397–403.

Keuthen NJ, Franklin ME, Bohne A, et al. Functional impairment associated with trichotillomania and implications for treatment development. Paper presented at: Trichotillomania: Psychopathology and Treatment Development Symposium, conducted at the 36th annual meeting of the Association for the Advancement of Behavior Therapy; November 2002; Reno, NV.

Keuthen NJ, O'Sullivan RL, Ricciardi JN, et al. The Massachusetts General Hospital (MGH) Hairpulling Scale:1. Development and factor analyses. *Psychother Psychosom* 1995;64:141–145.

Keutzer C. Kleptomania: a direct approach to treatment. *Br J Med Psychol* 1972;45:159–163.

Kim SW. Opioid antagonists in the treatment of impulse-control disorders. *J Clin Psychiatry* 1998;59(4):159–164.

Kim SW, Grant JE. Personality dimensions in pathological gambling disorder and obsessive compulsive disorder. *Psychiatr Res* 2001;104:205–212.

Kim SW, Grant JE, Adson DE, Remmel RP. A preliminary report on possible naltrexone and nonsteroidal analgesic interactions [letter]. *J Clin Psychopharmacol* 2001a;21:632–634.

Kim SW, Grant JE, Adson DE, Shin YC. Double-blind naltrexone and placebo comparison study in the treatment of pathological gambling. *Biol Psychiatry* 2001b;49(11):914–921.

Kim SW, Grant JE. An open naltrexone treatment study of pathological gambling disorder. *Int J Clin Psychopharmacol* 2001c;16:285–289.

Kim SW, Grant JE, Adson DE, Shin YC, Zaninelli R. A double-blind placebo-controlled study of the efficacy and safety of paroxetine in the treatment of pathological gambling. *J Clin Psychiatry* 2002;63:501–507.

Koepp MJ, Gunn RN, Lawrence AD, et al. Evidence for striatal dopamine release during a video game. *Nature* 1998;393(6682):266–268.

Kofoed L, Morgan TJ, Buchkowski J, Carr R. Dissociative Experiences Scale and MMPI–2 scores in video poker gamblers, other gamblers, and alcoholic controls. *J Nerv Ment Dis* 1997;185:58–60.

Koob GF. Drugs of abuse: anatomy, pharmacology and function of reward pathways. *Trends Pharmacol Sci* 1992;13:177–184.

Koob GF, Bloom FE. Cellular and molecular mechanisms of drug dependence. *Science* 1988;242:715–723.

Koran LM, Chuong HW, Bullock KD, Smith SC. Citalopram for compulsive shopping disorder: an open-label study followed by double-blind discontinuation. *J Clin Psychiatry* 2003;64(7):793–798.

Koran LM, Faber RJ, Aboujaoude E, Large MD, Serpe RT. Estimated prevalence of compulsive buying behavior in the United States. *Am J Psychiatry* 2006;163(10):1806–1812.

Koran LM, Aboujaoude EN, Gamel NN. Escitalopram treatment of kleptomania: an open-label trial followed by double-blind d3 continuation. *J Clin Psychiatry* 2007a; 68:422–427.

Koran LM, Aboujaoude EN, Solvason B, et al. Escitalopram for compulsive buying disorder: a double-blind discontinuation study. *J Clin Psychopharmacol* 2007b;27:225–227.

Kranzler HR, Burleson JA, Korner del Boca FK, Bohn MJ, Brown J, Liebowitz N. Placebo controlled trial of fluoxetine as an adjunct to relapse prevention in alcoholics. *Am J Psychiatry* 1995;152:391–397.

Krueger RF, Caspi A, Moffitt TE, Silva PA. The structure and stability of common mental disorders (DSM-III-R): a longitudinal-epidemiological study. *J Abnorm Psychol* 1998;107:216–227.

Krueger RF, Hicks BM, Patrick CJ, Carlson SR, Iacono WG, McGue M. Etiologic connections among substance dependence, antisocial behavior, and personality: modeling the externalizing spectrum. *J Abnorm Psychol* 2002;111:411–424.

Krueger THC, Schedlowski M, Meyer G. Cortisol and heart rate measures during casino gambling in relation to impulsivity. *Neuropsychobiology* 2005;52 (4):206–211.

Kumar G, Pepe D, Steer RA. Adolescent psychiatric inpatients' self-reported reasons for cutting themselves. *J Nerv Ment Dis* 2004;192:830–836.

Ladd GT, Petry NM. Gender differences among pathological gamblers seeking treatment. *Exp Clin Psychopharmacol* 2002;10:302–309.

Ladouceur R, Sylvain C, Boutin C, et al. Cognitive treatment of pathological gambling. *J Nerv Ment Dis* 2001;189:774–780.

Ladouceur R, Sylvain C, Boutin C, Lachance S, Doucet C, Leblond J. Group therapy for pathological gamblers: a cognitive approach. *Behav Res Ther* 2003;41:587–596.

Lappalainen J, Long JC, Eggert M, et al. Linkage of antisocial alcoholism to the serotonin 5-HT1B receptor gene in 2 populations. *Arch Gen Psychiatry* 1998;55:989–994.

Leckman JF, Grice DE, Boardman J, et al. Symptoms of obsessive compulsive disorder. *Am J Psychiatry* 1997; 154:911–917.

Ledgerwood DM, Petry NM. Gambling and suicidality in treatment-seeking pathological gamblers. *J Nerv Ment Dis* 2004;192(10):711–714.

Lejoyeux M, Arbaretaz M, McLoughlin M, Ades J. Impulse control disorders and depression. *J Nerv Ment Dis* 2002;190:310–314.

Lejoyeux M, Tassain V, Solomon J, Ades J. Study of compulsive buying in depressed patients. *J Clin Psychiatry* 1997;58(4):169–173.

Lejoyeux M, Bailly F, Moula H, et al. Study of compulsive buying in patients presenting obsessive-compulsive disorder. *Compr Psychiatry* 2005;46:105–110.

Lesieur HR, Rothschild J. Children of Gamblers Anonymous members. *J Gambl Behav* 1989;5:269–281.

Lim KO, Choi SJ, Pomara N, Wolkin A, Rotrosen JP. Reduced frontal white matter integrity in cocaine dependence: a controlled diffusion tensor imaging study. *Biol Psychiatry* 2002;51:890–895.

Lindberg N, Holi MM, Tani P, Virkkunen M. Looking for pyromania: characteristics of a consecutive sample of Finnish male criminals with histories of recidivist fire-setting between 1973 and 1993. *BMC Psychiatry* 2005;5:47.

Linden RD, Pope HG, Jonas JM. Pathological gambling and major affective disorder: preliminary findings. *J Clin Psychiatry* 1986;47:201–203.

Linehan MM, Tutek DA, Heard HL, et al. Interpersonal outcome of cognitive behavioral treatment for chronically suicidal borderline patients. *Am J Psychiatry* 1994;151:1771–1776.

Linnoila M, Virkkunen M, George T, Higley D. Impulse control disorders. *Int Clin Psychopharmacol* 1993;8(1, suppl):53–56.

Linnoila M, Virkkunen M, Scheinin M, Nuutila A, Rimon R, Goodwin FK. Low cerebrospinal fluid 5-hydroxyindoleacetic acid concentration differentiates impulsive from nonimpulsive violent behavior. *Life Sci* 1983;33(26):2609–2614.

Liu T, Potenza MN. Problematic internet use: clinical implications. *CNS Spectr* 2007;12:453–466.

Lloyd-Richardson EE, Perrine N, Dierker L, et al. Characteristics and functions of non-suicidal self-injury in a community sample of adolescents. *Psychol Med* 2007;12:1–10.

Lobo DS, Kennedy DL. The genetics of gambling and behavioral addictions. *CNS Spectr* 2006;11(12):931–939.

Lochner C, Hemmings SM, Kinnear CJ, et al. Cluster analysis of obsessive-compulsive spectrum disorders in patients with obsessive compulsive disorder: clinical and genetic correlates. *Compr Psychiatry* 2005;46:14–19.

London ED, Ernst M, Grant S, Bonson K, Weinstein A. Orbitofrontal cortex and human drug abuse: functional imaging. *Cereb Cortex* 2000;10(3):334–342.

Lorenz VC, Shuttlesworth DE. The impact of pathologic gambling on the spouse of the gambler. *J Community Psychiatry* 1983;11:67–75.

Lorenz VC, Yaffee RA. Pathological gamblers and psychosomatic, emotional and mental difficulties as reported by the spouse. *J Gambl Behav* 1988;4:13–26.

Makarchuk K, Hodgins DC, Peden N. Development of a brief intervention for concerned significant others of problem gamblers. *Addict Dis Treatment* 2002;1:126–134.

Marazitti D, Presta S, Pfanner C, et al. The biological basis of kleptomania and compulsive buying. Paper presented at: American College of Neuropsychopharmacology 39th annual meeting: December 2000; San Juan, PR.

Marks I. Behavioural (non-chemical) addictions. *Br J Addiction* 1990;85:1389–1394.

Mason BJ, Salvato FR, Williams LD, Ritvo EC, Cutler RB. A double-blind, placebo-controlled study of oral nalmefene for alcohol dependence. *Arch Gen Psychiatry* 1999;56:719–724.

Mataix-Cols D, van den Heuval OA. Common and distinct neural correlates of obsessive-compulsive and related disorders. *Psychiatr Clin North Am* 2006;29:391–410.

Mataix-Cols D, Rosario-Campos MC, Leckman JF. A multidimensional model of obsessive compulsive disorder. *Am J Psychiatry* 2005;162:228–238.

Matsunaga H, Kiriike N, Matsui T, Oya K, Okino K, Stein DJ. Impulsive disorders in Japanese adult patients with obsessive-compulsive disorder. *Compr Psychiatry* 2005;46:43–49.

McCarthy BW. Sexually compulsive men and inhibited sexual desire. *J Sex Marital Ther* 1994;20:200–209.

McConaghy N. Behavior completion mechanisms rather than primary drives maintain behavioral patterns. *Act Nerv Super (Praha)*1980;22:138–151.

McConaghy N, Armstrong MS, Blaszczynski A, Allcock C. Controlled comparison of aversive therapy and imaginal desensitization in compulsive gambling. *Br J Psychiatry* 1983;142:366–372.

McConaghy N, Blaszczynski A. Imaginal desensitization: a cost-effective treatment in two shoplifters and a binge-eater resistant to previous therapy. *Aust N Z J Psychiatry* 1988;22:78–82.

McConaghy N, Blaszczynski A, Frankova A. Comparison of imaginal desensitization with other behavioral treatments of pathological gambling: a two to nine year follow-up. *Br J Psychiatry* 1991;159:390–393.

McElroy SL, Hudson JI, Pope HG, Keck PE, Aizley HG. The DSM-III-R impulse control disorders not elsewhere classified: clinical characteristics and relationship to other psychiatric disorders. *Am J Psychiatry* 1992;149:318–327.

McElroy SL, Keck PE, Pope HG, Smith JM, Strakowski SM. Compulsive buying: a report of 20 cases. *J Clin Psychiatry* 1994;55:242–248.

McElroy SL, Pope HG, Hudson JI, Keck Jr PE, White KL. Kleptomania: a report of 20 cases. *Am J Psychiatry* 1991;148:652–657.

McElroy SL, Pope HG, Keck PE, Hudson JI, Phillips KA, Strakowski SM. Are impulse-control disorders related to bipolar disorder? *Compr Psychiatry* 1996;37:229–240.

McElroy SL, Soutullo CA, Beckman DA, Taylor P, Keck PE. DSM-IV intermittent explosive disorder: a report of 27 cases. *J Clin Psychiatry* 1998;59(4): 203–210.

McElroy SL, Arnold LM, Shapira NA, et al. Topiramate in the treatment of binge eating disorder associated with obesity: a randomized placebo-controlled trial. *Am J Psychiatry* 2003;160:255–256.

McElroy SL, Kotwal R. Binge eating. In: *Clinical Manual of Impulse Control Disorders*. Hollander E, Stein DJ (eds.). Washington, DC: American Psychiatric Publishing; 2006: 115–148.

McNeilly DP, Burke WJ. Stealing lately: a case of late-onset kleptomania. *Int J Geriatr Psychiatry* 1998;13:116–121.

Mehlman PT, Higley JD, Faucher I. Low CFS 5-HIAA concentrations and severe aggression and impaired impulse control in nonhuman primates. *Am J Psychiatry* 1995;151:1485–1491.

Meyer G, Hauffa BP, Schedlowski M, Pawlak C, Stadler MA, Exton MS. Casino gambling increases heart rate and salivary cortisol in regular gamblers. *Biol Psychiatry* 2000;48(9):948–953.

Meyers TJ. A contribution to the psychopathology of shoplifting. *J Forensic Sci* 1970;15:295–310.

Miguel EC, Leckman JF, Rauch S, et al. Obsessive-compulsive disorder phenotypes: implications for genetic studies. *Mol Psychiatry* 2005;10:258–275.

Mitchell JE, Burgard M, Faber R, et al. Cognitive behavioral therapy for compulsive buying disorder. *Behav Res Ther* 2006;44:1859–1865.

Moeller FG, Barratt ES, Dougherty DM, Schmitz JM, Swann AC. Psychiatric aspects of impulsivity. *Am J Psychiatry* 2001;158:1783–1793.

Morasco BJ, Pietrzak RH, Blanco C, Grant BF, Hasin D, Petry NM. Health problems and medical utilization associated with gambling disorders: results from the National Epidemiologic Survey on Alcohol and Related Conditions. *Psychosom Med* 2006;68(6):976–984.

Moreno I, Saiz-Ruiz J, Lopez-Ibor JJ. Serotonin and gambling dependence. *Human Psychopharmacol* 1991;6:9–12.

Moss HB, Yao JK, Panzak GL. Serotonergic responsivity and behavioral dimensions in antisocial personality disorder with substance abuse. *Biol Psychiatry* 1990;28(4):325–338.

Murphy DJ. *Customers and Thieves: An Ethnography of Shoplifting*. Brookfield, VT: Gower Press; 1986:85–98.

Nadir K, Schafe GE, LeDoux JE. Fear memories require protein synthesis in the amygdala for reconsolidation after retrieval. *Nature* 2000;406:722–726.

National Council of Welfare. *Gambling in Canada*. Ottawa: National Council on Welfare; 1996.

National Opinion Research Center. *Gambling Impact and Behavior Study: Report to the National Gambling Impact Study Commission*. Chicago, IL, National Opinion Research Center at the University of Chicago; 1999. Available at: http://www.norc.uchicago.edu/new/gamb-fin.htm.

Ninan PT, McElroy SL, Kane CP, et al. Placebo-controlled study of fluvoxamine in the treatment of patients with compulsive buying. *J Clin Psychopharmacol* 2000a;20(3):362–366.

Ninan PT, Rothbaum BO, Marsteller FA, Knight BT, Eccard MB. A placebo-controlled trial of cognitive-behavioral therapy and clomipramine in trichotillomania. *J Clin Psychiatry* 2000b;61:47–50.

Nock MK, Prinstein MJ. Contextual features and behavioral functions of self-mutilation among adolescents. *J Abnorm Psychol* 2005;114:140–146.

Nordin C, Eklundh T. Lower CSF taurine levels in male pathological gamblers than in healthy controls. *Hum Psychopharmacol* 1996;11(5):401–403.

Ocean G, Smith GJ. Social reward, conflict, and commitment: a theoretical model of gambling behavior. *J Gambl Stud* 1993;9:321–329.

Odlaug BL, Grant JE. Childhood-onset pathologic skin picking: clinical characteristics and psychiatric comorbidity. *Compr Psychiatry* 2007;48:388–393.

O'Guinn TC, Faber RJ. Compulsive buying: a phenomenological exploration. *J Consum Res* 1989;16:147–157.

Olivier B, Young LJ. Animal models of aggression. In: Charney D, Davis KL, Coyle JT, Nemeroff C, eds. *Neuropsychopharmacology: The 5th Generation of Progress*. Philadelphia, PA: Lippincott, Williams and Wilkins; 2002:1699–1708.

O'Malley SS, Jaffe AJ, Chang G, et al. Naltrexone and coping skills therapy for alcohol dependence: a controlled study. *Arch Gen Psychiatry* 1992;49:881–887.

O'Sullivan RL, Christenson GA, Stein DJ. Pharmacotherapy of trichotillomania. In: Stein DJ, Christenson GA, Hollander E, eds. *Trichotillomania*. Washington, DC: American Psychiatric Press; 1999:93–124.

Pallanti S, Baldini Rossi N, Sood E, Hollander E. Nefazodone treatment of pathological gambling: a prospective open-label controlled trial. *J Clin Psychiatry* 2002;63:1034–1039.

Pallanti S, DeCaria CM, Grant JE, Urpe M, Hollander E. Reliability and validity of the Pathological Gambling Modification of the Yale-Brown Obsessive-Compulsive Scale (PG-YBOCS). *J Gambl Stud* 2005;21:431–443.

Pallanti S, Quercioli L, Sood E, Hollander E. Lithium and valproate treatment of pathological gambling: a randomized single-blind study. *J Clin Psychiatry* 2002;63:559–564.

Pallanti S, Rossi NB, Hollander E. Pathological gambling. In Hollander E, Stein DJ, eds. *Clinical Manual of Impulse Control Disorders*. American Psychiatric Publishing; 2006:251–289.

Perez de Castro I, Ibanez A, Saiz-Ruiz J, Fernandez-Piqueras J. Genetic contribution to pathological gambling: possible association between a functional DNA polymorphism at the serotonin transporter gene (5-HTT) and affected men. *Pharmacogenetics* 1999;9(3):397–400.

Perez de Castro I, Ibanez A, Torres P, Saiz-Ruiz J, Fernandez-Piqueras J. Genetic association study between pathological gambling and a functional DNA polymorphism at the D4 receptor gene. *Pharmacogenetics* 1997;7(5):345–348.

Petry NM. *Pathological Gambling: Etiology, Comorbidity, and Treatment*. Washington, DC: American Psychological Association; 2005.

Petry NM, Casarella T. Excessive discounting of delayed rewards in substance abuse with gambling problems. *Drug Alcohol Depend* 1999;56:25–32.

Petry NM, Kiluk BD. Suicidal ideation and suicide attempts in treatment-seeking pathological gamblers. *J Nerv Ment Dis* 2002;190:462–469.

Petry NM, Roll JM. A behavioral approach to understanding and treating pathological gambling. *Semin Clin Neuropsych* 2001;6:177–183.

Petry NM, Stinson FS, Grant BF. Comorbidity of DSM-IV pathological gambling and other psychiatric disorders: results from the National Epidemiologic Survey on Alcohol and Related Conditions. *J Clin Psychiatry* 2005;66(5):564–574.

Phelan J. Childhood kleptomania: two clinical case studies with implications for further research. *Psychol Education Interdiscip J* 2002;39:19–21.

Phillips AG, LePiane FG. Reinforcing effects of morphine microinjection onto the ventral tegmental area. *Pharmacol Biochem Behav* 1980;12:965–968.

Phillips KA, Taub SL. Skin picking as a symptom of body dysmorphic disorder. *Psychopharmacol Bull* 1995;31:279–288.

Potenza MN. The neurobiology of pathological gambling. *Sem Clin Neuropsychiatry* 2001;6:217–226.

Potenza MN. Advancing treatment strategies for pathological gambling. *J Gambl Stud* 2005;21:179–203.

Potenza MN. Should addictive disorders include non-substance-related conditions? *Addiction* 2006;101(1, suppl):142–151.

Potenza MN, Leung HC, Blumberg HP, et al. An FMRI Stroop task study of ventromedial prefrontal cortical function in pathological gamblers. *Am J Psychiatry* 2003;160:1990–1994.

Potenza MN, Steinberg MA, McLaughlin SD, Rounsaville BJ, O'Malley SS. Illegal behaviors in problem gambling: an analysis of data from a gambling helpline. *J Am Acad Psychiatry Law* 2000;28:389–403.

Potenza MN, Steinberg MA, McLaughlin SD, et al. Characteristics of tobacco-smoking problem gamblers calling a gambling helpline. *Am J Addict* 2004;13:471–493.

Potenza MN, Steinberg MA, McLaughlin SD, Wu R, Rounsaville BJ, O'Malley SS. Gender-related differences in the characteristics of problem gamblers using a gambling helpline. *Am J Psychiatry* 2001;158:1500–1505.

Potenza MN, Steinberg MA, Skudlarski P, et al. Gambling urges in pathological gambling: a functional magnetic resonance imaging study. *Arch Gen Psychiatry* 2003;60:828–836.

Potenza MN, Xian H, Shah K, et al. Shared genetic contributions to pathological gambling and major depression in men. *Arch Gen Psychiatry* 2005;62:1015–1021.

Presta S, Marazziti D, Dell'Osso L, Pfanner C, Pallanti S, Cassano GB. Kleptomania: clinical features and comorbidity in an Italian sample. *Compr Psychiatry* 2002;43:7–12.

Quadland MC. Compulsive sexual behavior: definition of a problem and an approach to treatment. *J Sex Marital Ther* 1985;11:121-132.

Ramirez LF, McCormick RA, Lowy MT. Plasma cortisol and depression in pathological gamblers. *Br J Psychiatry* 1988;153:684–686.

Rasmussen SA, Eisen JL. The epidemiology and clinical features of obsessive compulsive disorder. *Psychiatr Clin North Am* 1992;15:743–758.

Raymond NC, Coleman E, Miner MH. Psychiatric comorbidity and compulsive/impulsive traits in compulsive sexual behavior. *Compr Psychiatry* 2003;44(5): 370–380.

Raymond NC, Grant JE, Kim SW, Coleman E. Treatment of compulsive sexual behavior with naltrexone and serotonin reuptake inhibitors. *Int Clin Psychopharmacol* 2002;17:201–205.

Raymond NC, Lloyd M, Miner MH, Kim SW. Preliminary report on the development and validity of the Sexual Symptom Assessment Scale (SSAS). *Sexual Addiction and Compulsivity.* 2007;14:119–129.

Regier DA, Kaelber CT, Roper MT, Rae DS, Sartorius N. The ICD–10 clinical field trial for mental and behavioral disorders: results in Canada and the United States. *Am J Psychiatry* 1994;151:1340–1350.

Reuter J, Raedler T, Rose M, Hand I, Glascher J, Buchel C. Pathological gambling is linked to reduced activation of the mesolimbic reward system. *Nat Neurosci* 2005;8:147–148.

Ritchie EC, Huff TG. Psychiatric aspects of arsonists. *J Forensic Sci* 1999; 44:733–740.

Robbins E, Robbins L. Arson, with special reference to pyromania. *NY State J Med* 1967;67:795–798.

Rodham K, Hawton K, Evans E. Reasons for deliberate self-harm: comparison of self-poisoners and self-cutters in a community sample of adolescents. *J Am Acad Child Adolesc Psychiatry* 2004;43:80–87.

Rogers RD, Everitt BJ, Baldacchino A, et al. Dissociable deficits in the decision-making cognition of chronic amphetamine abusers, opiate abusers, patients with focal damage to prefrontal cortex, and tryptophan-depleted normal volunteers: evidence for monoaminergic mechanisms. *Neuropsychopharmacology* 1999;20:322–339.

Rosenthal R, Lorenz VC. The pathological gambler as criminal offender: comments on evaluation and treatment. *Clinical Forensic Psychiatry* 1992;15: 647–660.

Rothbaum BO, Ninan PT. The assessment of trichotillomania. *Behav Res Ther* 1994; 32:651–652.

Roy A, Adinoff B, Roehrich L, et al. Pathological gambling. A psychobiological study. *Arch Gen Psychiatry* 1988;45(4):369–373.

Roy A, De Jong J, Linnoila M. Extraversion in pathological gamblers. Correlates with indexes of noradrenergic function. *Arch Gen Psychiatry* 1989;46(8): 679–681.

Saiz-Ruiz J, Blanco C, Ibanez A, et al. Sertraline treatment of pathological gambling: a pilot study. *J Clin Psychiatry* 2005;66(1):28–33.

Samuels J, Shugart YY, Grados MA, et al. Significant linkage to compulsive hoarding on chromosome 14 in families with obsessive-compulsive disorder: results from the OCD Collaborative Genetics Study. *Am J Psychiatry* 2007;154: 493–499.

Sanavio. Obsessions and compulsions: the Padua Inventory. *Behav Res Ther* 1988;26:169–177.

Sarasalo E, Bergman B, Toth J. Personality traits and psychiatric and somatic morbidity among kleptomaniacs. *Acta Psychiatr Scand* 1996;94:358–364.

Sarasalo E, Bergman B, Toth J. Theft behavior and its consequences among kleptomaniacs and shoplifters—a comparative study. *Forensic Sci Int* 1997;86: 193–205.

Saudou F, Amara DA, Dierich A, et al. Enhanced aggressive behavior in mice lacking 5-HT1B receptor. *Science* 1994;265:1875–1878.

Saxena S. Is compulsive hoarding a genetically and neurobiologically discrete syndrome? Implications for diagnostic classification. *Am J Psychiatry* 2007;164: 380–384.

Saxena S, Rauch SL. Functional neuroimaging and the neuroanatomy of obsessive-compulsive disorder. *Psychiatr Clin North Am* 2000;23:563–586.

Schlosser S, Black DW, Blum N, Goldstein RB. The demography, phenomenology, and family history of 22 persons with compulsive hair pulling. *Ann Clin Psychiatry* 1994;6:147–152.

Schmitt LH, Harrison GA, Spargo RM. Variation in epinephrine and cortisol excretion rates associated with behavior in an Australian Aboriginal community. *Am J Phys Anthropol* 1998;106:249–253.

Segrave, K. *Shoplifting: A Social History.* Jefferson, NC: McFarland; 2001:3–28.

Shaffer HJ, Hall MN, Vander Bilt J. Estimating the prevalence of disordered gambling behavior in the United States and Canada: a research synthesis. *Am J Pub Health* 1999;89:1369–1376.

Shalev U, Grimm JW, Shaham Y. Neurobiology of relapse to heroin and cocaine seeking: a review. *Pharmacol Rev* 2002;54(1):1–42.

Shapira NA, Goldsmith TD, Keck PE, Khosla UM, McElroy SL. Psychiatric features of individuals with problematic internet use. *J Affect Disord* 2000;57:267–272.

Shapira NA, Lessig MC, Goldsmith TD, et al. Problematic Internet use: proposed classification and diagnostic criteria. *Depress Anxiety* 2003;17:207–216.

Sheehan DV. *The Anxiety Disease.* New York, NY: Scribner's; 1983.

Shinohara K, Yanagisawa A, Kagota Y, et al. Physiological changes in Pachinko players; beta-endorphin, catecholamines, immune system substances and heart rate. *Appl Human Sci* 1999;18(2):37–42.

Silver H, Goodman C, Knoll G, Isakov V, Modai I. Schizophrenia patients with history of severe violence differ from nonviolent schizophrenia patients in perception of emotions but not cognitive function. *J Clin Psychiatry* 2005;66(3):300–308.

Simeon D, Favazza AR. Self-injurious behaviors: phenomenology and assessment. In: *Self-Injurious Behaviors* (Simeon D, Hollander E, eds.). Washington, DC: American Psychiatric Publishing, Inc. 2001:1–28.

Simeon D, Stein DJ, Gross S, Islam N, Schmeidler J, Hollander E. A double-blind trial of fluoxetine in pathologic skin picking. *J Clin Psychiatry* 1997;58(8):341–347.

Simpson HB, Fallon BA. Obsessive-compulsive disorder: an overview. *J Psychiatr Pract* 2000;6:3–17.

Singh NN, Wahler RG, Adkins A, Myers RE. Soles of the feet: a mindfulness-based self-control intervention for aggression by an individual with mild mental retardation and mental illness. *Res Dev Disabil* 2003;24:158–169.

Slutske WS. Natural recovery and treatment-seeking in pathological gambling: results of two U.S. National surveys. *Am J Psychiatry* 2006;163:297–302.

Slutske WS, Eisen S, True WR, Lyons MJ, Goldberg J, Tsuang M. Common genetic vulnerability for pathological gambling and alcohol dependence in men. *Arch Gen Psychiatry* 2000;57(7):666–673.

Slutske WS, Eisen S, Xian H, et al. A twin study of the association between pathological gambling and antisocial personality disorder. *J Abnorm Psychol* 2001;110(2):297–308.

Snyder W. Decision-making with risk and uncertainty: the case of horse racing. *Am J Psychol* 1978;91:201–209.

Sokero TP, Melartin TK, Rystala J, Leskela US, Lestela-Mielonen PS, Isometsa ET. Suicidal ideation and attempts among psychiatric patients with major depressive disorder. *J Clin Psychiatry* 2003;64:1094–1100.

Specker SM, Carlson GA, Edmondson KM, Johnson PE, Marcotte M. Psychopathology in pathological gamblers seeking treatment. *J Gambl Stud* 1996;12:67–81.

Stanley MA, Cohen LJ. Trichotillomania and obsessive-compulsive disorder. In: Stein DJ, Christenson GA, Hollander E, eds. *Trichotillomania*. Washington, DC: American Psychiatric Publishing; 1999:225–261.

Stanley MA, Prather RC, Wagner AL, et al. Can the Yale-Brown Obsessive Compulsive Scale be used to assess trichotillomania? A preliminary report. *Behav Res Ther* 1993;31:171–177.

Steel Z, Blaszczynski A. The factorial structure of pathological gambling. *J Gambl Stud* 1996;12:3–20.

Skeketee G, Frost R. Compulsive hoarding: current status of the research. *Clin Psychol Rev* 2003;23:905–927.

Stewart SE, Jenike MJ, Keuthen NJ. Severe obsessive-compulsive disorder with and without comorbid hair pulling: comparisons and clinical implications. *J Clin Psychiatry* 2005;66:864–869.

Stinchfield R, Kushner MG, Winters KC. Alcohol use and prior substance abuse treatment in relation to gambling problem severity and gambling treatment outcome. *J Gambl Stud* 2005;21:273–297.

Streichenwein SM, Thornby JI. A long-term, double-blind, placebo-controlled crossover trial of the efficacy of fluoxetine for trichotillomania. *Am J Psychiatry* 1995;152(8):1192–1196.

Swedo SE, Leonard HL. Trichotillomania: an obsessive compulsive spectrum disorder? *Psychiatr Clin North Am* 1992;15:777–790.

Swedo SE, Leonard HL, Rapoport JL. A double-blind comparison of clomipramine and desipramine in the treatment of trichotillomania (hair pulling). *N Engl J Med* 1989;321(8):497–501.

Sylvain C, Ladouceur R, Boisvert JM. Cognitive and behavioral treatment of pathological gambling: a controlled study. *J Consult Clin Psychol* 1997;65:727–732.

Taber JI, McCormick RA, Ramirez LF. The prevalence and impact of major life stressors among pathological gamblers. *Int J Addict* 1987;22:71–79.

Tavares H, Zilberman ML, Hodgins DC, el-Guebaly N. Comparison of craving between pathological gamblers and alcoholics. *Alcohol Clin Exp Res* 2005;29:1427–1431.

Templer DI, Kaiser G, Siscoe K. Correlates of pathological gambling propensity in prison inmates. *Compr Psychiatry* 1993;34:347–351.

Teng EJ, Woods DW, Twohig MP. Habit reversal as a treatment for chronic skin picking: a pilot investigation. *Behav Modif* 2006;30:411–422.

Tepperman JH. The effectiveness of short-term group therapy upon the pathological gambler and wife. *J Gambl Behav* 1985;1:119–130.

Tsuang MT, Lyons MJ, Meyer JM, et al. Co-occurrence of abuse of different drugs in men. *Arch Gen Psychiatry* 1998;55:967–972.

Twohig MP, Hayes SC, Masuda A. A preliminary investigation of acceptance and commitment therapy as a treatment for chronic skin picking. *Behav Res Ther* 2006;44:1513–1522.

Van Ameringen M, Mancini C, Patterson B, et al. A randomized placebo controlled trial of olanzapine in trichotillomania. *European Neuropsychopharmacology* 2006;16(suppl):S452[poster].

van Minnen A, Hoogduin KA, Keijsers GP, Hellenbrand I, Hendriks GJ. Treatment of trichotillomania with behavioral therapy or fluoxetine: a randomized, waiting-list controlled study. *Arch Gen Psychiatry* 2003; 60:517–522.

van Wolfswinkel L, van Ree JM. Effects of morphine and naloxone on thresholds of ventral tegmental electrical self-stimulation. *Naunyn-Schmiedebergs Arch of Pharmacol* 1985;330:84–92.

Virkkunen M, Goldman D, Nielsen DA. Low brain serotonin turnover rate (low CSF 5-HIAA) and impulsive violence. *J Psychiatr Neurosci* 1995;20:271–275.

Vitaro F, Ferland F, Jacques C, Ladouceur R. Gambling, substance use, and impulsivity during adolescence. *Psychol Addict Behav* 1998;12:185–194.

Volberg RA. The prevalence and demographics of pathological gamblers: implications for public health. *Am J Pub Health* 1994;84:237–240.

Volkow ND, Wang GJ, et al. Relationship between subjective effects of cocaine and dopamine transporter occupancy. *Nature* 1997;386(6627):827–830.

Volpicelli JR, Alterman AI, Hayashida M, O'Brien CP. Naltrexone in the treatment of alcohol dependence. *Arch Gen Psychiatry* 1992;49:876–880.

Wainberg ML, Muench F, Morgenstern J, et al. A double-blind study of citalopram versus placebo in the treatment of compulsive sexual behaviors in gay and bisexual men. *J Clin Psychiatry* 2006;67(12):1968–1973.

Walker MB. Irrational thinking among slot machine players. *J Gambl Stud* 1992;8:245–261.

Walker M, Toneatto T, Potenza MN, et al. A framework for reporting outcomes in problem gambling treatment research: the Banff, Alberta consensus. *Addiction* 2006;101:504–511.

Warshaw MG, Massion AO, Peterson LG, Pratt LA, Keller MB. Suicidal behavior in patients with panic disorder: retrospective and prospective data. *J Affect Disord* 1995; 34:235–247.

Weil F. Irresistible impulse: psychiatric viewpoint. *Med Law* 1989;8(5):463–469.

Weintraub D, Siderowf AD, Potenza MN, et al. Dopamine agonist use is associated with impulse control disorders in Parkinson's disease. *Arch Neurol* 2006;63:969–973.

Welte J, Barnes G, Wieczorek W, Tidwell MC, Parker J. Alcohol and gambling pathology among U.S. adults: prevalence, demographic patterns and comorbidity. *J Stud Alcohol* 2001;62:706–712.

Wilhelm S, Keuthen NJ, Deckersbach T, et al. Self-injurious skin picking: clinical characteristics and comorbidity. *J Clin Psychiatry* 1999;60:454–459.

Winsberg ME, Cassic KS, Koran LM. Hoarding in obsessive-compulsive disorder: a report of 20 cases. *J Clin Psychiatry* 1999;60:591–597.

Winters KC, Rich T. A twin study of adult gambling behavior. *J Gambl Stud* 1998;14:213–225.

Woods DW, Flessner CA, Franklin ME, et al. The trichotillomania impact project (TIP): exploring phenomenology, functional impairment, and treatment utilization. *J Clin Psychiatry* 2006;67(12):1877–1888.

Woods DW, Wetterneck CT, Flessner CA. A controlled evaluation of acceptance and commitment therapy plus habit reversal for trichotillomania. *Behav Res Ther* 2005;Jul 21 [Epub ahead of print].

Wray I, Dickerson MG. Cessation of high frequency gambling sexual compulsions. *J Clin Psychiatry* 1986;47:201–203.

Wray I, Phil M, Dickerson MG. Cessation of high frequency gambling and withdrawal symptoms. *Br J Addiction* 1981;76:401–405.

Yen S, Shea MT, Pagano M, et al. Axis I and Axis II disorders as predictors of prospective suicide attempts: findings from the Collaborative Longitudinal Personality Disorders Study. *J Abnorm Psychol* 2003;112:375–381.

Zack M, Poulos CX. Amphetamine primes motivation to gamble and gambling-related semantic networks in problem gamblers. *Neuropsychopharmacology* 2004;29(1):195–207.

Zion MM, Tracy E, Abell N. Examining the relationship between spousal involvement in Gam-Anon and relapse behaviors in pathological gamblers. *J Gambl Stud* 1991;7:117–131.

Zuchner S, Cuccaro ML, Tran-Viet KN, et al. SLITRK1 mutations in trichotillomania. *Mol Psychiatry* 2006;11(10):887–889.

The Minnesota Impulse Disorders Interview

This is a clinician-administered screening instrument that has shown good reliability and validity in studies of adult (Grant et al., 2005) and adolescent (Grant et al., in press) psychiatric patients. The time to administer the interview varies but should only take approximately 20 minutes. A scoring sheet is also provided.

Minnesota Impulse Disorders Interview

General Information

1. (Check) _____ Male   _____ Female

2. (Check) _____ White   _____ Black   _____ Hispanic
             _____ Asian   _____ Native American
             _____ Other

3. How old are you? _____ (years)

4. What do you do for a living? _____

5. What is your sexual orientation / gender identity?
    _____ Heterosexual   _____ Bisexual   _____ Gay   _____ Transgender

6. What is your marital status?
    _____ Single
    _____ Married
    _____ Separated
    _____ Divorced
    _____ Widowed

7a. Do you have children? Y   N
    7b. (if yes) How many children do you have? _____
    7c. (if yes) How old are they? _____

8a. How many years of school have you completed? _____
    8b. (if more than high school) What is the highest degree
        that you have obtained? _____

9. What is your approximate yearly household income? _____

Buying Disorder Screen

1. Do you or others think that you have a problem with buying things too
    often or with spending too much money? Y   N
    1b. (if yes) Why? _____

2a. Do you ever experience an irresistible urge or uncontrollable need to buy
    things or mounting tension that can only be relieved by buying? Y   N
    2b. (if yes) Do these urges or thoughts about buying seem to be forced into
        your thinking or intrusive? Y   N
    2c. (if yes) Do you attempt to resist these urges or thoughts? Y   N

3a. Is buying followed by release of tension or a sense of gratification even if only for the moment? Y   N

4a. Has problem buying led to social, marital, family, financial, or work problems or caused you to experience significant distress? Y   N

    4b. (if yes) In which of these areas has there been a problem?

        Social _____

        Marital _____

        Family _____

        Financial _____

        Work _____

        Personal distress _____

        Other (specify) _____

    4c. (if yes) How has buying affected these areas?

    _____

    _____

(If yes to questions 1 and 4, go to complete buying disorder interview; if no to question 1 or 4, end module.)

Kleptomania Screen

1a. Have you ever stolen anything? Y N   (if no, skip to next module)

    1b. (if yes) When did this occur? _____

    1c. (if yes) What did you steal? _____

    1d. (if yes) Do you currently steal? Y N

    (if yes) Please describe your current pattern of stealing:

    _____

    1e. (subject demonstrates a recurrent pattern of theft not limited to a few isolated events)   Y   N (if no, end module)

    1f. Some people steal for their own personal use or for the value things might bring in selling or trading them. Others steal for no obvious reason to others or even themselves, with stealing seeming senseless or impulsive. Why do you steal?

    _____

    _____

    1g. What percentage of your stealing is for your own use, for sale or trade, and for no apparent reason?

        Steals for monetary value   _____%

        Steals for personal use   _____%

        Steals objects not necessary   _____%

        For personal use or for monetary value   _____%

2a. Do you experience an irresistible urge or uncontrollable need to steal things
     or mounting tension that can only be relieved by stealing? Y   N
     2b. (if yes) Do these urges or thoughts about stealing seem to be forced
          into your thinking or intrusive? Y   N
     2c. (if yes) Do you attempt to resist these urges or thoughts? Y   N

3a. Is stealing followed by release of tension or a sense of gratification even if
     only for the moment? Y   N

4a. Has stealing led to social, marital, family, financial, or work problems or
     caused you personal distress? Y   N
     4b. (if yes) In which of these areas has there been a problem?
          Social _____
          Marital _____
          Family _____
          Financial _____
          Work _____
          Personal distress _____
          Other (specify) _____
     4c. (if yes) How has stealing affected these areas?
          _____
          _____

Trichotillomania Screen

1.   Have you ever pulled out scalp, eyelash, eyebrow, pubic, or any other body
     hair other than for cosmetic reasons? (e.g., eyebrow plucking, pubic hair
     plucking for swimsuits, gray hair removal, facial hair removal) Y   N
     (if no, skip to next module)

2.   From the following list, please indicate which hair sites you have ever pulled
     from. (check only those not pulled exclusively for cosmetic reasons; check
     even if subject indicates that no visible loss has been evident)
     Scalp   _____
     Lashes   _____
     Brows   _____
     Pubic   _____
     Beard   _____
     Mustache   _____
     Legs   _____
     Arms   _____
     Axillary   _____
     Chest   _____
     Abdomen   _____

3. Has hair pulling ever resulted in visible hair loss such as hair thinning, bald patches, or in the case of eyelashes, gaps along the eyelid? Y   N(if no, end module)

4a. Do you ever experience a mounting or building tension or urge to pull hair prior to pulling hair from any site? Y   N
    4b. (if yes) Is this different from a more general tension or anxiety that might be attributable to stressors at the time? Y   N

5. Do you experience tension relief after pulling out hair even if only momentarily? Y   N

6. Do you experience a sense of pleasure or gratification after pulling out hair even if only momentarily? Y   N

Intermittent Explosive Disorder

The following includes questions about assaultiveness. Because the law requires me to report to the authorities threat of physical harm to others and child abuse, I strongly recommend that you not supply any more detail to questions other than that asked of you and that you answer all yes/no questions with a yes or no response only. By following these guidelines, none of your answers will be reportable. You may choose not to answer any or all of these questions.

1a. Have you ever lost control and assaulted someone or destroyed property? Y   N
    1b. (if yes) Has this happened on several occasions? Y   N
    1c. (if yes) Did you cause serious injury or destruction of property during these episodes? Y   N
    1d. Did you or others feel that these episodes were grossly out of proportion to the situation? Y   N
    1e. Are these episodes unlike you? Y   N
    1f. Are these episodes always associated with using alcohol or other psychoactive drugs? Y   N
    1g. At what age did you first experience this loss of control?

2. Are you often on the edge of losing control? Y   N

Pyromania Module

1a. Have you deliberately or purposefully set a fire on more than one occasion? Y   N   (if no, skip to next module)
    (if yes) Have more than one of these fires:

1b. not been set for monetary gain? Y N

1c. not been to conceal criminal activity? Y N

1d. not been out of anger or vengeance? Y N

1e. not been to improve your living circumstances? Y N
     (Note: Hallucinations, delusions not addressed in this module)

2.   Have you experienced any kind of urge or mounting tension prior to setting a fire? Y N

3.   Have certain mood changes made you feel like you had to set a fire? Y N

4.   Are you fascinated with, interested in, curious about, or attracted to fire, situations in which fires occur, things used to set fires, or the consequences of fires? Y N

5.   Do you experience pleasure, gratification, or relief when setting fires, watching fires or being involved with the aftermath of fires? Y N

Gambling Screen

1.   Do you gamble? Y N   (if no, skip to next module)

2.   Do you or others think that you have ever had a problem with gambling? Y N

3.   Have you ever felt guilty about the way you gamble or what happens when you gamble? Y N

4.   Have you often been preoccupied with gambling or obtaining money to gamble? Y N

5.   Have you frequently gambled larger amounts of money or over longer periods of time than you intended to? Y N

6.   Have you found that you need to increase the size or frequency of bets to obtain the same excitement? Y N

7.   Have you felt restless or irritable when you were unable to gamble? Y N

8.   Have you ever tried to stop gambling and had difficulty? Y N

9.   Have you ever decreased your involvement with, or quit some important social, work, or recreational activity in order to gamble? Y N

10. Have you ever continued to gamble despite having significant money, social, family, or occupational problems caused or exacerbated by gambling? Y N

11. Have you returned to gambling despite repeatedly losing money gambling, in an attempt to win back losses? Y   N

12. Have you frequently gambled when you were expected to meet social or occupational obligations? Y   N

Compulsive Sexual Behavior Screen

The following section includes questions about sexual behavior. The law requires us to report to the authorities acts of physical harm to others and child abuse. We strongly recommend that you do not supply answers to the questions below if your answers indicate that your sexual activities involve threatening others or sexual relationships with minors which you would not want reported. If you choose to answer only the yes/no questions, none of your answers will be reportable. You may choose not to answer any or all of these questions.

1. Do you or others that you know think that you have a problem with being overly preoccupied with some aspect of your sexuality or being overly sexually active? Y   N

2a. Do you have repetitive sexual fantasies which you feel are out of your control or cause you distress? Y   N
    2b. (if yes) Can you give me examples? Y   N (if yes) Please describe this:

    _____

    _____

    _____

    2c. (if yes) Does the above fantasy frequently intrude into your mind?
        Y   N
    2d. (if yes) Do you try to resist thinking about this (above) fantasy? Y   N
    2e. (if yes) When you are having the fantasy, does it cause you to feel good or bad about yourself? _____ Good _____ Bad
    2f. Do you feel ashamed about having had the fantasy after the fact?
        Y   N

3a. Do you have repetitive sexual urges which you feel are out of your control or cause you distress? Y   N
    3b. (if yes) Can you give me examples? Y   N (if yes) Please describe this:

    _____

    _____

    _____

    3c. (if yes) Do the above urges frequently intrude into your mind? Y   N
    3d. (if yes) Do you try to resist thinking about the above urges? Y   N

3e. (if yes) When you are having the urges, do they cause you to feel good or bad about yourself? _____ Good _____ Bad

3f. (if yes) Do you feel ashamed about having had these urges after the fact? Y   N

4a. Do you engage in repetitive sexual behavior which you feel is out of control or causes you distress? Y   N

4b. (if yes) Can you give me examples? Y   N (if yes) Please describe this:

_____

_____

_____

_____

4c. (if yes) Do thoughts of the above behaviors frequently intrude into your mind? Y   N

4d. (if yes) Do you try to resist engaging in this behavior? Y   N

4e. (if yes) When you are engaged in this behavior, does it cause you to feel good or bad about yourself? _____ Good _____ Bad

4f. Do you feel ashamed about having engaged in the behavior after the fact? Y   N

Scoring Sheet

Buying Disorder
Positive screen if the subject answers "yes" to 1a, 2a, 3a, **and** 4a

Kleptomania
Positive screen if the subject answers "yes" to 1a, 2a, 3a, **and** 4a

Trichotillomania
Positive screen if the subject answers "yes" to 1, 3, 4a, 5, **and** 6

Intermittent Explosive Disorder
Positive screen if the subject answers "yes" to 1a, 1b, 1c, **and** 1d; **in addition,** the subject must answer "no" to 1f

Pyromania
Positive screen if the subject answers "yes" to 1a, 2, 3, 4, **and** 5; **in addition,** the subject must answer "no" to 1b, 1c, 1d, and 1e

Pathological Gambling
Positive screen if the subject answers "yes" to 1, **and** to at least 5 of the rest of the questions

Compulsive Sexual Behavior
Positive screen if the subject answers "yes" to 1, 2a, 3a, **or** 4a

Referral Sources for the Treatment of Impulse Control Disorders

This is only a partial list of referral sources.

Midwest Region

Jon E. Grant, MD
Suck Won Kim, MD
Department of Psychiatry
University of Minnesota
Minneapolis, MN 55454
612–273–9736

Donald Black, MD
University of Iowa
College of Medicine
Psychiatry Research–MEB
Iowa City, IA 52242–1000
319–353–4431

Douglas Woods, PhD (*trichotillomania and pathological skin picking only*)
University of Wisconsin–Milwaukee
224 Garland Hall
2441 E. Hartford Avenue
Milwaukee, WI 53211
414–229–5335

Emil Coccaro, MD (*intermittent explosive disorder only*)
University of Chicago Medical Center

5841 S. Maryland Avenue
Chicago, IL 60637
773–834–4083

Susan McElroy, MD
University of Cincinnati College of Medicine
231 Albert Sabin Way
Cincinnati, OH 45267
513–558–1132

West Coast

Lorrin Koran, MD
Stanford University
300 Pasteur Drive
Stanford, CA 94305
650–498–9111

Timothy Fong, MD
Impulse Control Disorders Clinic
UCLA
760 Westwood Plaza, Room C9–440
Los Angeles, CA 90024
310–825–1479

East Coast

Nancy Keuthen, PhD (*trichotillomania and pathological skin picking only*)
Charles River Plaza
Simches Research Building
185 Cambridge St., Fl. 2
Boston, MA 02114
617–726–6766

Martin Kafka, MD (*sexual compulsivity only*)
Harvard Medical School
McLean Hospital
115 Mill Street
Belmont, MA 02478
617–855–3191

Eric Hollander, MD
Mount Sinai School of Medicine
One Gustave Levy Place, Box 1230
New York, NY 10029
212–241–3626

Marc Potenza, MD, PhD
Yale University
Connecticut Mental Health Center
Room S–104
34 Park Street
New Haven, CT 06519
203–974–7356

Martin Franklin, PhD (*trichotillomania only*)
University of Pennsylvania School of Medicine
3535 Market Street
Philadelphia, PA 19104
215–746–3327

Europe, South America, Middle East

Pinhas Dannon
Tel Aviv University
Tel Aviv, Israel

Stefano Pallanti, MD
University of Florence
Viale Ugo Bassi 1
50137
Florence
ITALY

Dr. Hermano Tavares
Instituto de Psiquiatria do Hospital das Clínicas
Faculdade de Medicina
Universidade de São Paulo

Rua Ovídio Pires de Campos s/n, São Paulo - SP, Brazil, CEP 05403-010
phone/fax: 55–11–30837816

For those with trichotillomania or pathological skin picking, please contact the
Trichotillomania Learning Center for more referrals at www.trich.org

Index